Public Deliberation

Public Deliberation

Pluralism, Complexity, and Democracy

James Bohman

The MIT Press
Cambridge, Massachusetts
London, England

Set in New Baskerville by The MIT Press.
Printed and bound in the United States of America.

Library of Congress Cataloging-in-Publication Data

Bohman, James.
  Public deliberation : pluralism, complexity, and democracy / James Bohman
    p.   cm. — (Studies in contemporary German social thought)
  Includes bibliographical references and index.
  ISBN 0-262-02410-1
  1. Democracy. 2. Pluralism (Social sciences) I. Title. II. Series.
JC423
321.8'01—dc20   96-599
                                                                      CIP

to my mother, Mary Rose Bohman, who taught me about justice, and to my daughter, Lena Gretchen Bohman, whom I hope to teach the same

Contents

Preface

This book is about deliberative democracy. I began working on it because of a significant gap that I saw in this promising new direction in contemporary democratic theory. Everyone was talking about deliberation, but no one was saying what it is or how it could work under real social conditions. The current theories are primarily procedural, and they base their accounts on ideal rather than actual conditions. On my view, this ideal approach is a mistake, since it makes it difficult to connect normative political theory to the practices of actual democracies and to real possibilities for democratic reform. It also only heightens the increasing skepticism in the social sciences about the practicality of democratic norms and ideals. In this book I want to answer the skepticism about the possibility of democratic politics that is now finding resonance even among proponents of Critical Theory and radical democracy.

Political skepticism has also found its way into everyday politics. While I was writing this book, Sheldon Hackney, the new chairman of the National Endowment for the Humanities, proposed a series of "town meetings" in which Americans could rethink the possibilities of a shared civic culture even while recognizing their new diversity. This proposal was met not only with skepticism but with virulent criticism from the Left and the Right. Soon after the proposal was made public, Richard Sennett called it "deeply wrongheaded" and even "a Serbian solution to the challenge of living with one another" (*New York Times* Op-Ed page, January 30, 1994). I want to show that such fears about the public sphere are not only as exaggerated as Sennett's rhetoric but are themselves deeply mistaken about how to meet the challenges of living together in a pluralist democracy. The opposite is true: it is through public deliberation that we can best preserve a cooperative, tolerant, and democratic form of pluralism. I will also show how public deliberation can go some way toward meeting other fundamental challenges to democratic politics, including the widening of social inequalities and the increasing complexity of social life.

Though I have long had an interest in democratic theory, the research for this book began during my year as an Alexander von Humboldt Fellow in Frankfurt under the sponsorship of Jürgen Habermas. I would like to thank Professor Habermas for his generous help at this stage of the project, as well the "Working Group on Legal Theory" in Frankfurt, whose members included Bernhard Peters, Klaus Günther, Ingeborg Maus, Lutz Wingert, Reiner Forst, and Kenneth Baynes during my year in Frankfurt. The group provided a very stimulating and challenging environment in which I first formulated many of these ideas. Work on the book was completed during a year-long sabbatical leave supported by Saint Louis University. I am grateful to Saint Louis University for research support over the last five years, including several Mellon Faculty Development Grants for travel to Germany and summer research. I would also like to thank the National Endowment for the Humanities for a Summer Research Grant on "Democracy and Cultural Pluralism." This grant not only allowed me to deepen my ideas on democratic pluralism but also enabled me to finish the book during the summer of 1994.

Many people have read much or all of the manuscript. I would especially like to thank Larry May, who also had a sabbatical during the same year. Without his willingness for long discussions and his patient reading of early drafts it would have been difficult for me to finish the book. Jack Knight's thorough reading of two drafts provided me with important insights; Jack especially helped me clarify issues related to chapters 1 and 3. Bill Rehg and Thomas McCarthy, too, provided important suggestions for chapter 2 and 4. Henry Richardson's and Mike Barber's willingness to make comments at the final stages helped to improve the book in many ways. Richard Dees helped by discussing issues of political liberalism. John Bowen and the members of the reading group on the public sphere associated with the Program for Social Thought and Analysis at Washington University in St. Louis provided a context for discussions of many of these problems, especially those of cultural pluralism in the public sphere. I also received helpful comments while delivering parts of the book as lectures to various philosophy departments, including those at Washington University in St. Louis (where I gave the tenth annual Spiegelberg lecture), Loyola University in Chicago, Purdue University, Denison University, the Free University of Berlin, and the University of Frankfurt, and to audiences at meetings of the Czech Academy of Sciences, the American Philosophical Association, the American Sociological Association, and the American Political Science Association. Suggestions and criticisms by anonymous reviewers for The MIT Press spurred many important revisions.

The book incorporates, in revised form, versions of previously published articles, and I gratefully acknowledge the work of the editors of the journals in which the articles appeared. Some of the general remarks on the appeal of deliberative democracy in the introduction are published in an article I co-authored with William Rehg for *The Journal of Political Philosophy*. A portion of chapter 2 was published in *Political Theory*. The beginning of chapter 4 was published (adapted for the South African context) in *Theoria*. Parts of the discussion of law, democracy, and complexity in chapter 4 were published in *Law and Society Review* and in *Constellations*. An earlier version of the discussion of radical social criticism that forms the middle part of chapter 5 was published in *Thesis Eleven*.

Above all, I want to thank Gretchen Arnold for inspiring me to examine the literature on social movements more closely; her criticisms, editorial help, and constant support are reflected in every page of the book.

Public Deliberation

Introduction: Deliberation and Democracy

Our government rests in public opinion. Whoever can change public opinion, can change the government, practically just so much.

—Abraham Lincoln

Majority rule, just as majority rule, is as foolish as its critics charge it with being. But it is never merely majority rule. . . . The means by which a majority comes to be a majority is the important thing: antecedent debates, the modification of views to meet the opinions of minorities. . . . The essential need, in other words, is the improvement of the methods and conditions of debate, discussion and persuasion.

—John Dewey

Critics of current democratic institutions, ranging from communitarians to radical democrats, share a remarkably consistent set of themes. They argue that current arrangements undermine the most important principles of democracy: contemporary political practices are based on a politics of self-interest that produces social fragmentation, they permit an unequal distribution of social and economic power that persistently disadvantages the poor and the powerless, and they presuppose institutions that depend almost entirely upon merely aggregative, episodic, and inflexible forms of decision making and that leave deep structural problems of social and economic renewal unresolved. Out of all these diagnoses comes the same remedy: public deliberation. It is not that citizens in many complex societies do not already have some opportunities for democratic deliberation, but that they seem unable to implement effective deliberation. A recurring image from the cable television network C-SPAN—members of the deliberative bodies of Congress delivering impassioned speeches to an empty chamber—epitomizes such deficiencies. Legislative bodies today seem less and less interested in deliberation, and their decisions seem more and more a matter of "mere" majority rule in Dewey's sense. Even the institutional devices of the U.S. Constitution that were designed to promote deliberation, such as the filibuster rule or the executive veto, do not promote better or more informed decision making; rather, they entrench the very "mischief of factions" they were meant to avoid. The now-common use of "focus groups" further undermines deliberation by tailoring political discourse to already-existing opinions, so that market strategies replace debate and discussion.

In this book I shall explore how it is that deliberative institutions can become more democratic through, as Dewey put it, "improvements in the methods and conditions of debate, discussion and persuasion."[1] Why do social critics from Dewey and Mill to Horkheimer and Habermas so closely tie the reforms of democratic institutions to improvements in deliberation? The simple answer is that such discussions of deliberation concern the way in which the practical reasoning of agents enters into political decision making. The call for more deliberation is, I will argue, a demand for a more rational political order in which decision making at least involves the public use of reason. According to this position, the legitimacy of decisions must be determined by the critical judgment of free and equal citizens.[2]

At the same time, a growing number of philosophers and social scientists criticize deliberative conceptions of democracy as unrealistic and impractical. The "facts" of modern society, particularly its pluralism and complexity, seem to be strong *prima facie* obstacles to deliberative democracy. Pluralism, these critics argue, undermines deliberation by producing intractable conflicts. Deliberation, it would seem, works only for relatively homogeneous groups who share many values and beliefs. The resurgence of nationalism and religious fanaticism makes such ideals of a "general will" or even public discussion seem more remote than ever. Furthermore, the size and the complexity of modern society seem to make most accounts of deliberation unrealistic, if not quaint. In town meetings, critics claim, people may be able to influence debate, but in institutions and organizations of the modern nation state such an expectation is unreasonable. Deliberation, too, seems to be elitist, more appropriate to university seminars and scientific communities than to the general public. Even if everyone could participate in deliberation, would not the more competent and better situated citizens tend to carry the day? What notion of political equality could make such arrangements work to the benefit of all rather than to the benefit of the most persuasive or, worse, to the benefit of those who know what they want and how to get it?

In this book I seek to respond to such skepticism and to defend public deliberation as a normative ideal and as a test for democratic legitimacy. To this end, I elaborate an account of public deliberation that is robust and practical enough to withstand skepticism about the prospects for deliberative arrangements under current conditions. Such a defense requires specifying what deliberation is, its normative presuppositions, and the informal and formal means by which it is best realized. It also requires an understanding of the social facts currently affecting the possibilities for deliberation: cultural pluralism, which produces potentially deep and persistent moral conflicts; large social inequalities, which make it difficult for many to participate effectively in public decisions; and social complexity, which makes it necessary for us to revise our models of what constitutes a forum for deliberation to include large and dispersed public spheres.

It has long been a hallmark of the Critical Theory of the Frankfurt School to provide just the sort of methodological combination of normative reflection and social scientific explanation that is needed to develop such a robust theory of public deliberation. This methodology is, however, not unique to Critical Theory narrowly understood. John Rawls's turn to a "political conception" of justice also begins with an inventory of social facts, the most important of which is "the fact of pluralism" (and the endemic social conflict that results from it). Similarly, Jürgen Habermas begins his theory of "deliberative politics" with a set of social facts, the most important of which is "unavoidable social complexity." Though Rawls and Habermas formulate different versions of the ideal "public use of reason," each of them seeks in his political theory to take into account the boundary conditions, or the descriptive social facts, under which such reason must operate. Accordingly, a theory is adequate if it recognizes both normative and factual constraints. My goal here is to develop an account of public deliberation that in this way contributes to the practical understanding of current political possibilities.[3]

This book spans the Anglo-American (primarily Rawlsian) and German (primarily Habermasian) literatures on the subject of deliberative democracy. Not only is there broad agreement on the desirability of public deliberation; there is also increasing agreement that democracy is justified to the extent that it makes possible the public use of common practical reason. The two traditions, I argue, face similar practical obstacles to realization and are open to the same sorts of skeptical objections. In response, both have made the same turn to social facts as part of their common methodology. Although their approaches are similar enough to be brought together fruitfully in dialogue, they have complementary weaknesses and strengths in their normative and descriptive components. In general, I locate my position between Rawls and Habermas: while more pluralistic than Habermas's account of discourse permits, it allows a wider and more dynamic role for critical public reason than Rawls's liberal neutrality allows. However, it shares with both Rawls and Habermas not only an emphasis on public reason in deliberation but also a common methodology and a strong emphasis on interrelated normative, descriptive, and practical concerns. A theory of deliberative democracy must be adequate on all three levels if it is to be a guide to political practice and reform.

Public Deliberation: A Preliminary Definition

What is deliberative democracy? First and foremost, democracy implies public deliberation in some form.[4] The deliberation of citizens is necessary if decisions are not to be merely imposed upon them. Consent is, after all, the main feature of democracy. That citizens give themselves their own laws not only makes the laws legitimate but also provides the citizens with reasons to be obligated to obey them. According to most proponents of deliberative democracy, political decision making is legitimate insofar as its policies are produced in a process of public discussion and debate in which citizens and their representatives, going beyond mere self-interest and limited points of view, reflect on the general interest or on their common good.[5] For this reason, many communitarian critics call for public deliberation as a means of producing a shared vision and for transforming citizens' limited and self-interested perspectives. Other defenders of deliberation, including Habermas and Rawls, are skeptical of such Rousseauian and "civic republican" variants of democracy. According to such criticisms, these interpretations of deliberative democracy suggest that political decisions should express the substantive values and traditions of a homogeneous political community or a "general will"—claims that are not readily plausible in contemporary pluralist democracies.[6] The challenge for a deliberative theory, then, is to show how the core idea of egalitarian democracy—that legitimate laws are authored by the citizens who are subject to them—can still be credible in complex and pluralist societies.

All deliberative models of democratic legitimacy are strongly normative in the particular sense that they all reject the reduction of politics and decision making to instrumental and strategic rationality. These uses of reason are constrained by the glare of publicity and by potential revisability in future deliberation. Some "pluralistic" theories of politics make competition the central mechanism of democracy. Social-choice theories, to cite another example, typically conceive rational public choice as the aggregation of individual preferences; the paradoxes afflicting this approach are well known.[7] For a deliberative theory, in contrast, it is crucial that citizens (and their representatives) test their interests and reasons in a public forum before they decide. The deliberative process forces citizens to justify their decisions and opinions by appealing to common interests or by arguing in terms of reasons that "all could accept" in public debate.[8] Merely stating that a given preference or belief is one's own will not, by itself, sway others to one's opinion.[9] As a result, the ensuing collective decision should in some sense be justified by public reasons—that is, reasons that are generally convincing to everyone participating in the process of deliberation. Whether or not such a decision is ultimately for the good of everyone is another matter. Outcomes can thus be considered democratic either if citizens themselves are involved in the deliberation or if representatives make decisions that all citizens *would* agree to if given time, knowledge, a chance to be heard, and a disposition to make their reasons "answerable" to one another.[10] Needless to say, this standard of agreement is hard to achieve and is usually considered a counterfactual and regulative ideal.

Whatever its precise formulation, such a conception of democracy presupposes an account of how the *process* of public deliberation makes the reasons for a decision more rational and its outcomes more fair. The reasons given must primarily meet the conditions of publicity; that is, they must be convincing to everyone. Because of this emphasis on reasons, the quality of deliberation is crucial to determining the reasonableness of an outcome or a decision. It is not surprising, then, that some theorists call their accounts of deliberation "epistemic" or "rational" in a broad sense: deliberation improves outcomes insofar as it helps citizens construct an interpretation of the decision and its consequence in light of what all those affected think about the matter at hand. According to this conception of democracy, a legitimate political system should foster deliberation and thus increase the chances of arriving at correct (or valid, fair, or true) decisions.[11] It is the prospect of improving the quality of the reasons for public decisions while maintaining egalitarian standards that, according to my view, makes deliberative democracy more attractive than its competitors.

But the emphasis on epistemic considerations in justifying deliberation should not be narrowly construed. One need not think of the correct decision as a truth "out there," somehow independent of the processes and procedures that discover it. In fact, there are many different accounts of such outcomes and procedures: some concern the common good; for others it is the rational or unanimous character of the agreement or consensus; for some it is the impartial viewpoint constructed by all in the very process of deliberation. Some deliberative theorists defend the claim that procedural ideals, rather than outcomes, constitute the decisive parameters for democratic legitimacy.[12] Others emphasize that deliberation either constructs or discovers the common good. Here one should not think of the common good in overly substantive terms, as though political deliberation primarily involved an authentic appropriation of already-shared values or political ideals. Though some shared agreements may be part of the picture (as a background of political culture required to get deliberation off the ground), they are never specific enough to capture the complexity of deliberation in contemporary institutions. Nor should deliberative theories be considered one-sidedly rationalistic. Many different "self-governing capacities" are necessary if citizens are to participate effectively in public deliberation and dialogue, including understanding, imagining, valuing, desiring, storytelling, and the use of rhetoric and argumentation.[13] Of course, deliberative theories are criticized on all these counts.

Because arguments must be articulated to defend the reasons for or against a decision in public, most deliberative theorists (beginning with John Dewey) have tended to emphasize their place in the methods of discussion and debate. But it is their use and not their logical form that is important: they are employed in what Kant calls "the public use of reason." In this context, Habermas's "discourse theory of democracy" can be seen as an epistemic account of the public use of reason that is both procedural and complex, for it explains the rationality of deliberation in terms of ideal reason-giving procedures. This account starts with the idea that beliefs and actions have a rational character insofar as they can be supported publicly by good reasons. The exchange of reasons takes place in a *discourse* in which participants strive to reach agreement solely on the basis of the better argument, free of coercion and open to all competent speakers.[14] Similarly, Rawls defends an "impure proceduralism" and argues that good reasons in deliberation must appeal to the "public basis of justification" for settling differences. In deliberation, citizens exercise their moral powers as free and equal persons. The exercise of political power is proper only within the framework of a constitution, "the essentials of which all citizens as free and equal may be reasonably expected to endorse in light of the principles and ideals common to their human reason."[15]

Whether defined in terms of discourse or common human reason, it is this general account of the public use of reason that I wish to defend in this book, with some modifications. In democratic deliberation, citizens address one another with their public reasons in the give and take of free and open dialogue. Even if they do not succeed in convincing others with their reasons, citizens may expect reasonable uptake and consideration for their opinions in this dialogue so long as they address and answer the concerns and opinions of others. The measure of such opinions is the "verdict" of "free citizens," who address their public reasons to an unlimited audience. It is precisely this universality that is the advantage of the distinctly public account of democratic deliberation, as opposed to the theories that limit deliberation to a community of like-minded citizens. Deliberation is thus a "public" rather than a "collective" or a group-specific activity. By the same token, however, the very lack of appeal to preexisting agreements and shared values presents a dilemma for the public use of reason: the norm of publicity can be either too strong or too weak. If too strong, it can presuppose too much and exclude many citizens; if too weak, it demands too little and offers no solutions to the pressing problems of contemporary democracy.

Given such doubts about its practicality, defenders of such an ideal of public reason must answer the political skeptic. Not only is there skepticism about deliberative arrangements; there is skepticism about democracy itself in the face of the overwhelming social facts of pluralism, inequality, and complexity. A long line of such skeptics among social theorists, from Max Weber to Niklas Luhmann, think that even representative democracy is obsolete to the extent that it is no longer a realistic implementation of democratic ideals under modern conditions. Devices of representation and the idea of a legislature standing in for deliberating citizens (which was to transform the classical doctrines of democracy and make them appropriate to modern conditions of size and complexity) are now thought to be nothing more than "institutional fictions."[16] Walter Lippmann challenged Dewey's deliberative ideal by calling the public a "phantom," suggesting that realism and rationality required that politics be left to the experts.

As I shall argue in the next section, such skepticism about democracy is the product of insufficient reflection upon and insufficient balance between considerations of political norms and social facts. Even defenders of more radical interpretations of democratic ideals, such as Marx and the early Frankfurt School, have had difficulty giving equal weight to the normative and descriptive features necessary for an adequate theory of deliberation. Their skepticism toward all existing forms of democracy has led to impractical attempts to apply demanding forms of participation in every area of social life and has lent a utopian cast to their positive democratic ideals.

There are two possible ways to answer such skepticism. On the one hand, Marx thought that if we encounter social facts that cannot be reconciled with democratic ideals we must change the facts to conform to the norms. But if norms such as full participation, equal respect, and unanimous agreement are impractical, this method is a nonstarter. On the other hand, Rawls thinks that principles often have to be changed so that it is at least possible to realize them under current circumstances. Although it seems more practical, this method errs in the opposite direction. Too many accommodations to social facts may produce useful practical principles and stable institutions, but at a high price for democracy.[17] Thus, an adequate political theory must combine facts and norms in the appropriate way. It must avoid the overly ideal and the overly accommodationalist horns of the dilemma while using a historical and political approach to constructing practical norms for actual deliberation. My approach balances this emphasis on social facts with the practical ideal of the public use of reason. It does not abandon the content of the ideals of deliberative democracy; it defends and reinterprets them so that they are feasible in societies as pluralistic and complex as our own.

Democracy, Criticism, and Skepticism: Social Facts and the Political Conception of Public Deliberation

One strand of democratic theory seeks to make the skeptic's objections harmless by arguing that they apply only to *current* democratic arrangements, which fail to live up to the norms they invoke. Such a critical theory of democracy contrasts the democratic norms of equality and autonomy with the facts about how they are implemented in the whole of a society and its practices. This dialectic has long been the basis for theories that call for "radical" or (as in Marx) "real" democracy.[18] The demand to consider actual circumstances motivated Marx's radical criticism of constitutionally guaranteed civil rights.[19] Marx juxtaposed the distinctly political rights guaranteed in various modern constitutions and the reality of civil society, showing that within existing social institutions civil rights are not achievable by all citizens. But such "disillusioning" criticism may devalue rights altogether and quickly turn into a corrosive skepticism toward constitutional constraints and even toward democratic principles.

The dialectic of facts and norms becomes self-defeating in many critical theories of democracy, leading to skepticism about the practicality of democracy. Rawls and Habermas have provided a way around this predicament: both accept that democratic ideals are constrained by the social facts of "pluralism" and "unavoidable social complexity." Whether or not they (like Marx) claim to be radical democrats, their main contribution to a critical theory of democracy is methodological. Their strategies of justification avoid normative skepticism while making social and historical facts and constraints relevant to political justification.

This general approach finds a way between the skeptical emphasis on social facts and the purely normative justification of democracy. A similar method of argument emerges in Rawls's shift from a Kantian theory of justice to the "political conception" of political liberalism. As Rawls puts it, the distinguishing mark of such a "political conception" is that it takes into account "the specific social and historical conditions of a modern democratic society." The conditions "require us" to regard principles of justice in a certain way "if such a conception is to be both practical and consistent with the limits of democratic politics."[20] Here I take this fundamental methodological lesson to heart; I consider a broad range of social facts and historical conditions that require us to see deliberative democracy in a certain way if it is to be both practical and consistent with the limits of democratic politics.

But, as the work of Rawls and others shows, the normative and factual sides of political reflection are not easily integrated. I shall briefly examine these recurring difficulties in critical theories of politics and illustrate them in the swings back and forth between skeptical and normative positions in the Frankfurt School.

When considering how normative ideals can be practical under current social and historical conditions, a critical theory of society aims at a political conception of justice. As Horkheimer defined it in his programmatic writings as director of the Frankfurt School's Institute for Social Research, a theory is critical if it fits three criteria: it must be descriptive (i.e., based on the best available empirical evidence concerning social conditions); it must be critical, in that its evaluations must be normatively justified; and it must also be practical, in that it can show how the transformation of the circumstances it criticizes is possible.[21] Such a theory "has as its object human beings as producers of their own historical form of life"; its goal is "the emancipation of human beings from the circumstances that enslave them."[22]

These same criteria apply to the critical theory of democracy. But democratic practice has a special place in Horkheimer's program for critical reflection, since he believed that the goal of emancipation required that human beings consensually choose and control the social conditions of their lives to the fullest possible extent. Thus, democratization relates to *all* circumstances that limit human emancipation. The political orientation of the Frankfurt School's critical theory has therefore been toward "true" consensus and autonomy—toward the transformation of capitalism into "real democracy." Like Marx, Horkheimer did not leave liberal institutions unaltered: democratic institutions should no longer be aggregative or based on rational self-interest; rather, they should be participatory and based on richer notions of reason and solidarity. And, much like some communitarians of today, Horkheimer criticized the modern political subject as abstract, detached, and ahistorical; whatever freedom and autonomy actors have as democratic citizens, it is only as "definite individuals" in relation to the equal freedom of others and in historically specific communities.

The facts about modern society that were most important to the Frankfurt School's account of democracy were its increasing rationalization and its effects on the autonomous moral personality. In this historical-social theory, these dominant processes of modern society preclude the realization of the political ideals of autonomy and democracy. But this inference need not follow from their analysis. Rather than promote skepticism, a complementary analysis of personality and societal structures could lend empirical support to prospects for further democratization. The Frankfurt School's actual empirical analysis of fascism still depends on the *democratic* personality as the contrasting type of psychic structure. In both *The Authoritarian Personality* and *Dialectic of Enlightenment*, resistance to such social effects has retreated to the micro level, in the continued capacities for the identification with others. But these works give up on the idea of "real" democracy, since the facts indicate the absence of social conditions necessary for democracy at all.[23] What is missing is any account of the social activity of deliberation.

By rejecting such holistic and one-dimensional explanations of rationalization, Habermas attempts to base a radical democratic critique of existing institutions on a normative account of political justification. In *Legitimation Crisis* Habermas argues that the demands of advanced capitalism limit the scope and the significance of democratic institutions and norms. Much like Horkheimer's argument that majority rule is a form of "subjectivism," Habermas regards current democratic practice's exclusive emphasis on periodic elections and voting to be an indication of its merely "formal" character.[24] To this reduced form of democracy, Habermas opposes "substantive" democracy, which emphasizes the "genuine participation of citizens in political will formation."[25] Rather than self-interested rationality, "substantive" democracy is based on a theory of practical rationality by which conflicts are settled in a consensual manner. Here Habermas's argument takes a purely normative turn: such a theory provides procedural criteria for testing decisions, but it says little about how the participation it demands could be institutionalized.

Because of the epistemological character of this theory of rationality, Habermas has been suspicious of attempts to apply it or its counterfactual constructs (such as the ideal speech situation) *directly* to the structure of political institutions. He has consistently argued that Marx and Rousseau, with their shared conviction that the general will can be achieved only in a direct, republican form of democracy, failed to see this problem. For example, by failing to see that the ideal agreement of the social contract specifies a certain procedural type of justification, Rousseau confused "the introduction of a new principle of legitimacy" with "proposals for institutionalizing just rule."[26] Habermas argues that democratic principles need not be applied everywhere in the same way, as defenders of communitarian, participatory, or "council" democracy might have it.

Habermas makes this point even more strongly in his most systematic treatment of democratic theory, in *Between Facts and Norms*. Democracy, he argues, cannot organize society as a whole "for the simple reason that democratic procedure must be embedded in contexts it cannot itself regulate."[27] These contexts are products of social complexity. According to Habermas, no normative conception of politics or law can be developed independently of a descriptively adequate model of the complexity of contemporary society, lest it fall prey to the impotent prescriptivism of the Kantian moral ought noted by Hegel and others.[28] Without this descriptive component, these norms become abstract and empty ideals rather than reconstructions of the rationality of actual practices. Moreover, directly applying such norms ignores further "unavoidable" social facts, including the "systemic constraints" on the information and decision costs in the deliberative process; asymmetries of competence, expertise, and the availability of information; the limits of public attention; and other scarcities of deliberative resources.[29]

Such an account of social complexity, however realistic it may be, eliminates two possible conceptions of publicity that are typical of radical democratic theories: that it is possible for the sovereign will of the people and its decision-making power to constitute the whole of society, and that a society formed out of purely communicative association is possible. Both of these mistakes have been made in the Rousseauian and Marxian variants of radical democracy. Habermas is not objecting to these ideals themselves so much as he is objecting to their lack of institutional mediation (although little is said about the character of legal and political institutions) and their overburdening of public deliberation. Modern complexity opens up new possibilities for both private and political autonomy and for the communicative and discursive structuring of many areas of life. But under these conditions, and under cultural conditions of the pluralization of forms of life, discursive democracy requires the mediation of political and legal institutions. They compensate for "the cognitive indeterminacy, motivational insecurity and the limited coordinating power of moral norms and informal norms of action in general."[30] Habermas admits that modern societies can also be overcomplex and undemocratic, especially when illegitimate forms of power increasingly accumulate in large institutions. Even without these pathological forms, modern societies can no longer be entirely organized along democratic lines.[31]

The question is whether anything remains of radical democratic theory's critical contrast between facts and norms once these realistic arguments about social complexity and the accompanying critique of ideals of participation are the descriptive starting point. Hence, Habermas's sociological analysis once again revives a form of political skepticism, now directed at the radical democratic ideals of Marxism and of Critical Theory. The potentials for democracy are now so limited by social and historical constraints that an open public sphere cannot ensure that citizens will influence the outcomes of institutional procedures. As a result, Habermas's recent writings are marked by an increasingly pessimistic tone concerning the possibility of transforming current forms of constitutional democracy. One of my main goals is to show that a theory of deliberative democracy can recognize pluralism and complexity and still defend the democratic ideals of the autonomy and sovereignty of citizens. But it can do so only if it transforms Habermas's underlying assumptions, which juxtapose counterfactual regulative ideals with pessimistic analyses of social facts.

Recent arguments in Anglo-American political theory take a more balanced approach to this shortcoming of many normative political theories. Habermas accuses these theories of being "sociologically naive" with regard to their practical component. Yet both Habermas and Rawls agree on most of the facts of modern society, including what Rawls calls "the fact of oppression." This fact implies that democracy cannot eliminate power under these circumstances: within the limits of democratic politics, "coercive law" (for Habermas) or "the oppressive use of state power" (for Rawls) is required to maintain social unity or integration.[32] For Rawls, these limits are in part defined by other social facts: the fact of reasonable pluralism and the fact that a democratic regime is enduring and secure only if it is "willingly and freely supported by at least a substantial majority of its politically active citizens."[33] Thus, for Rawls the conception of justice must take into account these facts of "political culture"; for Habermas they must consider the differentiation of modern institutions and their mechanism of social integration as basic requirements of any practical theory of legitimacy. But it is Rawls and not Habermas who draws the proper conclusion: these social facts do not change the method of justification; rather, they change the practical aims of a political theory. These aims, Rawls insists, should be understood pragmatically and depend on the structure of the society the theory addresses.[34]

My argument here is that a stronger practical conception of deliberative democracy can be had by reexamining the normative idealizations and assumptions of some deliberative theories. Besides giving a more prominent place to the practical side of political theory, a much more minimal account of justification is required if we turn to actual deliberation. Thus, the guiding anti-skeptical strategy of this book is to begin with only those normative assumptions necessary for the process of deliberation—a process in which citizens attempt to convince others to adopt certain policies on the basis of public reasons as they emerge in the give and take of deliberative dialogue. In contrast with the theories that I reject, my argument begins with a detailed account of how public deliberation actually works and then develops the normative constraints that deliberative institutions must embody. In each subsequent chapter, I shall introduce various facts of modern social structure that make normative and institutional demands on deliberation. For example, without the normative constraints needed to make political exclusion impossible, persistent social inequalities make it unlikely that those who lack resources and capacities will participate effectively in public dialogue. This social fact demands corrective measures for democratic inclusion.

My strategy is closer to Rawls's than to Habermas's constructivism, yet it differs from Rawls to the extent that it does not attempt to recapture the content of liberalism as the public basis for justification. Since we need not adopt all of liberalism to get public deliberation off the ground, my assumptions are even more minimal than Rawls's "political" conception. By not building in too many assumptions about how democracy works, I not only discuss actual deliberation but also avoid the dilemmas that plague liberalism and communitarianism. Above all, I broaden the descriptive component of deliberative theories to include other facts about the modern state and about market institutions, including social and economic inequalities, cultural biases, and the complexity, scale, and size of modern institutions.

On the Possibility of Public Deliberation: A Sketch of the Main Argument

The persistent tension in recent constructivist and reconstructivist approaches discussed in the last section can best be represented as follows: although the norms they endorse are based on rule by "real consensus" or "the agreement of free and equal persons," the facts and trends they uncover tend to make the realization of these ideals increasingly improbable. For all his attempts to reformulate a critical theory without its empirical overgeneralizations and normative deficits, Habermas's dual method has not successfully avoided the sociological skepticism about democracy that has plagued the Frankfurt School. Yet he still calls his theory of democracy "deliberative politics," clearly aligning himself with political forms that emphasize public deliberation and participation.[35]

There is now a large and diverse literature defending various conceptions of "deliberative democracy." The central accomplishment of these theories, on which I shall build, is to elaborate a set of necessary conditions for an "ideal procedure" of democratic deliberation. Though sometimes enumerated as a set of basic rights, these conditions actually reflect basic normative requirements and constraints on deliberation: the inclusion of everyone affected by a decision, substantial political equality including equal opportunities to participate in deliberation, equality in methods of decision making and in determining the agenda, the free and open exchange of information and reasons sufficient to acquire an understanding of both the issue in question and the opinions of others, and so on.[36] These norms not only make possible a discursive public space but are best understood as specifying what is to go on within it: how deliberation is best promoted by methods and conditions of debate, discussion, and persuasion, the nature of which constitutes what Dewey calls "*the problem of the public.*"

Properly reformulated, such normative conditions may become robust enough to withstand skepticism. Whether they have any practical import remains another question. But the method I employ does not begin with an ideal procedure. Although useful for the purpose of critically evaluating some deliberative processes and outcomes, such an approach is inherently counterfactual and theoretically inadequate, especially with regard to the descriptive task of showing how deliberation is possible and the practical task of showing when it is successful. Rather, a more empirical, practical, and Deweyan approach ought to begin with an account of how deliberation works—that is, with a fine-grained analysis of how reasons become publicly convincing in deliberative dialogue.

Most of the previous theories of deliberative democracy construct different versions of the same proceduralist argument: first construct the right egalitarian procedure and then show why decisions made in light of it will tend to be fair. Ideal proceduralism is supposed to solve various philosophical problems, such as giving a deliberative account of rights and a criterion of fairness; however, it leaves the core of the theory of deliberative democracy relatively unanalyzed. For all their talk about deliberation, few theorists or philosophers describe it at all, and few of those who describe it do so in sufficient detail to make clear why it is democratic, what putting it into practice would mean, or how it is possible under the social conditions of pluralistic and complex societies. Rather than procedural, the account developed here is dialogical in that the exchange of public reasons in the give and take of dialogue makes speakers answerable and accountable to one another. In such a process, citizens may have the reasonable expectation that they may affect the outcome of deliberation or revise unacceptable outcomes in the future.

In chapter 1, I shall offer just such a richer, fine-grained account of public deliberation, the two main features of which are that deliberation is a dialogical process and that it is public to the extent that it is a joint social activity involving all citizens. This sort of account departs from Habermas's communication-centered theory. By looking at how actual deliberation produces publicly convincing reasons, I reject the more common approach of justifying the norms of deliberation through elaborating an "ideal procedure." Along with proceduralism, I reject models that analyze constitutions as irrevocable precommitments that provide the best way to establish basic norms. Since deliberation extends to the normative framework for deliberation, it too can be revised according to the public reasons of participants in deliberation.

After developing this non-proceduralist account of how public deliberation actually works to promote agreements and cooperation, I shall turn to the major challenges facing deliberative democracy as a practical ideal: social facts concerning cultural pluralism that endanger deliberation with deep and seemingly unresolvable conflicts (chapter 2); social inequalities that undermine the public character of deliberation and make it reproduce and reinforce the advantages of those who possess sufficient cultural resources and political capacities to get what they want (chapter 3); social complexity, which threatens to overwhelm deliberation and make its decisions irrelevant (chapter 4); and community-wide biases and ideologies, which restrict public deliberation and institutional abilities to deal with problems and conflicts (chapter 5). Each of these facts represents a challenge to the very possibility of free, equal, open, rational deliberation and to the basic conditions necessary for democratically legitimate decision making.

Each of the aforementioned facts potentially threatens the possibility of successful deliberation and hence of deliberative democracy as a realizable ideal. Answering these challenges also provides a way of responding to the excesses of past attempts to achieve more extensive democracy: pluralism checks the coercive qualities of the general will, political equality answers the charge of elitism, and the sovereignty of the public preserves self-rule without excessive rationalism or overcomplexity. In each case, I try to be realistic about such social facts without being skeptical, and to be normative in orientation while insisting on sociological descriptions that illuminate the real potentials for deliberation in current practices and institutions. Taken together, these arguments make a cumulative case that takes the sting out of political skepticism toward democracy, which is usually based on one or more of these considerations.

First, cultural pluralism could lead to political skepticism about deliberation. Given the multiethnic, multicultural character of most modern nation states, deliberation has to be able to settle conflicts of moral values and principles among diverse groups. As I shall argue, even second-order solutions, such as practices of adjudication, could fall to such skepticism, since moral conflicts in pluralist societies may be about the very nature of principles of public justification. Public reason itself is increasingly open to public contestation. In general terms, the solution I offer here is to make the public use of reason more dynamic and pluralistic. Even the notion of agreement in deliberation must be pluralistic. I argue that the model of compromise must be expanded to apply to a deliberative democracy that is consistent with political equality and with shared citizenship marked by participation in a common public sphere. Besides expanding the notion of public reason beyond its Kantian limitations, this chapter provides an argument against postmodern skeptics, such as Jean-François Lyotard, who deny that consensus can be reconciled with pluralism.[37]

Second, large social inequalities, which are widening in our society, can also give rise to political skepticism about democracy. Rather than promote equality, deliberative arrangements seem to favor the best off (who stand to be the most effective in public debate) and to disadvantage the worst off (who might not have the reasonable expectation to influence the decisions by which they are the most affected). As a solution, I adapt Amartya Sen's account of economic inequalities to the political domain, emphasizing the capacities and the cultural resources needed for adequate political functioning.[38] I also offer various deliberative mechanisms that correct for the effects of social inequalities. These mechanisms ensure that all salient positions enter into public debate, and current discussions of campaign finance reform offer an example of such proposals at a practical level. Should these measures fail, collective action and solidarity will play a large role in correcting unfair disadvantages in currently structured public deliberation.

Third, social complexity leads to political skepticism to the extent that it seems to make deliberation and popular sovereignty seem obsolete, especially if modeled on face-to-face assemblies and town meetings. At the beginning of the twentieth century, such difficulties led proponents of "realistic theories" of democracy, from Max Weber to Walter Lippmann, to speak of a "phantom public" that was to be replaced by scientific experts and professional politicians. In this argument, I reject Habermas's two-track solution to the problems of complexity. In its place, I develop a modified version of the familiar "dualist" model of democracy, so that popular sovereignty is reinterpreted as the rule by deliberative majorities formed out of the public sphere. The dual solution must be applied to all political institutions, particularly bureaucratic and administrative ones. According to my argument, public opinion does indeed rule through deliberative majorities, and precisely in the sense that both Lincoln and Dewey articulate in the epigrams that begin this chapter.

Finally, the inevitable presence of community-wide biases and ideology could lead to political skepticism about the flexibility of democratic institutions and their capacities for innovation and change. Here the political speech of social critics and the effects of public actors at critical historical moments serve to open the possibility for innovation in the public sphere. Sometimes such innovation calls for new possibilities that change the relationship between the public and political institutions. In order to see how deliberation can promote democratic change, it is important to see the constant interplay between the publics that form institutions, which publics are in turn organized by those institutions—that is, the interplay between emerging publics and their demands for institutional change. Such moments include periods of what Bruce Ackerman has called a "constitutional politics"[39] (or, in the case of new international social problems and civil society, a "cosmopolitan politics"). Not only do new issues and topics come to the fore in such periods of change; the very public framework and the methods of deliberation may be changed by collective actors that emerge from the civic public sphere.

As I see it, this effort to rethink the potential for democracy in terms of public deliberation clearly continues the legacy of the Frankfurt School. In its initial phases, critical social theory developed a clear and radical orientation to democratic theory through the ideal of a self-organized, free society that expresses human needs and powers in its totality. This model is inadequate not only in light of the spectacle of the rapid disintegration of state socialism but also in light of the social facts of pluralism and complexity. Radical democracy no longer means the total transformation of society; rather, it means a piecemeal project of reform that builds upon the constitutional and institutional achievements of the past. In this reformist democracy, the role of the social critic is to show the potentials and the limits of the public and autonomous employment of practical reason. In light of the goals of deliberative politics, public reason is exercised not only in the state and its representatives but also in the public sphere of free and equal citizens. In the American civil rights movement, for example, citizens collectively changed the character of the legal interpretation of the Constitution and its guarantees of political equality. To the extent that deliberative democracy is defined by its link to radical democratic and reformist politics, its practical aim is a more extensive form of democracy—that is, one with greater scope for public decision making and self-rule. I want to show that the theory of deliberative democracy provides the most compelling normative, descriptive, and practical basis for this task.

In the rest of the book, I shall answer the specific objections that lead to political skepticism about extending democracy in this way in complex and pluralistic societies. I shall not undertake a general justification of democracy itself, although I shall argue that democracy alone makes it more likely that decisions will be reasonable and that free and equal citizens will be able to accept them. My main line of argument is that democratic principles (such as self-rule, public deliberation, and the equal participation of all those affected by a decision) and the innovative effects of new publics not only are applicable to the large-scale institutions of modern societies such as ours but also can still be increased in scope, even though they remain insufficiently realized owing to the unequal distribution of power, resources, and capacities. It is certainly true that democracy is the real "unfinished project of modernity" (as Habermas has put it), and not because we need to abolish mass society or dismantle its large institutions. This is not to say that a theory of deliberative democracy leaves social conditions as they are and adapts to them. Some social conditions will have to be corrected if these ideals are to be achieved; large social inequalities are inconsistent with public forms of deliberation in egalitarian institutions. Nonetheless, if such ideals are not to lose their normative force, they must at least be possible; as Kant puts it, "ought implies can." The legacy of Critical Theory and political liberalism can be extended by a theory of deliberative democracy that establishes how such an ideal is practical, given the structure and the culture of modern society. Far from being impediments to deliberative democracy, pluralism and complexity may promote free, equal, and rational deliberation in vibrant and cosmopolitan public spheres. This task requires not only political imagination but also—and perhaps most of all—more public deliberation about the nature of democracy.

1

What Is Public Deliberation? A Dialogical Account

Deliberation was thought by Aristotle to be the paradigmatic activity of political virtue and self-rule. Only those who can deliberate well can maintain their own self-government. But, like direct democracy, the Aristotelian deliberative ideal presupposed a small and homogeneous political community. Deliberation is no doubt made easier if citizens already agree about most matters of value and belief. But modern democracies expanded the exercise of deliberation to diverse communities that included all as politcally equals, regardless of creed, status, or culture. In this form, it has a long and noble history, including the constitutional assemblies of France and the United States and New England town meetings. But some see in these more exemplary cases the proof that well-functioning deliberative arrangements are either transient or rare. Deliberation seems to be limited to the constituting power of the founding moments of institutions, rather than exercised in the ordinary politics of the already-constituted forms of political power. Can deliberation function as the governing ideal of complex, pluralistic, and yet stable modern societies? The increasing globalization of culture and power belies the assumptions of the standard models of civic deliberation.

For all these potential obstacles, modern constitutional democracies have opened up space for many forms of public deliberation. Certainly the rights enshrined in them, such as freedom of speech, expression, association, and inquiry, are all necessary conditions for successful deliberation. Such rights, too, are exercised in shared practices with others, including debate, discussion, and writing directed to the audience of all free and equal citizens. But even though such rights are found in many documents, including the U.S. Constitution and the UN Declaration of Universal Human Rights, the institutions they have created are now less often forums for deliberation and more often locations for strategic gamesmanship. Rights may make deliberation possible, in part by setting limits upon it, but they tell us neither what deliberation is nor how it is best conducted under current conditions and constraints.

Do these facts mean that deliberation, like direct citizen participation in all political decisions, is no longer possible? Do modern societies lack the unity necessary for deliberative practices? Is such a society no more than a union of social unions? In light of the argument made in the introduction, the deliberative ideal must at least be plausible with respect to the relevant social and historical facts. Three models appear, *prima facie*, to be plausible candidates: precommitment, proceduralist, and dialogical accounts of deliberation. Each model speaks to some of the facts. We could simply avoid deliberating, especially about contentious issues, and "precommit" ourselves irrevocably to a binding set of rules and a defined public agenda. Though minimal in its assumptions, the precommitment model hardly seems a realistic option in view of the ongoing demands and conflicts in democratic political life. For many, the fact of pluralism makes some form of proceduralism the only desirable option, since it avoids making overly strong and substantive assumptions about agreement among citizens. Despite all their practical strengths, I reject both of these options. Instead of precommitment and proceduralism, I argue for an account of deliberation based on dialogue, since it is only in dialogue with others—in speaking to them, answering them, and taking up their views—that the many diverse capacities for deliberation are exercised jointly. Public dialogue is possible, even with those with whom we disagree and with others who are not literally present before us.

The aim of this chapter is to give a general account of public deliberation that is appropriate to contemporary democratic institutions and their public spheres. For all the talk of deliberation among democratic theorists, few tell us what it actually is. Too many proponents of deliberation are satisfied with merely describing some very general procedural conditions and rules. Often it is thought to be sufficient to show that deliberation fulfills the requirements of political equality by maximizing the opportunities for deliberation and the number of citizens who take advantage of them. Although this is certainly true, there is little discussion of what makes deliberation public, what it can really accomplish, and when it is actually successful. Deliberation in the sense examined here is interpersonal; it concerns the process of forming a public reason—one that everyone in the deliberative process finds acceptable. A fine-grained analysis of this process is necessary to show that the reasons produced for decisions not only are more convincing than reasons that have not undergone the scrutiny of public testing in free and open public dialogue of all citizens but also are likely to be epistemically superior to them.

Such practical reasoning has been normatively reconstructed in various ways, with Aristotle on one side and Kant on the other. Such a reconstruction is complicated by the fact that various contexts demand different types of deliberation: moral, goal-directed, individual, interpersonal, and so on. Deliberation in democracies is interpersonal in a specific, political sense: it is public. In democratic polities, all citizens are equally empowered and authorized to participate in deliberation and reasoning about decisions that affect their lives together. As citizens, they are given equal voice in the process of deliberation and in the mechanisms that affect decisions. Democratic citizenship confers political equality, whereby citizens have the same civil rights, equal standing before the law, and equal voice in making decisions. My account presupposes broad political equality, although in chapter 3 I examine what sort of equality is demanded for deliberation to be genuinely public.

"Public" here refers not just to the *way* citizens deliberate but also to the *type of reasons* they give in deliberating. "The public" denotes not only the body of citizens but also the existence of overlapping spheres of decision making, discussion, and information pooling that should in principle be open to everyone. It also refers to the reasons offered for deliberation within a public sphere, which have a specific scope; that is, they must be convincing to everyone. This fact about democratic deliberation provides a minimal standard for what constitutes an agreement among free and equal citizens. Citizens deliberate in order to find and construct what T. M. Scanlon calls "informed, unforced general agreement," or, alternatively, what Jürgen Habermas calls "uncoerced consensus"; both are descriptions of the same minimal condition for the democratic legitimacy of deliberative outcomes.[1] It means that the only things that ought to be convincing are the reasons offered by or to fellow citizens who also freely exercise their deliberative capacities.

The public character of a reason depends on its intended audience. Citizens deliberate together before the audience of all other citizens, who must be addressed as political equals. This audience sets certain constraints on reasons that are public. They must be communicated in such a way that any other citizen might be able to understand them, accept them, and freely respond to them on his or her own terms.[2] Reasons formed in this way are more likely to result in decisions that everyone may consider legitimate in a special sense: even if there is no unanimity, citizens agree sufficiently to continue to cooperate in deliberation. Illegitimate political decisions, which often cause injury and disadvantage to many citizens, are made precisely for *non-public* reasons and in non-public ways. They are not addressed to an audience of politically equal citizens.

In light of this characterization of what publicity entails for political deliberation, freedom and equality are thus the primary tests of public reason, and a non-public reason is precisely one that violates these norms by excluding some citizens, by restricting the audience of communication, or by addressing citizens with reasons that do not require their assent. On the basis of these norms, unreasonable opinions are excluded; citizens have to address their reasons to the "gallery" of the public at large, which includes groups who may be the target of the deliberators' prejudices and who may be disadvantaged under their deliberative schemes. Even in small groups, people are aware that many of their statements could not be made public: they violate not only norms of civility but also the norms of public discourse that make it possible to communicate with the implicit audience of all other citizens.[3]

But publicity also has an epistemic import: deliberation improves the quality of political justification and decision making by subjecting them to a wide range of possible alternative opinions. But, surely, it may be objected, not all public decisions will necessarily be better than non-public decisions, especially when there are community-wide errors and prejudices. And these decisions will not necessarily be more efficient or always promote better overall consequences or social utility. Consider how risk averse the public is in comparison with experts. Even if decisions made by a public were not always as reliable as decisions that would be made by its best-informed members, public deliberation could still be positively defended on other grounds: one could simply argue that it is constitutive of the autonomy of citizens. Although self-expression is a political value, this is not my argument here. Rather, I argue that the best defense of public deliberation is that it is more likely to improve the epistemic quality of the justifications for political decisions. When deliberation is carried out in an open public forum, the *quality* of the reasons is likely to improve. In such a forum, public opinion is more likely to be formed on the basis of all relevant perspectives, interests, and information and less likely to exclude legitimate interests, relevant knowledge, or appropriate dissenting opinions. Improving the quality of the reasons employed in political justification will ultimately affect the quality of the outcomes that they produce: reasons will be more public, in the sense that they reflect the broader input of all the deliberators who are affected.

With this goal in mind, the following is my initial definition of public deliberation: a dialogical process of exchanging reasons for the purpose of resolving problematic situations that cannot be settled without interpersonal coordination and cooperation. On this definition, deliberation is not so much a form of discourse or argumentation as a joint, cooperative activity. This definition elaborates the proper aim, necessary conditions, and scope of public deliberation. Reconstructing an idealized version of such a process is useful for some critical purposes, especially since it can highlight deficiencies in existing deliberative arrangements. However, one of the main advantages of seeing deliberation primarily as a cooperative activity is that the standard of publicity need not depend on strong idealizations that do not refer to any actual deliberation.[4]

I argue below that such a cooperation-based and non-proceduralist account of public deliberation provides both an epistemic and a moral basis for democratic participation in complex societies. Many similar "cognitivist" defenses of deliberation fail to make it consistent with participatory democracy and instead propose alternative and more restricted institutions and decision-making mechanisms to improve the quality of reasons. On the one hand, some democratic theorists think that deliberation can be improved only at the price of participation. Among others, Madison and Mill thought that various mechanisms of representation were needed to improve upon public opinion and abilities. On the other hand, some theorists conclude that democracy can be defended only at the price of deliberation. Many rational-choice theorists argue that voting eliminates the need for deliberation—that, owing to the problems of coordination at a more substantive level, voting is the only egalitarian way to ensure that everyone has about the same say in large and complex societies. I do not dispute the advantages of both voting and representation as political devices, but I do not think that they exhaust the democratic possibilities of complex and pluralistic societies. Indeed, there is good historical evidence that such devices do not always solve the problems they are supposed to solve: representative institutions do not necessarily improve upon public opinion (as Madison thought), and voting does not resolve the problems of diverse preferences and giving everyone an equal say in complex societies.[5]

For most "realistic" theories of democracy, it is an easy step to argue that the failures of "simple" devices of aggregation and representation necessarily imply that deliberation, with its even more demanding requirements, faces still greater obstacles. This quick dismissal is made easier by the failure of many proponents of stronger, participatory forms of democracy to specify the cognitive mechanisms operating in *actual* public deliberation. Before turning to those mechanisms, in the next section I offer arguments for a non-proceduralist justification of public deliberation. It is based on the give and take of open and inclusive dialogue, in which speakers offer reasons, receive uptake, and provide answers to one another.

Ideal Proceduralism and the Problem of Participation

As I use the term here, radical democracy has two components, one consisting of critical standards and the other consisting of guiding positive ideals. The critical standards are methodological: that democratic ideals (and their philosophical reconstruction) must be constantly tested against the actual social facts of political culture and institutions. The positive ideal is the participation of all citizens in decision making, widely dispersing power in society. Even if deliberation takes place in representative bodies, it still involves the deliberation of all citizens. Such bodies remain deliberative only if citizens vote for and choose their representatives on the basis of participation in public debate and discussion of issues.

Political skeptics and realists suggest that these participatory ideals face a number of difficulties when they are applied to complex societies: conflicts between equality and deliberation, between informal public opinion and institutionalized decision making, and between popular sovereignty and social complexity. Typically, participatory and deliberative solutions to these problems place great weight on their effects on citizens. Two different conceptions of participation have emerged as plausible ways to overcome the inadequacies of mere procedural opportunities, aggregative voting, and merely negative rights. On the one hand, civic republicans propose that participation itself has strong educative effects and is thus able to transform interests and preferences so as to produce a shared conception of the common good.[6] On the other hand, proceduralists are skeptical of the capacity of deliberation to produce the transformation necessary to overcome social fragmentation and to create a commitment to shared values. All that is needed is to specify the conditions that everyone would agree would be likely to produce decisions backed by broadly public reasons; then some deliberative procedure could be constructed to embody these conditions of publicity.

Rather than follow either the proceduralist or the civic republican line of argument, I want to propose a third general defense of participatory democracy, one that overcomes the weaknesses of these more common approaches. Deliberative theories of political participation say either too much or too little. Civic republicans either presuppose such overlapping virtues and values that democracy is unnecessary, or they offer us no assistance in specifying how to resolve conflicts and disagreements about values.[7] Proceduralists either idealize so much that they no longer provide any way to guide political practice, or they do too little to indicate how "participants themselves" can successfully work out these problems "democratically" under the procedural constraints. As an alternative, I propose an account of the actual processes of public deliberation that is not only more informative for current democratic institutions but also less open to the standard objections concerning the impossibility of democratic participation under current social conditions. To the degree that my account considers both of these factors, it defends a version of "radical-egalitarian," or participatory, democracy.

Democracies face a number of difficulties that do not yield easily to collective social action, including potential obstacles of scale, cultural diversity, and persistent social inequalities. Such difficulties generally lead democratic theorists to introduce two institutional mediations as a way to realize the ideals of their normative analysis: the state and civil society. The formal institutions of the constitutional state are often seen as the only way to implement basic norms such as civil and human rights, and an informal sphere of voluntary associations in civil society is supposed to make up for all the conditions of democratic life that formal institutions cannot fulfill. But where do people deliberate together? Although the existence of *both* state institutions and civil society is a necessary feature of a democratic society, together they are not yet sufficient for public deliberation.[8] It is hard to see why different groups in civil society could arrive at an agreement about how to implement constitutional essentials or about the public bases of justification for state policies. Moreover, many groups in civil society might want to resist the incursions of market forces or other powerful large institutions. Nor is it clear how civil society could avoid collapsing into competitive pluralism for institutional resources without some overarching shared system of values or public agreements unifying its diverse voluntary associations.

In response to the diversity of values and the absence of a shared conception of the good life, many liberal and radical democratic theorists appeal to *ideal procedures* as distinctive of democratic justification. Such proceduralist views usually require a "neutral" state that maintains the conditions of deliberation, such as strict boundaries for reasonable moral conflict. But only a very narrow range of issues can be settled by appeal to "pure" procedures, and such solutions refer precisely to non-deliberative decision-making mechanisms (such as coin tosses and lotteries). In cases in which procedures alone are decisive (as in "pure" proceduralism), it becomes difficult to explain why participants find the *outcomes* of their deliberations convincing and binding.[9] Indeed, an advantage of strict proceduralist justifications is that they may be applied to any issue whatsoever, but in most cases egalitarian decision makers regard them as second best and need a reason to apply them. For example, no good grounds or non-question-begging criteria can justify such results, as the case of egalitarian queues for scarce resources makes clear. But there is no practical reason to limit political decision making to cases in which pure procedural criteria are sufficient. Almost every issue on the public agenda today, including affirmative action, abortion, and welfare policy, involves questions of value and principle for most citizens. Nor should a theory of public deliberation be satisfied by merely spelling out ideal conditions of procedural equality without reference to the social conditions in which such procedures operate.

The main shortcoming of procedural accounts is that they require overly narrow definitions of deliberation. In dialogue and communication, procedures alone do not define standards of fairness or rationality. Consider a procedure that permits every individual in a group to have his or her say. Even with the equal chance to speak, not every speaker will be able to influence the outcome of deliberation in his or her favor. Since open and informal procedures such as simple turn taking do not preclude strategic manipulation, it is necessary to consider the effectiveness of the speaker, and not just the opportunity to have one's reasons considered. Owing to the wide range of cases in which procedural grounds provide no reason to favor any one of a number of possible solutions, it is necessary to give a close description of why reflective agents might find reasons convincing after participating in public deliberation. If deliberation is a joint activity, as I will argue, then procedures alone, even ideally rational or intrinsically fair ones (such as coin tosses), do not capture the criteria and conditions of success in this activity.

Deliberative theorists have provided fairly detailed lists of necessary procedural conditions for political equality. Even if we acknowledge the differences between them, Joshua Cohen and Robert Dahl have supplied the most systematic lists of such procedural conditions.[10]

For Dahl these procedures outline "the general features of the democratic process"; for Cohen, the "framework for free public deliberation." Dahl's list centers on the decision-making process: equal votes (in the decisive stage when outcomes are determined), equal effective participation (in the process of making decisions), equal opportunity to discover and validate reasons, final control of citizens over the agenda, and inclusiveness (of all adult citizens).[11] Cohen's list is directly concerned with the process of deliberation: deliberation ought to take argumentative form, as the exchange of reasons in light of available information, and must remain open to future revision. These conditions are ensured procedurally: through equal allocation of votes, equality of opportunity, and so on. Habermas's ideal speech situation supplies a similar list. However, even if these conditions are necessary for deliberative equality, they fail to specify when a reason is publicly convincing.

No such list can be complete, because it is always tied to historically specific institutions. Nevertheless, these general conditions for deliberation and decision making, or any similar set, apply to any arrangement in which collective decisions are to be made by public reasoning and discussion. They are necessary but not sufficient conditions that tell us a lot about why decisions often fail to be democratically legitimate and why deliberation in some circumstances cannot be democratic. But do they tell us how or when public deliberation may in fact succeed? Proceduralism cannot answer this sort of question, because it pays insufficient attention to what it is that these rules and conditions are supposed to enable to occur in deliberation and among those deliberating.

Proceduralists credit the generality of these conditions to the way they identify procedures of discourse (that is, of argumentation and discussion). Deliberation is better described as primarily a particular social activity that can be performed only through public discourse, and thus as an activity it has its own standards and criteria of success not identical with those of discourse. The proceduralist accounts of deliberation given by Cohen, Dahl, and Habermas are not wrong; however, they lack an account of the process of deliberation, and thus they cannot provide criteria for its success. On my view, deliberation is a joint social activity, embedded in the social action of dialogue— the give and take of reasons. Such deliberation is typically initiated in and about a specific social context. It begins with a problematic situation in which coordination breaks down; it succeeds when actors once again are able to cooperate. A successful outcome of deliberation is acceptable to all, but in a weaker sense than demanded by procedural theories: success is measured not by the strong requirement that all can agree with the outcome but by the weaker requirement that agents are sufficiently convinced to continue their ongoing cooperation. An outcome of an actual decision is acceptable when the reasons behind it are sufficient to motivate the cooperation of all those deliberating.

What are the precise criteria of success for public deliberation? Deliberation succeeds to the extent that participants in the joint activity recognize that they have contributed to and influenced the outcome, even when they disagree with it. Certain types of influence would not be sufficient to induce cooperation; for example, a group may influence a decision in ways that are unfavorable to it simply because of widespread prejudices and biases against its members. In many elections, the mere fact that a minority group supports a candidate may influence some members of the majority to cast their votes for another. Deliberative dialogue seeks to minimize this type of endogenous and non-public influence and replace it with the influence of contributions to ongoing public debate. Given that a dialogue is free and open, each actor or group of actors cooperates in deliberation because they reasonably expect that their reasonable views will be incorporated into the decision in some respect that is favorable (or at least not unfavorable) to them. Procedures alone describe some very general discursive conditions that enable deliberation to succeed as a joint activity, not success itself. Some such conditions may constrain certain bad outcomes and untenable reasons, but they do not specify how in any particular case agents themselves discover outcomes that legitimately resolve the problematic situations. The structure of deliberation as a joint activity brings out these features. Conversation is, similarly, a joint activity that must be actively maintained by participants, here under norms of sociability. Unlike conversation, however, the activity of deliberation is public not only in the sense that the audience to which contributions are directed must remain unrestricted but also in the sense that the joint activity of deliberation must also be organized so that all citizens may take part in the activity and in so doing test and maintain its public character. These conditions were not met in the case of the minority group discussed above.

In the next two sections, I argue that only a richer description of the process of deliberation can explain the convincing character of public reasons. The starting point for my reconstruction of democratic deliberation is somewhat different than the one adopted by most deliberative theorists: it is the question of why reasons offered in deliberation are convincing to others. In particular, a reason becomes publicly convincing through the operation of "dialogical mechanisms"—not because it is merely the outcome of a fair procedure, or because certain types of reasons were used in justification, or because certain issues were excluded. It is through these dialogical mechanisms that agents achieve success in their deliberative activity. Such a dialogical account answers the weaknesses of the more common proceduralist and precommitment models that I discuss below.

The aim of this account is to develop a corresponding general criterion for democratic legitimacy. Unanimity is too strong a criterion for democratic agreement; instead, all that is necessary is continued cooperation in an ongoing dialogical process of settling common problems and conflicts. Before I turn to the description of these mechanisms, I propose a general account of the type of deliberation involved in democracy, in which actual citizens make public use of their reason. This account will be based on the possibilities of dialogue rather than discourse or argumentation, since it is through dialogue that deliberation becomes "public" and decisions legitimate. The analysis of discourse concerns what arguments or types of justification may be publicly convincing; by contrast, the analysis of dialogue concerns how public interaction produces those practical effects on participants that make reasons "convincing."

Deliberation, Democracy, and Publicity: On the Public Use of Reason

I argued in the introduction that "deliberative" theorists must defend the once popular and now quixotic ideals of participatory democracy.[12] Deliberative theories are generally also contractarian to the extent that their criterion for political legitimacy is rational agreement among free and equal citizens. As Kant put it, a political order is legitimate to the extent that it permits each citizen "to express his objection or veto without let or hindrance."[13] Such a demanding standard of legitimacy may seem an impossible ideal, permitting a lone dissenter to declare well-justified decisions illegitimate. However, I want to show how such a standard can in fact guide a deliberative politics that is based on *public* agreement. The central task for a deliberative theory of democracy is to show how the norm of publicity provides the basis for just those agreements that pass the stringent test Kant envisioned. On my view, reasons backing a political decision are public when they are convincing enough to motivate each citizen, even a dissenter, to continue to cooperate in deliberation even after the decision has been made. For reasons to be of this sort, they must be produced and tested in free and rational deliberation in which citizens have equal standing and effective voice. I call these the *non-tyranny, equality,* and *publicity* conditions.

Any democratic theory must specify some means for forming agreements. No matter how minimal this mechanism may be, it must share some of the common features and constraints of all forms of democracy. Whether they do so through mechanisms that aggregate votes or through active participation, citizens in a democracy freely agree to the rules and goals of their common life. At the very least, these mechanisms for producing agreement must be so constructed that the decisions made through them are not tyrannous (that is, are not dependent on illegitimate coercion or advantage that grants some groups undue influence). Thus, the first qualification on democratic agreements is that they fulfill what James Fishkin calls the "non-tyranny constraint."[14] As a minimal constraint, non-tyranny establishes institutional requirements for constraining the distribution of power and is typically achieved via separation of powers or via legally guaranteed rights. Non-tyranny must be built into the process of deliberation, especially in view of the dangers of majority rule. Non-tyranny has to apply not only to the product but also to the process of deliberation, making it more likely that decisions will be made in light of broadly convincing reasons rather than based on power asymmetries. Non-tyranny ensures that decisions actually reflect the deliberative process, that no group automatically succeeds, and that no group must accept a decision for which it bears an exclusive burden.

Whatever specific deliberative institutions or devices citizens employ to frame decisions, they must embody a further standard: political equality. Certainly, democratic equality is a contested concept, and I shall offer my own account in the next chapter. But regardless of its content, a norm of equality has to be operative in democratic deliberation and decision making. For example, if the decision-making process is defined in terms of discussion and debate, then every citizen must have an equal chance to speak and to employ the full range of expressions available to everyone else; everyone must also have equal access to all relevant arenas for debate and discussion, as well as equal standing and opportunities in the decision-making process. If we define these conditions of standing and access in terms of rights, then all must have the *same* rights; most central to deliberation are rights to equal freedom of expression, conscience, and association. If the process is defined so that voting is its decision procedure, all citizens' votes must be counted equally. In each case, the equality condition governing democracy minimally ensures equal standing and consideration for every citizen. Though the equality condition is often counterfactual, it must be capable of being realized in actual deliberation. Thus, these ideal standards become thresholds or filtering requirements in the design of deliberative institutions. Equality within deliberation must be strong enough to ensure the inclusion of all citizens in deliberation and the exclusion of extra-political or endogenous forms of influence, such as power, wealth, and preexisting social inequalities. For example, equality conditions filter out undue influence, threats, and non-public bargaining.[15]

A related problem for deliberative equality is that participants enter into deliberation with unequal resources, capacities, and social positions. If large enough, such differences could affect outcomes non-democratically, even with formal guarantees of "one person, one vote." Since the main deliberative process I shall defend is dialogical, the appropriate conditions of equality in it concern expanding opportunities and access to deliberative arenas, implementing the sort of dialogue that remains free and open, and establishing threshold requirements necessary for effective voice in making one's reasons count in the course of discussion.

Even though these ideals are demanding enough, equality and non-tyranny are sufficient only to make deliberation minimally democratic. A further condition must be introduced to make it fully democratic: publicity. Like non-tyranny and equality, this condition applies to both the process and the outcome of deliberation and hence has multiple meanings. Publicity applies both to the social space in which deliberation takes place and to the type of reasons offered by citizens in it. We may distinguish a weaker and a stronger sense of publicity. When applied to a contribution to deliberation, publicity means only that speakers' intentions must be avowable in the sense that they could be made known. When applied to the political process, weak publicity requires that any attempt to influence deliberation, such as through side agreements, actually be known to everyone. But, in a stronger sense, publicity is a norm of dialogue ensuring that all speakers can participate effectively in the arena of debate and discussion. Strong publicity applies to the type of reason that could be formed in such an arena or forum, in which all can expect that others will be answerable to them.[16] When decisions are reached, strong and weak publicity can also be applied as a standard by which to judge the quality of an agreement. Agreements have "weak" publicity if they meet certain minimal procedural conditions; they have "strong" publicity if the deliberative process actually shapes the decision and if its justification is in fact known by all citizens. A free press ensures "weak" publicity; well-ordered deliberative bodies form agreements with strong publicity. In any case, publicity admits of degrees, and any democratic mechanism requires strong publicity for decisions to be legitimate.

From Weak to Strong Publicity: Impartiality and the Public Sphere

Whereas equality and non-tyranny refer to the standing of citizens in deliberation, publicity constitutes and governs the social space necessary for democratic deliberation: the public sphere. Publicity works on three levels: it creates the social space for deliberation, it governs processes of deliberation and the reasons produced in them, and it provides a standard by which to judge agreements.[17] In many deliberative situations, what citizens deliberate about is also public in that it concerns matters of the common good or shared features of social life. But it is not the content of the issues that determines their public character, since whether something is a matter for collective concern is itself a deliberative issue. More important is the public character of the reasons addressed to others in deliberation. That is, the reasons offered to convince others must be formulated in such a way that all deliberators can understand and potentially accept them. If this scope of communication cannot be achieved, the issue at hand is not one for public decision making. It is reasonable to assume that some issues and domains of life ought not to be subject to public scrutiny; such a social space for privacy in deliberative democracy serves as a location for individual liberty, but also for experiments in living with self-selecting members. Although the same rights of participation also permit some citizens to refuse to deliberate, privacy does not ensure that the public decisions made in any individual's voluntary absence are not still binding on that individual.

Contract law provides an example of weak, or minimal, publicity: a contract is enforceable only if all its clauses are publicly known. When applied to a polity, weak publicity simply means that the rules governing the political life and the justification of these rules are publicly known, acknowledged, and interpreted. This restriction suggests that even "weak" publicity has broad implications: it requires that only policies or rules that can be publicly known and endorsed be implemented, particularly if these rules and policies will be used in subsequent deliberation. Weak publicity ensures that decisions are at least candidates for acceptance by all and are at least open to deliberative input from all. Weak publicity does not make deliberation strategy-proof, but at least it constrains those strategic moves that are non-avowable.

Ordinary language suggests that publicity can also be a stronger standard. We may require not only that a policy be known to those it affects but also that it be comprehensible to them. In the first place, publicity here denotes a kind of general comprehensibility and intelligibility of the form of communication. Political discussion in large, pluralistic societies cannot succeed in producing cooperation without publicity in this sense. This public is an unrestricted audience, or gallery, comprising all citizens. Here Kant's odd use of the private-public distinction refers to differences in forms of communication in this sense. Kant considers communication "private" when it is directed at a specific and restricted audience.[18] For this reason, appeals to authority or to religious belief are non-public; they are convincing only to those who have accepted such claims already. Political communication on a non-public basis may fail, since the conditions of its success require that its audience be restricted in its beliefs.[19] Contesting such restrictive assumptions makes deliberation public.

Kant proposes the use of public reason as an alternative to the limits of authority. As O'Nora O'Neill puts it: "A communication that presupposes some authority other than that of reason may fail to communicate with those who are not subject to that authority; they can interpret it, if at all, only on the hypothesis of some claim that they reject."[20] Publicity is then a condition for successful communication once we assume that no person or office is authorized to make specific claims. Instead of basing communication upon such restrictive presuppositions, the "public use of reason" addresses "the world at large" and appeals to justifications that anyone may accept. In this way, even the same reason that is at first directed to a restricted audience by appeal to authority could indeed be made a public reason and thus potentially convincing even to those who do not share a particular set of beliefs. Here 'publicity' refers to the pragmatic presuppositions of communication and not its actual audience; a conversation among friends may be just as public as the reasoned inquiry of the scientific community.

"Public" reasons are convincing on this account precisely because they are unrestricted in two senses. First, they are directed to an unrestricted and hence inclusive audience. Such reasons must be formulated not only to be comprehensible to such an audience but also to be testable by them. Second, and more important, such reasons must be convincing in the absence of restrictions in communication between audience and speaker, in the dialogue in which assent and dissent are expressed. The public use of reason in this stronger sense is thus not only dialogical; it is also self-reflective or recursive in any important sense for deliberation. Its use in communication makes it possible to disclose the limitations and restrictions on both reasons and the deliberative process itself. It is in light of this self-reflective character of the public use of reason that Kant argued that publicity and enlightenment are interconnected. The absence of restrictions permits participants in dialogue to be self-critical. When deliberators become suspicious of previously accepted reasons and of the genuinely public character of their communication with one another, they then have new possibilities: they can consider alternative viewpoints and new reasons and thus reject entire forms of justification; or they may become aware of the hidden operation of power, prejudice, and authority in their own communication and beliefs.

As Kant describes public reason, reaching an unrestricted audience requires the capacities for consistent and "enlarged thought" and for "unprejudiced thinking," all of which depend on a capacity "to think from the standpoint of everyone else" and to revise one's judgments accordingly.[21] Each of these "maxims of common human understanding" captures some necessary condition for the public use of reason: that each abstract from his or her point of view and "adopt the viewpoints of all others," or that each "think consistently" in revising shared beliefs in light of new reasons being offered.[22] For all their detail, Kant's maxims lack a clearly public mechanism for such reflection. In Habermas's intersubjective and proceduralist revision of the Kantian publicity, discourse becomes the medium of public deliberation.

By discourse, Habermas means second-order communication about communication; this reflective level of communication takes place in arguments, pragmatically understood as a speaker's making good on a hearer's demand to provide the warrant for a particular claim. It is in the accountability demanded in such second-order communication that speakers are forced to adopt the standards of publicity, as they respond to requests by others to make their contributions at least comprehensible and potentially acceptable. Such intelligibility is required for argumentation, in which the justification of some claim is itself the explicit theme of communication.[23] The weakness of this discursive version of the intersubjective turn in public reason is that Habermas does not go far enough for democratic theory: this shift away from the Kantian version of publicity still attempts to reconstruct the regulative ideals of convergence, unanimity, and impartiality in political terms. In the rest of this section I shall argue against these ideals as presuppositions of public deliberation. Although they may sometimes characterize its outcomes, they are not necessary presuppositions of democratic discussion or public argumentation.

For all its weaknesses and all its formalism, Habermas's discursive account at least gets us started in characterizing what actual public deliberation entails. According to this account, deliberation requires a special form of communication that begins when extant forms of communication and shared understandings are strained or even break down. Moral and political deliberation, in particular, is oriented toward resolving *problematic situations*, such as an unsolved problem in achieving the goals of a practice or an unresolved conflict about the interpretation of a particular goal or norm. In such situations, we cannot simply "go on" as before. On the account I shall develop here, the primary aims of deliberation are to resolve such conflicts and to restore cooperation among actors and coordination of their activities. Instead of his Kantian emphasis on impartial justification, I emphasize Habermas's less formal claim that rationality emerges in such communication, "especially in difficult situations."[24]

Habermas argues that publicity is not anything exceptional in social life but, rather, is one of its pervasive features, built upon the "infrastructure of communication." Actors coordinate their everyday activities via the mechanisms of communication, by accepting or rejecting offers or claims made in speech. These "validity claims" entail obligations that make the acceptance of a speech act binding. According to this type of analysis of speech acts, speakers and hearers establish mutual expectations for future interaction by offering or by accepting a promise. The basis for the binding character of such obligations is the expectation that speakers will be able to bring forth reasons that "warrant" their speech acts and redeem their claims when called upon by others to do so. When communication breaks down, this supposition must actually be redeemed if interaction is to be restored. Discourse is thus a social mechanism for coordinating action, and the distinction among types of discourse forms "the frame or categorical scaffolding that serves to order problematic situations" that need to be agreed upon explicitly.[25] Various forms of argumentation deal with standard and recurring problems and gradually specialize into institutions such as law and science. But such specialized and cumulative forms are not the proper model for deliberation in problematic situations; they are also ongoing forms of communication which also break down in new problematic situations and whose practices and norms can be challenged. Thus, the routinization and standardization of acceptable reasons in specialized discourses do not exhaust the potential of the public sphere's issues and problem-solving mechanisms; such discourses must still be made public and thus cannot be the paradigmatic case of resolving problematic situations by public reason.

In order to overcome this weakness, we must distinguish between two forms of second-order or reflective communication: discourse and dialogue. In specialized argumentation, speakers may develop generalized accounts of how certain claims may be warranted. In ordinary deliberation, by contrast, various claims are often mixed together so that it is difficult to tell in advance what *type* of reason will be convincing in any particular situation. Public deliberation at this level is dialogical rather than discursive in the strict sense. It emerges whenever second-order communication, the exchange and testing of reasons, is needed to resolve atypical and non-standard problematic situations or breakdowns of coordination; but usually there is no well-established means for resolving such problems, or these means themselves are called into question. The conditions for the activity of dialogue are more important than argumentation *per se* to understanding how public reasons are convincing under such circumstances. Argumentation is deliberative only when it is dialogical, in the give and take of arguments among speakers.

Before going on to these differences, I shall first describe what my account shares with Habermas's discursive model of deliberation. After describing deliberation as a dialogical, joint activity, I shall criticize the two other dominant models of deliberation: proceduralism and precommitment. Although my model owes much to Habermas's conception of communicative rationality, his account of publicity demands too much from discursive forms of justification and impartiality. The current models of deliberation are based on restrictive and inadequate conceptions of publicity, and none of them can capture the full range of problems of *actual* deliberation in complex societies.

However, I will also show that each of them captures one aspect of an adequate notion of publicity. From Habermas it is the generalization of structures of communication, the understanding of deliberation as joint activity from precommitment models; from proceduralism it is the specification of fair terms of participation in which everyone has equal standing. All these models demand the presence of a well-functioning public sphere as the social location of deliberative activity.

Rather than simply providing generalized maxims of public judgment, Habermas makes explicit the way in which the general and unavoidable structure of communication becomes the basis of public discourse. On this view, publicity refers "neither to the function nor to the contents of everyday communication but to the social space that it generates."[26] The linguistically constituted space of interaction under such communicative presuppositions can be extended to a variety of contexts, including writing and other media. In every case, a communication is public to the extent to which it abstracts from the spatial and indexical features of face-to-face interaction. Through the extending of ordinary communication, new temporal dimensions of deliberation emerge. The medium of writing permits just such a temporal extension, which Habermas shows to be crucial to the creation of the early modern public sphere. The temporal delay between an audience's reception and its response enables deliberation to create a different kind of audience: a non-simultaneous public of readers and critics. Taken together, all such extended and decontextualized forms of communication can be generalized into a "public sphere" that is open to an unlimited audience of communication.[27] The public sphere provides the practical implementation that a radical democratic theory often lacks; for democratic control over complex institutions, deliberation requires a spatially and temporally extended form of publicity.

The generalization of communication in the public sphere has two practical effects. The generalization beyond specific contexts and beyond the personal characteristics of speakers produces both greater abstractness and ambiguity. On the one hand, this generalization reduces the influence of "private" features of communication, such as the authority of individual speakers. On the other hand, it increases demands for constant interpretation and explication, producing less culturally specific vocabularies and dispersing widely shared specialized vocabularies. The contextual presuppositions of ordinary coordination in naive communication are often suspended when deliberation takes place in the public sphere, permitting a space for the reflective forms of communication that public deliberation requires.

The conception of the public sphere helps to explicate the conditions of democratic deliberation. It also suggests a narrowly Kantian interpretation of the nature of decontextualized, public communication. Neo-Kantian accounts of public deliberation, such as those proposed by Habermas and Rawls, are overly rationalistic in two ways. First, Kantian cognitivism ties the rationality of public communication specifically to argumentation—to the logic of specialized discourses that make reasons of a particular type convincing in specific domains. On these assumptions, the generalization and the abstraction that occur in the public sphere invariably point toward formal and specialized forms of discourse, rather than toward a deliberative notion of political debate among citizens with diverse and even conflicting viewpoints and standards. However, public debate need not be specialized in this sense, especially if it is to be inclusive. Natural science provides a good example of specialized argumentation; its aims seem to demand more agreement among participants than do other practices, at least at the level of shared background beliefs in the form of entrenched theories. Impartiality in political debate does not provide an analogous set of strong constraints; it is only one of many considerations that may make a reason publicly convincing.

Because of the variety of possible problematic situations to be resolved, the use of public reason in politics cannot be limited to a single type of knowledge or to a single set of reasons. Rather, it should include a variety of possible public reasons, including pragmatic goals, considerations of justice, and cultural self-understandings. Excluding whole types of reasons from political discussion for epistemic reasons would violate political equality. Such exclusions could filter out reasonable objections and make it more difficult for those citizens who wish to challenge the currently accepted practices and views. Rather than serving as a model for public deliberation, specialized discourses are better seen as restricted to formal institutions, such as court proceedings. In such cases, procedural rules can limit the public use of reason by directing participants to very specific types of reasons; formal court proceedings, for example, may be guided by strict rules of evidence to protect the rights of the vulnerable. Other attempts to limit political discourse through formal constraints introduce needlessly limiting and highly artificial "conversational" constraints, including restrictions on the information and topics favored by some recent forms of liberalism.[28]

The second, and deeper, problem concerns impartiality as a requirement for public reasons. Impartiality is not identical with publicity. For example, expressive communication can be publicly convincing without being impartial in the strict sense; my needs remain mine even if they are publicly comprehensible. As in the case of proceduralist considerations for equal opportunity, impartiality is not always the most salient feature of public deliberation on conflicting demands. As Scanlon shows, urgency may take precedence in time-indexed decisions when claims are otherwise equal.[29] The decision to give priority to urgent claims over other considerations (such as efficiency) is a decision to be made in deliberation, one that cannot be settled by formal or impartial considerations alone.

Why do more Kantian democratic theorists give priority to impartiality? Here again, it is because formal institutions are a misleading model for unconstrained public reason. In such institutions, impartiality works as a filtering mechanism—most importantly as a constraint on adjudication. Judges supposedly make decisions under special constraints of coherence and completeness, motivated by the constraints of making the reasons for their decisions public as well as by the coherence constraints of precedent. But judicial decisions are a special case and ought not to be generalized into the model for all public deliberation.[30] Habermas takes adjudication as his model when he discusses what makes a reason publicly convincing: it is impartiality, he claims, that "lends reasons their consensus producing force."[31] Otherwise, Habermas believes, differently situated agents are not convinced for the *same* reasons, and hence no consensus is actually reached. This strict requirement of consensus does not apply to public deliberation any more than a particular interpretation of impartiality or of the liberal separation of the right and the good.[32]

As in most liberal versions of deliberative democracy, Habermas unnecessarily narrows the range of convincing reasons in ways that are especially problematic for vibrant political deliberation in pluralistic societies. Public reasons are not always convincing simply because they are impartial; moreover, discussions about what counts as strict impartiality may be difficult to resolve in circumstances of cultural diversity and social inequality. There is also no telling in advance of deliberation just what standard of impartiality can be achieved or how best to constrain strategic partiality. Moreover, some reasons may convince conflicting parties because they are sufficiently abstract and vague, not because of their impartial qualities; other reasons may be convincing only when they reflect the shared experiences of the parties in deliberation. Most of all, impartiality is only one of the many types of reasons that are convincing under conditions of publicity.

As an alternative to explicating the convincing character of public reasons by impartiality, I propose a less restrictive (and ultimately less singular) conception of strong publicity: publicity does not consist of the full knowledge of all relevant reasons and interests; rather, it is the particular way in which reasons are offered so that they can be communicated to others and elicit answers from them. To offer a reason is to call for a response from others; if the potential audience of this response is unrestricted and general, both the reason and the audience to which it is directed may be called "public." A "public" in this sense is to be distinguished from a "collective," since generalized communication does not require any specific set of identical or shared first-order beliefs or values (although they do make conflicts more readily resolvable). The public sphere does not require a collective consciousness or even a community, although both may emerge out of public practices. However, in order to sustain such a public sphere and such a process of reflection over time—one that is not merely episodic or evanescent in communicative interaction—requires some common framework. Such a framework of formal and informal conventions, ongoing agreements, and explicit laws makes possible continued and sustained public deliberation. This framework must itself be warranted by public reasons, and central to this form of reflexive public justification is that the framework enable deliberation itself. To do so, the framework must constantly be open to new reasons and revisions.

In this section I have developed the dialogical conception of publicity at work in deliberative democracy and contrasted it with specialized discourses (such as science and law) and with liberal ideas of neutrality and impartiality. Before turning to the details of my dialogical account of deliberation (the main aim of which is to explain why reasons can become convincing as public reasons), let me briefly consider two alternative models of deliberation that have some proponents among deliberative theorists: precommitment and pure proceduralism. Precommitment models describe the rationality of deliberative processes in terms of their being governed by irrevocable constraints (usually embodied in constitutional "rights"); ideal proceduralist models see procedural rules and constraints by themselves as sufficient for the rationality of deliberation. I shall argue that these models presuppose sameness of belief and desires in ways that make them inappropriate for ongoing political debate. Neither can, in principle, give an adequate account of the process by which the framework of deliberation is revised. Finally, I shall illustrate the practical superiority of my dialogical model for the problems posed by what Martha Minnow calls "the dilemmas of difference"—dilemmas that require us to think about deliberation in new ways.[33]

Alternative Models of Deliberation: Joint Activity versus Proceduralism and Precommitment

Precommitment models regard the rules of democratic self-government as a strategy for achieving social cooperation, i.e., as self-limiting or self-restraining behavior. Such strategies are needed to produce stable cooperation among factional and self-interested creatures, whether human beings or Kant's "race of devils." In politics, constitutions or charters may be considered prior agreements to irrevocable constraints: just as Ulysses tied himself to the mast to avoid the calls of the Sirens, so, too, citizens constrain themselves through their constitutions to avoid conflicts.[34] As Jon Elster puts it, "societies as well as individuals have found it useful to bind themselves, e.g., through a constitution"[35] in order to solve problems of their imperfect rationality and weakness of will. Samuel Freeman construes the agreement reached in Rawls's original position similarly as "a joint precommitment to certain principles,"[36] which then become an "irrevocable" public basis for justification. In a more deliberative vein,

Elster argues that engaging in dialogue at all involves "a precommit-ment to a rational decision."[37]

The analogy between precommitments and constitutions raises two problems. How is it that such agreements could be reached in the first place? Even if established, how much of a role could strict pre-commitments play in ongoing social life? The agreement to such commitments would itself have to be unanimous and thus depend on a rather strong consensus about the goals of political life. Thus, Freeman regards such agreements as appealing to a "shared social in-terest," in that "each individual desires the same object, a background of social institutions."[38] On the basis of this shared desire, Freeman sees democratic governance as a "joint undertaking where each is held by others to his decision, thereby ensuring the perpetuity and ir-revocability of the principles agreed to."[39]

Although my view of deliberation shares with proceduralist models an emphasis on the conditions of communication in the public sphere, it shares with precommitment models an emphasis on politics as a "joint undertaking." Indeed, the general conditions for both public communication and joint deliberative activity must be constitutionally secured. However, on the assumptions of the precommitment model, the joint activity of politics is based on second-order strategic behav-ior rather than on a certain type of public dialogue and planning. Although both can bind future common actions, they do so in im-portantly different ways, making dialogue typical of the planning of joint activities of which precommitment is a special case. In this case, the joint activity works only to the extent that the commitment is ir-revocable, and it is irrevocable to the extent that compliance ensures the mutual benefit.

It is difficult to imagine that those who are currently disadvan-taged in such an activity will want to continue any such arrangement, unless stability is an overriding value. As in impartiality, precommit-ment stands or falls on the strong assumption that all citizens have the same desire for the same object, and that they share the goal of having some institutional background for politics. Surely the desire for a shared political life depends on the agents' conceptions and hence cannot be assumed to be identical among all deliberators.[40] Even if citizens have identical desires, these desires may change once

they begin to deliberate about institutions and their general principles. If the required precommitments are too specific, many citizens
will not cooperate in deliberation; if the commitments are too general, they will not be a basis on which conflicts may be avoided and
strategic behavior limited. The basic problem is that joint precommitments work only if they set up an enforcement mechanism for
holding others to their commitments.[41] Given that non-tyranny requires that citizens be the enforcers of their own commitments, the
original problem simply repeats itself in cases of conflict with those
who find the original agreement unacceptable. The special cases in
which precommitments can be made effective cannot be generalized
to all democratic deliberation. The sole argument for them—that
they are the only way to fulfill the different desires for a shared political life—is hard to establish empirically.

Precommitments are also insufficient to take into account the dynamic and recursive qualities of deliberation in which citizens acquire more commitments and revise others. But most of all,
precommitments of this sort depend on an identity of beliefs and
desires that is an unnecessarily strong political assumption. In view of
this fact, it would be hard to see why precommitment is necessary in
the first place. It may be true that some laws function as precommitments, as when industries are prohibited from making fluorocarbons.
But precommitments do not help settle either conflicts of interest or
disputes about principles that occur when people have sufficiently different beliefs and desires. The belief in the finality of constitutional
essentials also simply ignores their constant dialogical respecification
and renegotiation in all currently existing forms of democracy.

These revisions may be only substantive, leaving the procedural
framework intact, exactly as the joint precommitment requires.
However, this does not accord with the facts of stable democratic
practice. According to Bruce Ackerman, this sort of revision of constitutional essentials is a constant feature of American history: constitutional revisions in Reconstruction and the New Deal "were creative
procedurally no less than substantively."[42] Besides the interpretation
of particular civil rights' being expanded in the former and property
rights' being narrowed in the latter, the revision process itself was altered to give more power to national-level institutions over the states.

The Federalist doctrine of the separation of powers changed in comparable ways, shifting from the earlier division of powers between nation and state to a separation of powers within the institutions of national government. Similar revisions of constitutional essentials, and not the gradual recognition of some precommitment in the Constitution, also characterize the more recent civil rights movement. In order to remain democratic, even a stable constitutional democracy must be capable of revising existing commitments and creating a new institutional framework in times of crisis. In different periods, different branches of government have been more responsive to the public voice than others and thereby have acquired more political power—enough so that Ackerman can call them different "constitutional regimes."[43] This dynamism is necessary to keep democratic institutions rooted in the needs and the public will of the citizens, which previous regimes frustrated and left unfulfilled.

At best, precommitments are specific devices that may take some issues off the public agenda for brief periods. As such, they are sometimes democratic and sometimes not: they can protect minorities and their rights, but they can also entrench majorities and their power over minorities. Judging precommitments requires some independent criteria, and it seems unwise to make them immune from revision. If constitutions are meant to be precommitment devices, they are rather badly designed for that purpose. It is better to see them as providing ordinary commitments of planning and its constraints on future action than as establishing irrevocable decisions.[44] Just as the plans of individual agents help them coordinate their many desires and goals as new situations and contingencies arise, constitutions embody future-oriented intentions, plans, and norms that help to coordinate the open-ended joint activity of deliberation.

Procedural models do not have the twin problems of postulating the unanimity of desires and the interpretive finality of norms that plague precommitments. As opposed to such commitments, procedures can pass deliberative and self-referential tests, and they can be reflexively revised to promote better and more successful deliberation. Proceduralist theories are also neither instrumentalist nor strategic; they are oriented to fairness rather than to specific types of results or outcomes. Rather than as precommitment devices, proceduralists

view constitutions as specifying well-defined social decision procedures, i.e., "a set of rules that describes an institutional mechanism
through which decisions are actually made."[45] But the very formal
character of procedures makes them open to objections similar to the
ones I raised against the precommitment model: procedures are not
self-justifying and need to be applied in further deliberation.
Whenever they are interpreted and applied, procedures still need a
point, and that point is deliberation. They promote deliberation only
if its basic character can be independently specified apart from the
procedures. Formal procedures are self-referentially justified only if
they make deliberation more public; otherwise, merely following a
procedure, no matter how fair, will not influence the quality of the
agreement reached or the reasons that support it.

Proceduralist justifications of democracy have a further shortcoming, one that makes them overemphasize constitutional issues: they
confuse public justification with the design of institutions that enable discourse and deliberation to take place. I have already argued
that the reasonableness of a procedure does not always provide a
convincing reason for endorsing any particular decision.[46] Rather
than provide the basis for public justification, procedures make explicit some conditions of democratic deliberation, such as instituting constraints on preexisting social inequalities. Procedural
considerations, however, do not always illuminate the ways in which
advantaged citizens can exploit fair democratic arrangements, nor
can they illuminate why disadvantaged groups ought to continue to
cooperate (unless supplemented with an account of public deliberation as a joint activity in which everyone reasonably expects to influence outcomes). Since they must be interpreted anew in each
deliberation situation, procedures are too underdetermining to guide
the deliberative practice of their application. Merely appealing to
rules or procedures is hardly sufficient, because the task of deliberation is to apply these norms to new situations and contexts.

Let me now turn to an example that illustrates both my criticisms
of these other views and the advantages of a more dynamic and dialogical deliberation. Perhaps the best illustration of the differences between a joint-activity model of actual deliberation and proceduralist
and precommitment models is one that I have already alluded to:

the role of public deliberation in developing and expanding constitutionally protected rights since the New Deal. In the 1930s, in conjunction with the development of new protections and entitlements for workers, Congress passed new laws to solve social conflicts that were irresolvable under the laissez faire interpretation of property rights. In 1937, after a period of great resistance, the Supreme Court justices appointed by President Franklin Roosevelt upheld these protections and overturned precedents long held to be irrevocable and immune from government intervention and regulation. Before the New Deal, the property-oriented understanding of constitutional liberties made them the legal tools for keeping many inequalities off the public agenda, including associative rights of workers to organize into unions. In the infamous *Lochner* decision, the Court repudiated a 1905 law that attempted to "limit" working hours to 60 hours a week.

How did this understanding of rights and procedures change? The experience of the Depression changed the public understanding of such rights. These changes also led legislators to refashion the institutional framework of government and to effectively abandon the cumbersome and easily subverted federalist process as the only way for the body of citizens to voice their demands for constitutional revision.[47] The New Deal also ended a certain understanding of the rule of law by gradually extending rights beyond merely formal ideals of equality and by introducing corrective ideals of political equality. Indeed, corrective amendments to the Constitution emerged out of the lived experience of the Civil War and Reconstruction; in the New Deal, working-class and poor citizens "sought to avail themselves of the amendment," to generalize its protections out of their original experiential contexts.[48] Similar problematic situations led other groups to challenge narrow interpretations of various procedural opportunities and civil rights, to the extent that they presupposed inequalities of gender and race in the identity of citizens; these changes led to different welfare and employment practices through the increased inclusion of people adversely affected by the previous deliberative framework and agenda. In these cases deliberation substantially enriched the content of basic political conceptions of rights and protections precisely because existing procedural opportunities open to all did not serve the purpose of bringing about equal consideration of the concerns of all citizens in the political process.

I shall now turn to a non-Kantian account of the deliberative process and of how it can produce convincing public reasons even in the absence of specialized argumentation, unanimity, and impartiality. It is hard to see how these strict normative requirements can be made consistent with the principles of a working democracy. I shall argue that deliberation demands a unique form of cooperative activity that can continue even when there is conflict. It requires neither the unanimous agreement of all nor some aggregative agreement of each, but a distributive ideal of agreement that accords to each his own motivation for cooperating in processes of public judgment. A dialogical account of deliberation best captures the ongoing process of reinterpreting norms and procedures in light of new experiences and problematic situations.

The Dialogical Process of Public Deliberation

In what sense is democratic cooperation rational? Broadly defined, rationality in this context concerns not the content of beliefs but "how actors use and acquire knowledge."[49] This definition implies that social practices are rational to the extent that they promote the acquisition and the use of knowledge. Various democratic theorists have tried to identify one or another feature of political discourses or institutions as the core of the rationality of democratic practices, often on the model of public justification in science, law, or morality; however, political deliberation is more complex than this description of their rationality indicates. Deliberative politics has no single domain; it includes such diverse activities as formulating and achieving collective goals, making policy decisions about means and ends, resolving conflicts of interest and principle, and solving problems as they emerge in ongoing social life.[50] Public deliberation therefore has to take many forms. Still, these activities are democratic to the extent that they are consistent with equality, non-tyranny, and publicity.

The diversity of the political domain makes the starting point of legitimacy quite broad: decisions need only be justified by some public reason. Deliberation is generally about solving typical problems with the resources available to political institutions. Proceduralism is correct in that publicity cannot be a determinate criterion for specific decisions. When initiated in problematic situations, deliberation assumes that social life is ongoing and sometimes fragile. Rather than form a new consensus whenever coordination breaks down, it is better to see public deliberation as itself a joint, cooperative form of social action. This shift to cooperative action as the proper model for deliberation not only makes sense of how political problems are actually solved, if they can be; it also makes better sense of the requirements for the political agreements that emerge in complex and diverse societies. Rather than being another appeal to practices as the basis of shared agreements, deliberation depends on a different aspect of social action: the accountability of intelligible action to others and the reflexive ability of actors to continue cooperation by extending accountability to all actors and to new situations.[51]

When extended beyond routine contexts, public accountability is measured in terms of its ongoing practical accomplishments. Even in everyday life, accountability is demanded in situations where expectations and coordination have broken down. When someone we know refuses to return a greeting, we may demand a justification if the possibility of future interaction is to be repaired. This ongoing accomplishment can become reflexive and recursive in public deliberation, which also has its particular sort of expectations and forms of accountability. A public utterance must be intelligible and answerable to the objections of others; if it is not, actors may lose their public standing as accountable to an indefinite audience. The public space closes.

Deliberative accountability can be linked to any number of complex coordinating mechanisms, such as those in formal institutional settings that extend the potential for being answerable to others to contexts broader than face-to-face interaction. The process of public deliberation brings together two social capacities that are crucial to establishing cooperation: the ongoing accountability of actors in problematic situations and the actors' capacity to engage in the generalized communication of the public sphere. At a minimum, public accountability demands a political public sphere in all institutions in which policies become answerable to the public.

Mutual expectations and accountability work in two distinct ways in everyday social actions: not only as bases for coordinating action but also as means for challenging and sanctioning other actors when such coordination breaks down. It is precisely such a framework of expectations (and not just the structure of communication) that public deliberation reflexively generalizes out of specific contexts to new problematic situations. The practice of public deliberation creates a new reflexive and recursive basis for general expectations, often made explicit in the charters of associations in the form of rules of order and (most important) in constitutions, with their procedures, rights, and divisions of powers. Such practice is recursive to the extent that its framework can be used to change the practices of accountability. A constitution's rules and rights are themselves available for renegotiation and reinterpretation in ongoing social life; adequate deliberation requires such a common public framework with planned recursive properties sufficient to make it open, accessible, and dynamic.[52] We may include here all practices of revising democratic decisions, such as judicial review and legislative change. But, most of all, revision begins with mutual demands for the accountability of actors in the public sphere.

In view of these general properties of a reflexive framework of public accountability, it is possible to specify how reasons offered in deliberation become convincing and effectively repair a problematic situation. As a joint activity, deliberation produces outcomes in a non-aggregative way. Even if this activity itself were to be analyzed once again as requiring the same "we intention" of each actor, it would leave unclear whether this intention could be accomplished.[53] As an alternative to both collectivist and individualist analyses, John Searle and others have proposed an alternative account of cooperative activity that is both intersubjective and public.[54] Public deliberation is one of the many cooperative activities that demands a plural rather than a collective or an individual agent or subject. One cannot perform it by oneself, since individual deliberation has a different structure; nor is it necessarily performed only by a unanimous group. Joint activities are performed only by plural subjects, consisting of autonomous individuals. Much like game playing, public deliberation is structured in such a way that each of a plurality of distinct actors cooperates by responding to and influencing the others.

The goal of public deliberation is to solve a problem together with others who have distinct perspectives and interests, a process that must begin with a shared definition of the problem. This sort of highly contested activity requires the constraints of regularized historical practices, which may be loosely organized in implicit conventions or tightly organized by formal rules. Within these settings, actors engage in problem-solving activities that they could not do alone. Electing a president or passing some legislation is much like playing in a jazz trio or building an automobile in a factory: one's specific intention is only a part of the larger outcome of a shared activity that is not entirely within any individual's control. As any listener of jazz can attest, such shared and improvised activity easily fails for lack of coordination. When it succeeds, deliberation produces a shared intention that is acceptable to a plurality of the agents who participate in the activity of forming it. In deliberative democracy, voting could be regarded by citizens as a method for forming joint intentions.

In such cases, shared intentions can be explained as a parts-whole relation in which the means are individual but the goal is defined by the interaction of the group. The outcome, if public, may be "subjectless," as Habermas has put it, in the sense that it does not accord with anyone's particular beliefs or desires.[55] Each among a plurality of deliberating agents can accept such a goal or outcome to the extent that he can recognize his own intentions as part of the deliberative activity, even if it is not directly a part of its specific outcome. Like a good jazz trio, deliberation succeeds only when each individual maintains his or her distinctiveness and the group its plurality; cohesion is only a by-product of each person's distinctive contribution.

But the analogy between deliberation and joint social actions is not a perfect one. Not all such actions have the special reflexive features of public deliberation. These features are specific to dialogical communication. Unlike a joint activity that is engaged in to achieve some collective goal, the success of a dialogue cannot always be specified in a means-ends way. The outcomes of a dialogue are often unforeseeable from the perspective of any particular actor. Even if a dialogue is supposed to produce an agreement, it cannot easily be predicted how or when such agreement will be produced. Heightening a conflict sometimes helps to resolve it; sharp and clear disagreements may actually promote deliberation better than premature attempts at consensus. These considerations show that cooperative instrumental activities "presuppose community"[56] whereas dialogue does not. Nor can we predict in advance of the dialogue the content of "the kind of reasons we are prepared to recognize" as legitimate, other than that they are public.[57] Public reasons simply continue the cooperative dialogue.[58]

Dialogical Mechanisms in Public Deliberation

Dialogue is a particular joint action with the special characteristics necessary for deliberation. We cannot engage in it by ourselves, and our particular contributions form a part of a whole that we cannot determine or fully direct. Often dialogue is a means to an end, as when I convince you through dialogue to give me a ride home; but it need not have some external purpose or intended result. Very often it takes place on the background of shared values and beliefs, but it also serves to sharpen disagreements about them. It can produce insight, understanding, or even love, but it can also fail and produce the very opposite.

Public deliberation is dialogue with a particular goal. It attempts to overcome a problematic situation by solving a problem or resolving a conflict. The joint activity through which deliberation takes place within the public sphere is dialogical and not merely discursive. Discourses employ specific regulative standards of justification, and they are typically structured toward one sort of claim or another. For example, scientific discourses are oriented toward claims of truth, whereas legal discourses are constrained by the arguments and claims that are consistent with the body of law. By contrast, dialogue is the mere give and take of reasons. It does not necessarily aim to produce well-justified claims; rather, it aims to produce claims that are wide enough in scope and sufficiently justified to be accountable to an indefinite public of fellow citizens.

Discourse takes place in actual dialogue. Nonetheless, discourse and dialogue must be distinguished along several dimensions. Such distinctions separate my dialogical view from Habermas's discursive account of deliberative politics. First, deliberation is dialogical, because it does not suspend the constraints of action. It works when a plurality of agents who act together try to convince one another to coordinate their activities in particular ways. Second, discourse is more demanding than dialogue; as second-order communication, it presupposes idealizations, most of which presuppose unanimous agreement on basic rules and standards of rational justification.[59] Third, discourses are open only in principle, since the presuppositions necessary for active participation may be quite high. Dialogue does not require specific epistemic expertise and is open to all citizens who wish to shape the outcome of deliberation.

Discourse and dialogue do have features in common. First, justification is at stake in each. In dialogue, however, what is crucial to justification is that it be convincing to others, who incorporate this proffered reason and respond to it in subsequent interaction. Second, each form of communication takes up agents' reasons. Nonetheless, dialogues are not constrained in the same way that discourses are: there is an exchange of reasons back and forth, and sometimes these reasons conflict. This back-and-forth exchange of reasons can ramify beyond the initial opposition in each speaker's response. At the same time, dialogue always must be maintained by each speaker's being accountable to others for his or her contributions.

In dialogue there is movement. Each speaker incorporates and reinterprets the other's contributions in his or her own. After a sufficient length of time, speakers begin to use expressions that they did not employ before; the process of trying to convince others may alter not only one's own mode of expression but also the reasons one finds convincing. One often hears oneself say things when made accountable to other specific actors that one might not have endorsed otherwise. This back-and-forth movement is part of the more general process of interpretation, as when we propose interpretations of a text and revise them through further readings of the text.[60] Novel reinterpretations signify the success of a dialogue, measured in the uptake of other points of view and reasons into speakers' own interpretations of the ongoing course of discussion.[61] Following J. L. Austin, I shall call this process "securing uptake" in dialogue.

But political deliberation is not just the mutual interpretation of one another's contributions. It takes place within a framework of accountable social interaction that is reflexively called into question as it is being used. Various equilibrium models, including Rawlsian reflective equilibrium and the Piagetian concept of learning, have been proposed to capture this dynamic process of reflection and revision. The important feature that these models capture is that the deliberative situation is dynamic and open ended. Resolutions of problematic situations can become relatively permanent when new or revised institutions emerge from successful problem solving and coordination of action,[62] but at the level of the analysis of public deliberation we need not presuppose that formal institutions already exist or that the deliberative situation will always produce some equilibrium point toward which interests and reasons converge. Various dialogical mechanisms at work in public deliberation are not always concerned with restoring equilibrium and with balancing reasons as much as they are with revising the common understandings that are operative in ongoing cooperative activity.

Here I can only provide an open-ended list of such mechanisms for restoring ongoing joint activity. My list of five such mechanisms does not exhaust the possibilities of public deliberation based on the process of giving reasons and answering others in dialogue. The common thread to all these mechanisms is that they produce "deliberative uptake" among all participants in deliberation—that is, they promote deliberation on reasons addressed to others, who are expected to respond to them in dialogue. This uptake is directly expressed in the interaction of dialogue, in give and take of various sorts.

(1) Rawls's conception of reflective equilibrium provides a model for the first type of dialogical mechanism: speakers work to make *explicit* what is *latent* in their common understandings, shared intuitions and ongoing activities. By plumbing the depths of their common understandings, agents employ "shared notions and principles" that are thought to be part of "public culture."[63] The movement of exchanging and disputing interpretations of this common culture can make these principles explicit, often in novel ways. In order to meet the threshold requirements of public deliberation, however, a purely hermeneutic description of this process must be modified. Not just any continuation of the normative framework of deliberation is democratic. As opposed to the tradition-guided model of interpreting the content of shared assumptions, here the questioner (and thus the dissenter) has priority in demanding justifications for ongoing

practices and interpretations. The epistemic gain here is that reasons backed by tradition can become less convincing when made explicit, especially if they are purported to be natural. Formulating such reasons with sufficient detail is often enough to reveal the arbitrary and conventional character of the justification. But most of all, making reasons explicit requires answering the specific objections of the dissenter; if they cannot be answered, they fail to meet the tests of publicity. Dialogues of this sort can work the other way, too. Disputes about different interests can be resolved when the solution is shown to be part of a larger context of principles, such as those that make explicit the demands of political equality. For example, shifting dialogues about interests and values to the level of principle may persuade currently advantaged members to take on burdens that their principles require. When such dialogical mechanisms are employed, deliberation comes to an end once the partners in the dialogue have explicated their common understandings sufficiently to see some mutually intelligible answer to their problems. This dialogical mechanism is appropriate when there is already a large degree of consensus, when there are shared values, and when there is little social inequality. In these cases, moving from an implicit and unformulated level of general agreement to an explicit one is likely to produce publicly convincing reasons. This is perhaps the most common sort of deliberation within established institutions with explicit charters and constitutions and a long history of their interpretation. The contribution of such explicit formulations is that they provide a new ongoing framework for interpretation, reestablished at a sufficient depth of common commitment or at a higher level of abstract principle (to use the most common metaphors that describe how these mechanisms work). Interpretive mechanisms work best within an already-accepted framework, such as a legal tradition, which can then be modified by new interpretations.

(2) Perhaps one of the most common dialogical mechanisms not dependent on shared values and commitments is back-and-forth exchanges around differences in biographical and collective historical experiences. Different biographical experiences may reveal the limits and the perspectival character of the understandings shared by many

in the political community. Such discrepancies are particularly important in the interpretation of needs, where the instances of norms are usually identified with prototypical members of the groups of a polity, including race, gender, or class features. Such prototypes operate in the routine interpretations of institutional actors. This dialogical mechanism involves more than simply hearing someone's confessional discourse or listening to someone's self-expression: in these cases uptake is minimal and dependent upon the listener's own capacities for empathy or identification. Rather, through the give and take of dialogue the limits of the hearer's understandings become clear as the dialogue shifts between the experiences of the life histories of individuals or groups and the current framework of understandings and norms. The outcome creates new categories or expands old ones in order to incorporate these life histories and their new experiences. For example, it is precisely through a deliberative process of this sort that the biased and normalizing assumptions of the welfare state have become clear. A "normal" household is assumed in the law, particularly in terms of how economic needs are interpreted. The same can be said for time schedules and day care provisions in the "normal" workplace. The feminist movement has challenged such assumptions by articulating their full implications along with a broader alternative framework. Consciousness-raising groups deliberate in the same way, as do social movements that struggle over need interpretations.[64] These dialogical mechanisms are appropriate for building solidarity and mutual recognition. Though not a means of solving problems, they create the conditions necessary to resolve disputes about personal and cultural identity, as in the cases of racism and sexism. Their success can be measured in terms of opening up space for deliberation about a broader range of identities and experiences.

(3) Public deliberation often concerns how to apply a given norm or principle to a particular case. The dialogical mechanism typically used in policy issues of this sort is the give and take between a general norm and its concrete specification. Such deliberation has the general structure of what Klaus Günther has called "discourses of application."[65] Such discourses do not aim at the justification of some

general norm, but at its proper use in particular conflicts or in new social situations. Such a dialogue might, for example, be concerned with whether it is proper to define a problematic situation as a violation of a civil right. The back-and-forth dialogue between members of the group and representatives of the institution will concern how to define the situation relative to some general norm (here a right) and the relevant respects that make the norm applicable. This dialogue also takes the form of a dialectic between institutional norms and social reality in which citizens compare justifiable rights claims with factual inequalities. In cases of complex norms, such as the legal norm "treat like cases equally and unlike cases unequally," specifying the relevant features of a situation becomes the issue, as when different speakers offer ways in which it is like and unlike other accepted interpretations. Henry Richardson argues that this greater specification of an abstract and general norm often returns to the "rational motivation" for adopting the norm in the first place.[66] The "fact of the matter" about such motivation is not necessarily decisive; rather, a particular application becomes convincing only relative to the alternatives that come up in the dialogical exchange and comparisons among various possible specifications of the norm. The deliberative process here articulates alternative descriptions of the situation and is convincing relative to the appropriateness of that description. Owing to the reflective character of dialogues of this sort, the original norm can also acquire new relevant features. These dialogical mechanisms are appropriate when disputes continue even after shifting to the level of abstract principles; here what makes some solutions more acceptable than others is tied to judgments about descriptions of the situation.

(4) Another set of dialogical mechanisms related to the application of social norms could, following Charles Taylor, be called "articulation."[67] Here the dialectic is between a vague and abstract ideal and various proposals to make it richer and more comprehensive. It is not the specification of a norm that is at issue, but making its content richer and more complex. The way in which articulation can resolve conflicts also shows how it differs from the mechanisms of reflective equilibrium. Articulation can resolve conflicts by incorporating the

opposing claims as component parts of a more elaborate proposal. This process not only modifies a framework but can also create new ones. Dewey often thinks of deliberation on this model as a dialectic of preservation and modification, and he employs deliberately Hegelian language in discussing it. Deliberation here attempts to articulate either the means or the goal of an action in such a way that all conflicting values and perspective are considered. This transforms "the original form" of the ideal, making it possible to fulfill it in a "sublimated fashion."[68] The practical reasoning that occurs in dialogues of this type aims at preserving the original goals of actors while modifying them by making them parts of a larger whole. Often what we take to be compromises are actually "sublimated" articulations of conflicts. Such dialogical mechanisms may produce solutions to conflicts by articulating greater complexity and differentiation of social spheres in which various universal principles apply; different spheres of choice may preserve liberty and privacy along with publicity. Sometimes the new articulation of the norm is actually more vague and abstract in order to encompass the new complex situations. Political conflicts such as those between the principles of liberty and equality certainly present this kind of public problem. In such cases, deliberators attempt to solve the problem at a higher level of articulation at which the conflict is no longer apparent or is embedded in larger social contexts. Michael Walzer calls these solutions the "art of separation," the artful employment of distinctions of social spheres and domains of value.[69]

(5) Some dialogical mechanisms employ the capacities for perspective taking and role taking implicit in communication—capacities for thinking from the standpoint of everyone else. The mechanism here is that of shifting and exchanging perspectives in the course of dialogue—shifting between speaking and listening. In order to convince you I may have to take your perspective, and vice versa. Even if I do not adopt your views, a change in perspective may cause me to modify my own reasons, particularly if they do not convince those who disagree with me. Such mechanisms build upon the sorts of cognition involved in resolving direct face-to-face conflicts.[70] In complex interactions there are multiple perspectives and roles, such as

the perspectives of organizational and institutional representatives or different perspectives related to the distribution of social knowledge. In deliberating on highly technical matters, knowledge is unequally distributed between lay and expert perspectives. Experts cannot assume that their special knowledge will have practical effects unless they can successfully take on the lay perspective; similarly, the layperson can take on the perspective of the expert by becoming a "well-informed citizen."[71] This type of perspective taking is typically performed by an informed public. The surprising effect of such a literate public sphere is that it reduces claims to expert authority. The question of the risks of nuclear power, no matter how small, has less to do with their exact assessment than with the moral and political aspects of their distribution among social groups or with how these groups evaluate them. The groups affected do not think in terms of the experts' aggregate risks but rather in terms of the irreplaceable values of their communities. Perspective taking of this sort can work against the occlusion of practical questions by the authority of experts. This mechanism need not be limited to taking the perspectives of actual persons in deliberation. There are also temporal perspectives, as when a deliberator advocates for the consideration of the perspective of future or past generations as virtual participants in a deliberation. Deliberation can produce bad decisions when it does not consider such temporal perspectives: it can be myopic in not considering the future at all, as is often the case in commercialist political cultures; or it can discount the present for the sake of some indefinite future, as is the case among Stalinist regimes.[72] When successful, temporal perspective taking broadens overly narrow horizons of discourse. It is also crucial in introducing new forms of expression and ways of looking at the consequences of social activities: the introduction of memory of the past and of the opportunities of future generations have produced new moral vocabularies and utopian visions into political discussions.[73] George Herbert Mead's discussion of perspective taking shows that this general ability depends upon the capacity to take a particular kind of perspective: not that of particular others, but that of the "generalized other." Perspective taking by itself contributes little to successful deliberation if participants are not able to coordinate all the various perspectives into one in a dialectical process of constant enrichment and new articulations. The introduction of this generalized perspective not only permits more complex forms of coordination but also permits the shift to a reflexive account of how discourse can construct generalized justifications for certain sorts of policies and decisions. Participants in democratic political cultures must be able to engage in public meta-level deliberation of this kind once legislative and judicial decisions are put up for public review and revision. Perspective taking of this sort aids deliberation by making reasons more convincing relative to the whole body of deliberators. The generalized perspective enables deliberators to see the cogency and intelligibility of reasons in new reflective ways, along with the multiple perspectives and views of others. Public dialogue cannot proceed without participants' successfully managing shifting perspectives and roles. Such abilities enable citizens to participate in a variety of truly open public spheres and arenas. Ackerman's assertion that "every citizen's reasons are as good as any other" ignores the limits of tolerance of democratic dialogue: my reasons are convincing only if they are addressed to and answerable by others.

The general structure of these dialogical mechanisms of public deliberation should now be clear: each provides an account of how reasons can secure uptake in deliberation. What is the purpose of this list of five such mechanisms? Although it is by no means exhaustive, it does establish that the dialogical exchange that is the basis of public deliberation employs a number of mechanisms by which reasons can become generally convincing. All the mechanisms discussed depend on symmetry and on other conditions that establish the general framework of equality, non-tyranny, and non-exclusion from the public sphere that is necessary for democratically formed agreements. Of course, violations of these conditions could readily bring the back-and-forth quality of dialogical deliberation to a standstill. For example, as anyone who has experienced asymmetries of power knows, inequalities of various kinds will reduce the need for more powerful participants to shift perspectives. Since unequal deliberators will not be able to participate effectively, their dissenting points of view will tend to be assimilated to the contributions of more effective participants. Thus, in chapter 3 I shall argue that social inequalities block the operation of dialogical mechanisms and thus undermine deliberation.

Besides inequalities, there are several other gaps in my account so far. I have not considered how to create conditions in which these mechanism can operate best, nor have I described the institutions that promote their use in situations of conflict. Furthermore, since deliberation takes place in the context of past decisions and is a temporally extended activity, coherence and consistency constrain the operation of these mechanisms for deliberation within institutional settings.[74] Without such consistency, the coordination of temporally extended and often spatially separated activities breaks down to such an extent that deliberation can cease to be public. Coherence in this process is an indication of its success or failure. In complex societies, the threat of such breakdown is best avoided through a division of deliberative labor and other social mechanisms; these designs deal with social complexity and open multiple avenues for public testing and for circumventing institutional blockages and accumulated advantages. Different spheres of activity and decision making should also emphasize the dialogical mechanisms that are appropriate to the problem situations in their domain.

Conclusion

In the preceding section I outlined a series of dialogical mechanisms employed in the process of public deliberation by agents who try to jointly construct publicly convincing reasons. These mechanisms identify the features of public deliberation that make it possible for deliberators to produce decisions supported by convincing public reasons. In conclusion, I want to illustrate the superiority of this dialogical view of public deliberation in solving problems posed by what Minnow calls "the dilemma of difference." These dilemmas are problems that can be dealt with democratically through specifications of the norm of equality.

Affirmative action is one of the more divisive political issues today. Such policies emerged as ways of dealing with persistent inequalities and past wrongs; they are not merely procedural claims. The deliberative situation within which these policies were formed employed the mechanism of compelling self-expression, which points out the discrepancy of some groups' experience and the collective interpretation of a problem; such policies were adopted through compelling biographical narratives that undermined the narrow interpretation of general legal norms. In arguing *Brown v. Board of Education,* Thurgood Marshall employed this remarkable strategy to show the specific effects of segregation on the life history of African-American children; the forceful presentation of these experiences, coupled with more general appeals to fairness, helped to bring school segregation under the norm of equal protection. This sort of non-procedural and non-formal expansion of the discourse on equality also occurred in debates about social welfare and public health. Here deliberation about the application of the law uncovered normalizing models and rigid social roles of the problem that limited solutions, just as the New Deal reinterpreted the corrective measures of Reconstruction.

Deliberation about these policies continues, incorporating a greater awareness of the diversity of needs within the welfare state. The most important change concerns the role of women in the family. Welfare-state policies have been "normalizing" in the Foucaultian sense, in that these policies presuppose and help to reproduce very particular sorts of households. With an increasing pluralization of household types, their diverse needs and problems go unmet. Similarly, equal-protection policies for the handicapped are supposed to enable participation in broad areas of social life. Effective participation goes beyond having formal access to giving the individuals affected the opportunity to articulate what the actual barriers are to them.[75]

Such a deliberative mechanism makes possible the articulation of what Minnow has called "unstated assumptions that make difference dilemmas seem intractable."[76] Once these presuppositions are made explicit, it is easier to see how the problematic situation could be reconceived and why the status quo versions of equality are not neutral. In particular, public deliberation of the sort described here makes decisions dependent on negotiating various possible axes of equality and difference. Active public deliberation can best apply the complex principle "treat like cases like, but different cases differently." Too narrow and too broad applications could be checked through the operation of dialogical mechanisms for the specification of general norms from various perspectives. Still, the explicit recognition of *all* differences in advance of implementing a policy or law is an impossible and meaningless demand. Deliberation discovers ways to deal with the specific differences within ongoing cooperative arrangements. In the case of welfare rights, the differences that are relevant now have most to do with the historical experiences of changing gender roles in the social division of labor.[77] This transformation changes the definition of the needs that have to be met in order to make all citizens politically equal and capable of functioning politically. These dilemmas of difference are exactly the sort of problematic situation that requires respecification and elaboration of a norm—here, the norm of equal rights. The dialectic between specificity and comprehensiveness in the application of basic norms can be found throughout the history of Constitutional revision and the various civil rights movements.

Such historical processes of transformation are made possible through the introduction of new public reasons to participatory deliberation, here by representatives in institutions and by social movements in the public sphere. In contrast to precommitment or proceduralist models, the solutions offered in long historical processes of deliberation fit a model of articulation: the basic contents of the constitutional framework are preserved within ever richer and more complex interpretations, in which increasingly diverse needs become component parts. But the achievement of a public redefinition of welfare rights and entitlements, particularly with respect to the gender of the recipient, required the more effective participation of women and minorities. It was only when those affected were able to articulate their needs and experiences in the public sphere that adequate reform could take place; no amount of counterfactual reflection could replace a dialogue in which the public sees the problems from the perspective of recipients. So, too, handicapped persons have articulated new understandings of unequal treatment. Such dilemmas of difference are not to be solved once and for all; they are a constant part of the process of deliberation which applies and enriches norms of equality in new historical contexts.[78]

This example of success also shows that public deliberation may become increasingly difficult as more concerns have to be considered and balanced. How is it that in a diverse and pluralistic polity citizens can deliberate together without collapsing into sheer conflict or a babble of incommensurable voices? Once the abilities for effective deliberation manifested in the public sphere become widely available in a society, new possibilities for cooperation emerge, along with new possibilities for deep and irreconcilable conflicts. But publicity and diversity are not opposing norms, since a public consists of a plural group. Not only has political reality lagged behind the ideals of public agreement; these ideals have lagged behind the reality of the new public sphere in pluralistic democracies. Perhaps the main challenge of deliberative democracy is to resolve the increasingly common conflicts without surrendering the political equality of citizens, the non-tyranny of outcomes, and the publicity of dialogue.

2

Public Deliberation and Cultural Pluralism

Although Rousseau may rightly be called a utopian with respect to his egalitarian ideals, he was a hardly naive one. In an important passage in his *Social Contract*, Rousseau discusses whether or not his proposals for legitimate government could ever be realized. He considers the strict social and natural conditions that are necessary for self-rule by citizens. The rare good fortune of finding a people who meet all these conditions implies that such egalitarian participatory democracy seldom occurs. Self-rule is possible, Rousseau admits, only on the following conditions: an appropriately sized political unit (indeed, one so small that all citizens can know one another), relative social equality (including equality of wealth, or at least no large inequalities so that no citizen can buy the votes or freedoms of another), and sufficient cultural homogeneity and community that there is not so much diversity of morals and customs as to engender persistent conflicts and "partial societies."[1] Moreover, Rousseau thought that certain propitious natural conditions were necessary, such as a climate favorable to agricultural self-sufficiency and a location with enough natural defenses so as to make military organizations and hierarchy unimportant.

Only a few places in Europe were fortunate enough to fulfill all these conditions. None of the large states with commercial economies qualified. The island of Corsica had some hope, but only if some "lawgiver" bestowed the right constitution on it. For the sort of basic political unit of most democracies today, none of these conditions hold: the nation states are large and complex, characterized by deep and growing inequalities, ethnically diverse, and culturally pluralistic. Does this mean that the dialogical form of public deliberation that I outlined in chapter 1 is impossible? For most critics of radical democracy, the same social conditions which Rousseau mentions may now be cited to declare participation and deliberation a utopian fiction.

In the next three chapters I shall examine the modern obstacles to deliberative democracy: cultural pluralism, social inequalities, and institutional complexity. I shall argue that none of these characteristically modern social conditions rules out the possibility of deliberative democracy. In the case of cultural pluralism, I shall argue, diversity can even improve the public use of reason and make democratic life more vibrant. But it can do so only if citizens can learn to deal with deep moral conflicts—conflicts that Rousseau and other radical democrats might have thought intractable.

Multiculturalism has become the watchword of many political debates. It is considered a cause either of the decline of democracy or of its renewal. The political problems of pluralism have moved to the center of much liberal political thought, including Rawls's recent account of a well-ordered democratic society. In *Political Liberalism* and in recent essays, the story Rawls tells us is that political liberalism emerges out of the conflicts between opposing moral doctrines, specifically the early modern wars of religion and the debates about religious tolerance. Such conflicts gave us a stark historical choice with which to begin political theory: either the endless conflict of competing transcendent visions of the good or equal liberty of conscience for all. "Political liberalism," Rawls claims, "starts by taking to heart the absolute depth of that irreconcilable latent conflict."[2] Conflicts of these sorts of values or "comprehensive doctrines" are "irreconcilable," since there is no "reasonable" or common basis for settling disagreements. Liberalism begins with the recognition that such disagreement is an enduring feature of contemporary societies and hence an ineliminable element of their political institutions.

But this social fact is itself historically variable. If anything, newer forms of cultural diversity have now produced conflicts and disagreements so deep and troubling that even our standard liberal solutions, modeled on religious liberty and tolerance, no longer seem adequate or stable. To borrow a distinction from Hume: many current disagreements are not merely conflicts of interest but conflicts of principle. Conflicts of principle, if deep enough, cannot be resolved through adjudication: what higher-order principles such as fairness consist of may be at stake. Democratic arrangements may only exacerbate these problems of pluralism. Since most nation states are now culturally as well as religiously diverse, citizens who deliberate together within them may not share the same collective aims, moral values, or world views. Are such conflicts also "irreconcilable"?

Following Rawls, we may distinguish the political conflicts of cultural pluralism in terms of their "depth." American citizens today debate about tax cuts. This debate assumes the same moral and political framework of the modern European nation state and the role of private property within it. This generally shared framework excludes neither conflicts of interest nor differences about the specific principles that best justify policies. Nonetheless, there is general agreement about the democratic procedures for settling such normative differences politically. Conflicts become "deep" when they challenge this basic framework of moral assumptions and political procedures, as when the Sioux tribe challenges the entire set of practices and procedures for settling disputes about past injustices through monetary compensation. More and more polities face such conflicts, particularly with regard to the political status of minority cultures.[3] The deep conflicts that often ensue make impossible a world without moral loss or legal coercion. Democratic polities, however, perish with too much loss or coercion and not enough common deliberation and discussion. These outcomes raise the following questions that are insufficiently addressed in political liberalism: What role does reason play in such deliberations, if standards of rationality are themselves subject to deeply conflicting interpretations? What sort of "public bases of justification" is adequate to such pluralism? In what follows, I want to argue that Rawls has not adequately resolved the dilemmas created by "irreconcilable values" that are the starting point of his political liberalism.

Two features of Rawls's political liberalism seem to preempt deep conflicts between cultural membership and democratic citizenship. First, the concept of an "overlapping consensus" may be thought to base the possibility of democracy on already-existing agreements and

antecedently shared values. As a matter of empirical fact, some "overlapping consensus" is usually all that is necessary for the political
practice of resolving most conflicts.[4] However, there is no reason to
believe that such a basis would be sufficient for a "political" conception of justice in complex and diverse modern societies.[5] Given sufficient diversity (and free expression and association), an "overlapping
consensus" that results when our doctrines happen to yield a restricted set of compatible interpretations is once again a minimal
condition, but hardly a sufficient basis, for a robust democratic practice. Moreover, even if there is an overlapping consensus about certain moral values, conflicts of principle about disputed issues are still
possible. Second, Rawls's "method of avoidance" suggests that such
conflicts about which no public agreement is possible might be left to
some pragmatic device, such as a "gag rule" or other precommitments. The point of such "self-binding" is to remove some topics
(such as fundamental rights and religious differences) from public
discussion under certain conditions.[6] But these devices are neither
democratic nor undemocratic; in practice they may as often as not
limit rather than enable democratic discussion and compromise, as
their frequent political use has shown.[7] Since precommitment and
other such devices are practical tools and possible outcomes in the
political process, it would be a mistake to interpret them as the core
of the rationality of democratic constitutions. It is certainly not rational to use these devices in every case.[8] Independent criteria of practical rationality or public reason are necessary to settle the issue. So
narrowly construed, neither overlapping consensus nor the method
of avoidance would be sufficient to settle the question of the public
basis of justification for solutions to deep cultural conflicts.

Given that neither overlapping consensus nor the method of avoidance solves the problem, I examine the implications of deep cultural
conflicts for Rawls's account of agreement among free and equal citizens. If we accept the social facts of pluralism and deep conflict,
then we must also wonder whether the scope of what is "reasonable
for all to accept" turns out to be so small as to be irrelevant for most
political disagreements. Yet the resolution to any conflict is legitimate
and democratic only to the extent that it can find free agreement
among all differently situated, but politically equal, deliberators. An

account of democratic agreement under these conditions still must be constructed. Such agreement is conceivable, I shall argue, only if it avoids the horns of a series of potential dilemmas. Deep conflicts pose *inter-group* dilemmas. I distinguish two types: liberal "each/all" dilemmas and communitarian "unity/plurality" dilemmas. After illustrating each type of dilemma in cases of actual cultural conflict, I shall consider the ways in which they might be overcome by the use of what Rawls calls "public reason." The problem, however, is that deep cultural conflict makes public reason itself essentially contestable, especially when moral and epistemic standards are inextricably intertwined.

I shall argue that deep conflicts only can be resolved publicly if political liberalism is revised in two ways: if the political conception of justice is made more dynamic and if public reason is made "plural" and not "singular." Both features are absent not only in Rawls but also in all other related Kantian treatments of the public use of reason, including Habermas's proceduralist notion of communicative reason. Habermas's recent concern with the effects of cultural pluralism on the liberal constitutional state goes some way toward fulfilling the first desideratum: by making public reason more dynamic, Habermas puts it to work in the process of constantly revising a common framework of political justification. Despite his explicit intention to go beyond Rawls and most liberals by affirming a plurality of cultural values in the face of nationalism and not "bracketing the pluralism of convictions and worldviews from the outset," I shall argue, Habermas's notion is still inconsistent with a pluralism of public standpoints and public reasons.[9] This is because a genuinely plural conception of public reason denies a single "public standpoint" for working out the reasonable moral compromises needed to resolve deep conflicts in pluralist democracies.

Deep Conflict: Liberal and Communitarian Dilemmas

Just how cultural pluralism produces "deep conflicts" can perhaps best be illustrated by the many problems concerning the unique legal status of Native Americans in the United States and Canada. As Will Kymlicka points out in *Liberalism, Community and Culture*, interpretations of their rights based on the idea of political inclusion fail to work for the simple reason that these interpretations are disputed by the Native Americans themselves. With the *Brown v. Board of Education* decision and the calls for the integration of all racial and ethnic groups into the political community with full and equal rights for all, the federal governments of the United States and Canada began to dismantle the system of differential treatment of Native Americans based on the reservation system.[10] Though the reservation system produced desperate and systemic poverty, groups like the American Indian Movement saw that it could be used for purposes of preserving cultural identity in the face of an overwhelming and invasive European culture. Given the enormous asymmetries of power in this case, the capacity of specifically Native American political communities to protect their culture and identity depends on their ability to make use of the extraordinary rights and powers already present in the reservation system for this end. Kymlicka describes the solution this way: "The reservations form special political jurisdictions over which Indian communities have guaranteed powers, and within which non-Indian Americans have restricted mobility, property, and voting rights."[11] Without these restrictions on otherwise universal rights and without these special powers not guaranteed in the Constitution, permanent minority cultures might disappear. Are such special powers and rights reasonable and legitimate, or are they violations of the constitutional guarantees to equal protection?

Deep conflicts do not emerge solely from special situations of ethnic and cultural minorities. Difficult political and legal issues emerge when well-established minority communities hold different belief systems, often for religious reasons. Such problems become deep conflicts when they are not just conflicts about particular beliefs or even principles but conflicts about principles of adjudication. Conflicts about animal sacrifice in religious rituals, no matter how abhorrent such sacrifice is to many, can still be resolved in terms of principles of the scope of religious liberty,[12] but in deeper conflicts such principles of adjudication are contested by citizens who are members of a cultural minority. Such conflicts occur in Christian Science refusal cases, which involve the refusal of parents to seek or allow conventional medical treatment of their children for treatable diseases. What makes such conflicts deep is not the conflicts between the "rights" of the parents and the "interests" of the state; rather, attempts at adjudication show that conflicting principles are at stake. It is all the more difficult to propose any kind of solution because of deep disagreements even about the "facts" of disease: since Christian Scientists dispute the distinction of mind and matter that is prevalent in medical science, they argue that even non-invasive diagnosis may "cause" a disease to occur.[13] Thus, even the "facts" are at stake in the conflict, since to recognize the medical "facts" of disease is to deny the moral beliefs of Christian Science. The intertwining of moral and epistemic reasons makes it difficult even to formulate any sort of compromise about the treatment of the children of Christian Scientists, since there seems to be no public basis for justification that would be acceptable to everyone.

These examples reveal quite well the persistent dilemmas of multicultural democracies. There are two such dilemmas. The first type I shall call the *communitarian dilemma*. On the one hand, the segmentation of distinct political jurisdictions (on analogy to the Native American case) without overarching common constitutional essentials and rights might sustain a semblance of political unity, but at the cost of disparate cultural communities that deliberate alongside of, rather than with, one another. On the other hand, not to recognize distinct cultural rights leads to forced integration and unity at the price of diversity. To force treatment of the children of Christian Scientists is effectively to undermine socializing them with these beliefs. Besides the case of Native American jurisdictions, we might also think of dilemmas created by communitarian responses to demands for multicultural education. On the one hand, the educational system might be regarded as a place in which students become citizens through being socialized in a common culture. However, this culture is not "common"; it is usually that of the majority group, as is clear in the case of France's policy of imposing French culture and language on recent immigrants via the educational system. On the other hand, the presence of groups with other moral viewpoints may heighten solidarity within groups at the price of exacerbating conflicts between them, eventually leading to balkanization of the curriculum among groups, schools, and communities. Thus, in this case there is a clear tradeoff between unity and plurality, and the unity of the larger political community clearly conflicts with the plurality and the integrity of smaller cultural groups.

I shall call this second tradeoff the *liberal dilemma*. This tradeoff is similar in structure to public-goods problems, such as voters' or contributors' dilemmas. Such dilemmas are by now familiar: what is good for all (e.g., less pollution) is not what is good for each (e.g., cheap gasoline). What is good for all groups in a society in some neutral sense (political inclusion through the same political equality and rights for all) is not necessarily good for each group (whose goals include the protection of their own minority cultures and identities). It is good for all groups to have freedom of mobility, but bad for some if this violates the good of maintaining cultural membership. The liberal dilemma emerges in various solutions to Native American rights proposed by the neutral, liberal state. Monetary solutions tend to benefit each member of the tribal group while providing no real protections or benefits for the cultural goals of the group as a whole. Land-based solutions giving large amounts of territory to tribal groups may be good for the group as a whole but may decrease freedom and increase poverty for individual members of the group. Given a sufficient number of such conflicts between general rights and cultural goals, what is good or rational for each group may be collectively self-defeating, and what is good for all may be self-defeating to each individual. In India, family law has been left to religious jurisdictions; this may be rational given the beliefs and goals of each group, but collectively it has meant that all of them have to recognize practices that are intolerable to each of them; what is good for all may be a neutral civil law, but that would defeat each of their collective goals. None of the groups could end up being able to socialize their members in domestic groups as they want (as is typically the case in religious toleration). Such examples can be multiplied in many diverse societies. For all to be included in the same way could undermine the conditions for cultural socialization into each group; for each to be included differently could undermine the political equality of all. Religious tolerance does not provide the proper analogy for these cases, since it is not a dilemma created by the agreed-upon basis for justification: the principle of political equality itself.

Following Rawls, the "public use of reason" seems ideally suited as the proper way for citizens to resolve such dilemmas and conflicts. On the Kantian account that Rawls endorses, public reasons can be distinguished from non-public reasons in terms of their scope: "Non-public reasons comprise the many reasons of civil society and belong to what I have called the 'background culture,' in contrast with the public political culture."[14] The model here is that citizens participate in political culture for the many different "reasons" that emerge in the groups, associations, and families that form civil society. Nonetheless, this plurality of forms of reason does not extend to public reason itself: ". . . there are many non-public reasons and but one public reason."[15] Rawls speaks of the single public reason as based on "common human reason," which includes the capacities and procedures of reason, such as drawing inferences, weighing evidence, and balancing competing considerations. By itself this least common denominator of reasoning is not enough. Public reason is also manifest as an "enlarged capacity for thought," to use Kant's phrase, which permits a critical and impartial process of deliberating and judging "from the standpoint of everyone else." It is precisely by appealing to public reason that a plurality of persons can resolve what Kant calls "the perplexities of opposing claims" in ways acceptable to all. Citizens are unreasonable to the extent that they do not exercise their common public reason and to the extent that they put forth reasons that do not have public scope. Public reasons in a pluralist society will not presuppose some particular conception of the good, or some comprehensive moral doctrine, since it is reasonable to assume that such reasons will not have public scope. If to be neutral in this sense is to avoid irreconcilable non-public moral claims, the public reasons will tend to be formal and procedural. Only as long as the limits on the nature and scope of public reasons remain uncontested is it possible to imagine a pluralist society that is a "union of social unions."

The "unity/plurality" dilemma shows strictly communitarian solutions to be non-starters unless they take on liberal features of a plurality of communities. Some forms of liberalism are more hospitable to diversity, particularly in versions that emphasize a shared, public political culture. In particular, the use of public reason seems to have a number of advantages for solving problems of cultural pluralism. It is not susceptible to the sorts of interpersonal dilemmas that, as Derek Parfit shows,[16] plague the individualist rationality of interest maximization. Nonetheless, I want to argue that new forms of these dilemmas appear. Indeed, without some modification of Rawls's political liberalism, public reason remains ensnared in both the liberal and the communitarian dilemma, especially in view of its role in supplying determinate answers to conflicts of these sorts. Kant himself realized this and viewed publicity quite minimally as a limit on coercive law and non-democratic sovereignty. That Rawls holds a stronger view is evident from what he says about the susceptibility of abortion and several other political conflicts to resolution by public reason.[17] I shall examine liberal and communitarian dilemmas of public reason in turn and then argue that they can be overcome only if we recognize that an account of the political uses of public reason must include a multiplicity of public standpoints. Political liberalism needs to assume that "public" reasons as well as "non-public" reasons may conflict deeply.

Public Reason and Citizenship in Political Liberalism

According to Rawls's account, citizens exercise public reason together by explaining to one another the reasons for the policies they advocate, and to determine whether a reason is a good one requires adopting an impartial and public standpoint in which all reasons, including those of others, are tested to determine which ones *all* citizens can be expected to endorse (that is, which "can be supported by the political values of public reason"[18]). But that there is such a unified standpoint assumes that there is one public standpoint in political life and not many different ones. Ideals of public reason usually imply convergence of opinions or interests in deliberation. But the formal and procedural character of these ideal constraints do not support the assumption of convergence toward a single public opinion, nor does the requirement of impartiality require that all adopt the same standpoint in deliberation. Even if individuals or groups each construe their public standpoint as appropriately abstracting from their concerns or interests, a variety of standards of impartiality or "individualized impartial concerns"[19] are inevitable in pluralist societies. The questioning of this assumption of singularity is in fact the core of many feminist criticisms of notions such as impartiality and the overly unitary forms of universality that they generate.[20]

Whatever abstraction from one's own point of view impartiality requires, it cannot be at the price of the plurality of potential preferences, norms, and values. If a society is diverse and divided, there is no one "public sphere," and indeed there is no one public but instead a plurality of them: the publics of different subgroups, cultures, and experts. We are back to Rousseau's problem of a plurality of "partial societies," each with its own version of the public standpoint that it can explain impartially to others.[21] These conflicts produce *inter-group* dilemmas.

As with such problems of unity and plurality, equally difficult each/all dilemmas emerge on the public level, especially if we recognize that different groups may construct their own versions of the public will. Here *intra-group* dilemmas take the form of conflicts between one's values qua citizen and one's values qua member of a cultural group; the case of conflicts between religious based domestic law and criminal procedure in India provides an extreme example. The two values may conflict. As citizens, we may think that it is reasonable for all to accept unrestricted rights for property ownership and voting as citizens; as members of a culture, we may think that such rights were unreasonable in light of general cultural goals which we would abandon if these rights are not restricted. This dilemma is faced by many Catholic public officials about abortion laws. Such dilemmas result from the democratic character of public discussion and decision making.

In order to be democratic, public discourses must take all interpretations into account. But this very feature leads precisely to each/all, inter-group dilemmas: if democratic discourses are entirely consistent, then public reason is little better off than individualist reason. What is collectively rational for all groups may be individually self-defeating for any one of them. Since norms (including norms of justification) are at stake here, the appeal to a higher level of abstraction does not work as it might if individuals were to take a broader perspective than their own interests. The dilemma could be resolved by introducing new constraints on self-determination (such as precommitments to political values), but these may violate the ideal of free agreement in some cases and may require revision in other cases when agents develop new conflicts and begin to see those as reflecting a particular public point of view. The problem is that many procedural conceptions of public reason do not yet provide a clear alternative for how to resolve such conflicts at a higher level of second-order principles.

Besides problems of inter- and intra-group plurality, a third problem of public reason emerges in its exercise in political institutions. In his discussion of the U.S. Supreme Court as the "exemplar of public reason," Rawls underestimates the unavoidable tendency of institutions to reduce diversity in two ways: by their cultural specificity and by the temporal constraints on decision making that they introduce. It is hard to see how public reason could be exercised without some formal institutions, especially if it is to be capable of guiding change over time. All such institutions, including those of public reason, are inevitably selective in various ways. Although bureaucracies and parliaments may be designed to be formal and general, when they are inhabited and interpreted by real actors they become historically and culturally specific. This cultural specificity may be the source of informal constraints that may restrict actual political communication and public deliberation—here we might think of the exclusionary effects of the formality of expert legal culture, which also ensures that the justices reason only in light of constitutional essentials. It is certainly clear from history that such restrictions at times lead the Supreme Court to adopt interpretations that all citizens may not reasonably accept. In these cases, public reason is actually being exercised by members of the larger public outside the institution who are not constraining their "reasons" in the same way. Yet this public's reason often finds consensus which the Court only later explicitly legitimizes and formalizes (as Bruce Ackerman shows to have happened in the case of the New Deal's revolution of constitutional interpretation[22]). In these cases, it follows that the existence of formal procedures and institutional restrictions to political values cannot eliminate democratic failures in pluralistic societies—failures that include the presence of permanent cultural minorities and social inequalities. In pluralist societies, there must be other exemplars of public reason than formal institutions if democracy is to work.

If these problems remain unsolved by Rawlsian public reason, how can Rawls's account be modified to deal with the myriad problems of cultural conflicts? Such a reconstruction has two steps: first, public reason must be made plural; second, public reason must become dynamic and historical. That is, a democratic solution to the two dilemmas of pluralism necessitates abandoning some of the restrictions on public reason that Rawls thinks follow from an "overlapping consensus" and from his assumption that there is "but one public reason." However, even if Habermas makes public reason more dynamic, as I shall show, his conception is no more pluralistic than Rawls's and hence also cannot deal with deep conflicts.

Plural versus Singular Public Reason: Democracy and Moral Compromise

These communitarian and liberal dilemmas of public reason point to a positive task for democratic theory: it must show that sustaining political deliberation is tied to resolving conflicts between plurality and publicity. Given that the plurality of comprehensive moral doctrines is constitutive of political liberalism, how can such conflicts be avoided in the public use of reason?

To begin with, there is a crucial ambiguity in the Kantian and neo-Kantian ways of conceiving of the use of public reason, and the failure to resolve this ambiguity has made Kantian pluralists like Rawls and Habermas unable to face squarely the problems of cultural pluralism. The only way to resolve these dilemmas, to the extent that they can be resolved, is to make a clear distinction between *singular* and *plural* public reason.[23] On the one hand, public reason is singular if it represents itself as a single norm of public deliberation; in light of this norm, agents come to agree upon some decision for the *same* publicly accessible reasons. As Rawls puts it: "There are many non-public reasons and but one public reason."[24] Habermas makes similar claims of a single universal standpoint as the idealizing presupposition of practical discourse. Its singularity is evident in his description of this standpoint as "an ideally extended we-perspective."[25] On the other hand, public reason is plural if a single norm of reasonableness is not presupposed in deliberation; thus, agents can come to an agreement with one another for *different* publicly accessible reasons. This sort of agreement is exhibited in granting differential rights to minority groups, as in the examples of land rights discussed above. Public reason is plural here because it does not presuppose a single public or impartial point of view. Though plural public reason also cannot resolve all inter-cultural conflicts, the problems for democratic theory are no longer conceptual; they are empirical. Such contestation depends not on unrecognized each/all dilemmas hidden within the standard of rationality but on real conflicts that are so deep and persistent that no common framework for deliberation and reflection can be constructed without loss or coercion.

In light of this preliminary definition of plural public reason, I would like to clarify why such a notion is important for contemporary democratic theory by contrasting it to the singular notion shared by Rawls and Habermas. I am not arguing that Rawls and Habermas have no room for pluralism in their normative political theories. Besides sharply distinguishing the right and the good, each tries to accommodate pluralism in a directly political way: Rawls in his notion of overlapping consensus, Habermas by means of the important roles he assigns to bargaining and negotiation in democratic politics. Contrary to some of the critics I cited above in constructing the dilemmas of public reason, I am not arguing against any role for unity in democratic polities. Democratic unity requires only that participants enter into public deliberation with everyone—with all citizens in the same public sphere.

Nonetheless, this *political* unity, I shall argue, does not require that there be "but one public reason." Rather, what is required in cases of deep conflict is a genuinely *moral* compromise in which plural public reason is exercised in the process of creating the framework for such an ongoing public consensus, now a minimal one that demands only the willingness to continue to cooperate. By showing how the reason of citizens can operate even in the absence of consensus, pluralizing public reason extends this type of reason to make it appropriate for the task of revising political norms and procedures. What follows is therefore an elaboration of the ideal of public reason in political life that permits, rather than denies or avoids, moral conflict and differences in democratic politics. This modification aims at precluding the fatal consequences of views of deliberation that are either too strong or too weak. In both versions, the ideal of public reason is simply an inappropriate standard for many important political conflicts, either because it excludes diversity or because it is uninformative. Rawls's version is too weak; Habermas's notion is too strong. Both are too restrictive in what counts as public agreement.

Dynamic and Pluralist Agreements

Rawls's "overlapping consensus" identifies the desired political characteristics: it is both pluralist and public. After all, a consensus is "overlapping" precisely because different and even opposing comprehensive moral doctrines may be reasonable in a public sense. All citizens may be able to agree with the public basis for political deliberation in light of moral values that they recognize within their own moral frameworks. Because the political framework of deliberation is moral or true for every citizen by his or her own lights, overlapping consensus is "not a compromise compelled by circumstances."[26] From the perspective of each comprehensive moral doctrine, the political values invoked in political argument are a shared part of their repertoire of moral reasons; to use Joshua Cohen's apt phrase, everyone appeals to "nothing but the truth but not to the whole truth."[27] Such restrictions on political deliberation make it possible for reasonable participants to respect the political autonomy of all and to recognize the proper limits of their own public reasons.

Put in this positive way, restrictions of this sort allow free public deliberation about issues that fall within these limits. The "method of avoidance" in overlapping consensus is also part of respecting the limits of public reason. Here, though, Rawls's conception is simply too weak for democratic deliberation, even for societies with "reasonable pluralism." It is too weak because it has nothing to say about deep disagreements and conflict, except that they should be "avoided" and removed from political deliberation. Not to accept such a solution is, by definition, unreasonable. Whereas Nazis and racists are unreasonable in this way, democratic groups want to deliberate in order to extend and modify reasonable political consensus when they disagree with one another. The abolitionist, feminist, and civil rights movements did so precisely through raising contentious issues that they deemed public. Indeed, often what is contentious in

these cases is the character of political life itself, as well as the meaning and scope of accepted political values. Thus, what is reasonable is
not the shared content of political values but the mutual recognition
of the deliberative liberties of others, the requirements of dialogue,
and the openness of one's own beliefs to revision. There is no reason
why these same suppositions could not be extended to contentious issues and deep conflicts.

Besides concerning the meaning and the scope of political values,
deep conflicts may concern standards of public reason and hence its
limits in deliberation. Understood by Rawls as a set of capacities,
"common human reason" and "guidelines of inquiry" are insufficient
to eliminate deep disagreements about how to assess evidence. Moral
and epistemic diversity often go hand in hand. If the differences in
frameworks for assessing evidence are sufficiently deep, then the appeal to a common human reason can still fail to produce agreement
even when agents are not irrational. When the "burdens of judgment" (to use Rawls's term) cannot be discharged, agents may have to
simply accept that in such cases there is no public basis of justification, and that there is a plurality of reasonable and defensible views
that cannot assessed comparatively. In this way, "reasonable persons
see that the burdens of judgment set limits on what may be reasonably justified to others, and so they endorse some form of liberty of
conscience and freedom of thought."[28]

For all the importance of establishing the possibility of "reasonable
pluralism" and the limits of public reason, it is nonetheless implausi-
ble to put the "values" of public reason beyond political contestation,
as Rawls does. Without a clear way to distinguish the reasonable and
the unreasonable such that all would agree, a public basis for justification cannot be expected to follow from wide agreement about facts
and the possession of common reasoning capacities. What is interesting for deep conflicts are cases in which we are asked to change
our modes of public justification. Boyle's debate with Hobbes was
not only about a particular piece of evidence (the existence of vacu-
ums) but also about a way to assess evidence (the validity and relevance of the mode of empirical justification in the practice of science,
with all its reasonable disagreements). Similarly, Ackerman traces several "revolutions" in which new interpretations and revisions of the

Constitution are tied to new forms of public justification and interpretation, as in the case of the equal protection guarantee of the Fourteenth Amendment that emerged out of the deep conflicts of the Reconstruction Era.[29] These historical facts show that public reason is dynamic and capable of transformation at the most basic levels of evidence, relevance, and inference.

A notion of public reason more closely tied to dialogue and communication may be more fruitful in dealing with such interlocking moral and epistemic conflicts. Habermas's account of deliberation that is without restriction of topics but is still public in scope takes us a step in this direction. It is more fruitful, especially for deep conflicts, since it lifts one of Rawls's restrictions on public reason: public reasons are not defined in terms of a shared "political conception." According to Habermas's idea of democratic deliberation, there is no way in advance of deliberation to tell which reasons are non-public. By broadening and making more dynamic and open-ended just what the burdens of reasonable judgment are, Habermas emphasizes two relevant features of communication for plural public reason: reflectiveness and inclusiveness. In dialogue, speakers can reflect, in public, on the conditions of communication under which they reach agreement. In doing so, they can alter and transform these conditions to become more inclusive in two ways. First, the membership of the communication community can become larger. More people can be included in deliberation in which collective decisions are made. Second, the "universe of discourse" becomes larger with the size of the discourse community and with the enlargement of the interpretive perspectives of its members. That is, giving everyone the opportunity to speak and make meaningful contributions to public debate and deliberation requires expanding the range of acceptable reasons and interpretations. In inclusive procedures of political communication and interpretation, deliberators may achieve mutual respect and accommodation as they exercise plural public reason.[30] With such inclusiveness and reflectiveness, unrestricted deliberation becomes possible. It is not just sectarians who challenge the public basis of justification, but also radical critics who want to expand the range of public reasons. In this way, the institutions of public reason become more dynamic and open to the challenges and complaints of minority groups as they reflexively learn and change their own normative foundations. The very dynamism exhibited in the history of the interpretation of the Constitution is impossible if we set the limits of public reason too narrowly and too quickly.

However, Habermas's account suffers from its own difficulties with regard to what counts as a public reason. Once he expands the range of available interpretations with more open and dynamic procedures, Habermas provides little normative guidance for settling the growing potential for conflicts of such a broader pool of public reasons. The problem is that Habermas's discussion of conflict places almost exclusive reliance on capacities for abstraction to solve problems of plurality, very much in the manner of democratic theories based on singular public reason. By abstraction I mean the capacity for impartiality and neutrality that Habermas identifies with the moral point of view. The only procedure besides abstraction that Habermas specifies is the "critical clarification of ethical values," but this lands him back in the same predicament as the conception of overlapping consensus.[31] Furthermore, he argues that argumentation required by any common deliberation also requires the same impartiality. The achievement of consensus in public deliberation depends on the discussion's being guided by an ideal of impartiality; this regulative ideal "lends reasons their consensus producing force."[32] Just as Rawls does, Habermas wants to distinguish impartial public reason from mere compromise, and he does so at the price of plurality. "Whereas parties can agree to a negotiated compromise for different reasons, the consensus brought about through argument must rest on identical reasons that are able to convince the parties in the same way."[33] This singularity can be seen in Habermas's conception of the relation between minority and majority opinions in democracies. Minorities, according to Habermas, give their temporary and conditional agreement until such a time as they can convince the majority of the correctness of the reasons for their particular view, toward which public opinion then converges.[34] Not only is this sameness of convictions required for the rationality of the deliberative process and the consensus it produces; it also must be presupposed by all deliberators who belong to the same public sphere.

This assumption of singularity depends on a model of consensus that is too strong for many contexts of political deliberation and discourse. To sustain deliberation in pluralistic contexts, it is necessary to distinguish two forms of agreement, one singular and the other plural. Much like Rawls, Habermas is here mistaken about the guiding role of the regulative ideal of a singular agreement: he demands that citizens converge, in the long run, on the same reasons, rather than agree for different reasons. Plural agreement merely requires continued cooperation in public deliberation, even with persistent disagreements. It is not that a singular agreement can never be reached through public justification in pluralist societies; rather, convergence is not itself a requirement of public reason or argumentation as such but an ideal of democratic citizenship. This ideal of common citizenship does not demand that all citizens agree for the same reasons; it demands only that they continue to cooperate and to compromise in the same process of public deliberation. In deep conflicts, such continued cooperation and thus common citizenship is precisely what is at stake. I want to argue that more minimal plural agreement (that is, ongoing cooperation and public reason giving) does not collapse public deliberation into the sort of compromise or *modus vivendi* that both Habermas and Rawls rightly reject. Once deliberation no longer relies exclusively on the ideals of a singular agreement, another form of compromise becomes the aim of political deliberation about conflicts: a compromise that is distinctly moral. How can such a compromise solve deep conflicts in ways that are not at best accommodation to circumstances or at worst surrender to existing unreason? Although there are many cases in which political compromise may be intolerable, in many others compromise is the only fair alternative.[35]

Political Conflict and Moral Compromise

Compromise in the ordinary sense is all about coming to an accommodation or making concessions. It involves tradeoffs and balances of interests—making concessions of one's own for equal ones by others. If these interests are backed by moral reasons, we often evaluate such tradeoffs or concessions as involving "compromising" one's beliefs or losing integrity; that is, we think that moral reasons should be overriding in all cases. Rawls's work offers us an example of an attempt to resolve conflicting principles. Indeed, we may think of his approach to justice as attempting to find a compromise between two principles that remain even after religious liberty is achieved: liberty and equality.[36] In this case we are dealing with a conflict of reasons of the same general type, but in the case of deep conflicts both sides have different types of reasons, each backed by a moral framework. Moreover, these frameworks do not have morally compatible ways of assessing evidence or of balancing reasons. In these cases, "common human reason" gets us no further; there is no other choice but to reach a compromise at a moral level. How is this to be done? Bargaining is always a possibility, but then democratic deliberation too often degenerates into a *modus vivendi*. Furthermore, bargaining is an inappropriate model for such conflicts, since it asks what cannot be done: if members of a culture could treat their deep commitments like negotiable interests or shifting preferences, there would be no deep conflict. Removing the contentious issues from the public agenda is also possible, but the parties have to agree to do so. This solution already requires a compromise: a public agreement to change the basis of political justification.

For deep conflicts, some form of public compromise is inescapable. Cultural disagreements do not only have their source in differences in value. Different cultural frameworks may assign various problems or issues to different forms of reason; these disputes are about justification and adjudication themselves and thus give rise to the need for the exercise of plural public reason. Considered apart from the threats of violence, the Rushdie affair is a good example of disagreements generated by differences in the classification of types of reasons. In Western liberal culture, freedom of expression is a "public" reason and blasphemy a "non-public" one; in the framework of a Shari'a-based Muslim culture the line between public and non-public reasons is not drawn in this way. The dispute is then deep, in the sense that moral and epistemic factors are so intertwined that no clear, antecedent basis for adjudication exists. Without a clear distinction of types of offense, the legitimate use of coercive power sanctioned by law will not divide up the same way in non-secular, Muslim culture. The framework of civil law could never be recognized as a culturally neutral, public arbiter without such a distinction.

Although my purpose here is only to show that such compromises are at least possible, I shall also sketch some acceptable compromises to deep cultural conflicts and show why they exemplify an adequate form of democratic agreement.[37] The process of reaching any compromise is the same for all its forms, including moral compromises: the give and take of discussion and debate. It is by virtue of this process that moral compromises are still compromises rather than mere coercion. However, moral compromises about deep conflicts are quite different from the standard cases of strategic bargaining or tradeoffs. Their structure is dialogical and hence requires some forum for public deliberation. Their aim or result is not the balancing of moral concessions from both sides but a change in the common framework for democratic deliberation. As in all compromises, the parties begin with opposing values and standards. However, here they do not merely "split the difference" fairly, nor do they find some impartial third position.[38] If standards of fairness and impartiality are at issue, the very procedures of compromise that appeal to them must be modified in public deliberation. In these cases of conflict, a compromise is formed as each party modifies his or her interpretation of the common framework, often modifying that framework itself in doing so.

In distinctly moral compromise, the parties do not modify the framework to achieve unanimity, although they may when conflicts are not so deep. Rather, they modify their conflicting interpretations of the framework so that each can recognize the other's moral values and standards as part of it. The framework is then common enough for each party to continue to cooperate and deliberate with the other. Nonetheless, it is still not already assumed to be the *same* framework, as would be true for an impartial agreement; in this way it remains plural. Certainly this give-and-take dialogue has to fulfill two functions if successful compromise is to be reached. First, it must expand the pool of available reasons as Habermas describes it, now in order to get beyond the incompatibility of current interpretations; second, it must be procedurally fair as Rawls describes it, but now in order to ensure that conflicting reasons are represented in some way in the new framework. This is the way constitutional assemblies have proceeded historically, producing not a single coherent set of principles but a complex patchwork of compromises and even conflicting values. This same vagueness and imprecision also applies to the framework of ongoing democratic practice.

Moral compromise about abortion in the United States may be possible, but only if the current framework of interpretation is changed. Ronald Dworkin proposes just such a moral compromise in his book *Life's Dominion*. He attempts to articulate a framework in which the "intrinsic value of human life" is recognized in such a way as to be consistent with the "procreative autonomy" of women.[39] Dworkin's proposal is a moral compromise in my sense: each side can find its moral reasons represented, interpreted, and assessed. It is far from the neutrality of the method of avoidance: citizens' values and conceptions of the good life are put up for public debate. The method of avoidance in this case would not promote public deliberation; it would produce communities in which there would be wider and wider discrepancy in the interpretations of the common framework and the standards of evaluation. Similarly, this solution would not depend on an overlapping consensus of antecedent values; it would, rather, require constructing a new and expanded framework for deliberating about differences. However, the result of the compromise is quite different from what Dworkin thinks it is. It describes only the general terms for a weak plural agreement, to which each side could assent for *different* reasons. It does not construct a common position on which both sides converge, nor does it produce a new shared consensus (as Dworkin seems to think it does). But such an agreement will often be the best available moral compromise to emerge in public deliberation.

Third-party mediation of conflicts may also provide stronger cases and illuminate the sorts of devices which promote plural consensus. In contrast with Dworkin's procedure, Jimmy Carter did not proceed by way of abstract principles in promoting the Camp David accords. He slowly constructed an alternative framework in communication facilitated by a changing negotiation text.[40] Once this device overcomes the initial incompatibilities, it may then be possible to deliberate in common about a new moral framework, with new rules of cooperation and new forms of justification. What is interesting about this procedure of compromise formation is that it does not require any kind of abstraction to an impersonal standpoint; each party can modify the text according to his or her own values and principles, and the result does not necessarily reduce the plurality of points of view in the same way as impartiality implies. The text is precisely the ongoing framework of deliberation, which each time must be modified enough to ensure continued cooperation by both sides. As in the case of abortion, the fact that there are alternative and even rival interpretations of basic moral conceptions within each of the conflicting groups further promotes the possibilities of compromise and of each side's adopting a different interpretation of the common framework.

Both sides in such a dispute may view any compromise, moral or not, as giving in to existing injustice, irrationality, and untruth. Even after a compromise is formed, not all participants will abandon their convictions. But enough will find it acceptable if the compromise reached genuinely fuses the existing frameworks and thus modifies both of them. The parties will accept the new framework for different moral reasons, in light of how common deliberation and dialogue with the conflicting view has changed their original beliefs. In the new vocabulary, fair comparison becomes possible. It is then no longer the case that participants have no choices other than the conflicting moral and epistemic values of the previous frameworks. Charles Taylor and others have argued that this is the structure of all intercultural understanding and comparative judgments.[41] But in this case the transformation in moral beliefs and standards of justification is not merely a general broadening of the horizon of understanding; it is a deliberative process of reflection on each of two conflicting sets of values and beliefs and of the construction of a third, alternative set. This is the way the Federalists and the Anti-Federalists together constructed the "dual democracy" of checks and balances in the Constitutional Assembly, a primary forum for moral compromise and for the public construction of new moral frameworks.

Pluralism, Inequality, and Majority Rule: Some Moral Compromises

I am, of course, describing the ideal exercise of plural public reason—the reason exercised in comparison, in which each party must recognize himself in the mutual interpretations and criticisms of the other parties. Such mutual comparison will produce plural agreements, since it avoids pervasive misunderstanding. This process of mutual interpretation provides the constraints on public deliberation that Kantians thought only strict impartiality made possible. Such weaker constraints still produce enough fairness and legitimacy for moral compromises, but not ultimate convergence or consensus. These rationality conditions make it possible for different cultural groups to deliberate together in one democratic public sphere, rather than separately, alongside one another. Revision of the common framework is therefore guided not only by the demands of public reason for mutual recognition but also by the regulative ideal of democratic citizenship. I take the solutions of restrictions on property and mobility rights of non-Native Americans on reservations described by Kymlicka to be adequate compromises of this sort (as far as they go). However, similar restrictions of rights of free expression and speech would not be acceptable moral compromises, since they make impossible the very use of plural public reason needed for political compromise within these communities. Only certain circumstances of inequality and minority status make such compromises reasonable modifications of basic constitutional principles; rights of cultural membership do not reasonably override the political rights necessary for common citizenship, and certainly not rights of free speech.

Whereas plurality is a condition for the uses of public reason that I have been describing, cultural survival by itself is not a goal that is necessarily accomplished by plural public reason. Indeed, the restrictions on rights of mobility proposed in the reservation policies discussed above are fair only because this compromise is for the sake of a disadvantaged minority within a larger and pluralistic political community. The same policies would be unfair under different circumstances (depending, for example, on considerations such as the extent of social inequalities, the presence of other minorities, or whether one community has constituted the original legal framework of a nation state). On the nation-state level, restrictive language and immigration policies cannot be justified for this reason—certainly not to protect particular cultures or even to protect diversity. Current political or religious values should not determine immigration status, as they might for a policy guided by an antecedent overlapping consensus. Pluralistic institutions are inclusive enough to make cultural membership irrelevant for public immigration criteria, except in cases where there are independent moral reasons such as asylum from persecution. Plural public reason promotes common deliberation about conflicts, not about the collective goals of particular cultures. Public reason works to transform the cultural framework of each culture through mutual criticism and interpretation, and hence will be resisted by anyone interested in dogmatism. Indeed, public reason promotes critical reflection on one's own culture, and open and pluralistic public forums inevitably change the beliefs and identities of their participants as they incorporate the new reasons and novel justifications of others. This sort of deliberation still demands the public use of reason by citizens, even when plural. The prospect of moral compromises should promote this pluralist deliberation, which inevitably spills over into deliberation within each community.

Moral Compromise, Social Inequalities, and Majority Rule: Voting Rights and Persistent Minorities

Deliberation and citizenship are particularly significant when compromises are made in situations of unequal minorities, such as in the Native American example with which I began. While significant, the compromise itself may be inadequate owing to the situation of deliberation in which it was formed. It was not until the Meech Lake agreements that Native Americans had anything like equal deliberative standing in revising the common framework in Canada, and to date nothing similar to Meech Lake has occurred in the United States.[42] Nonetheless, the particular compromise concerning political jurisdiction is fair as far as it goes: it considers the cultural values involved and the specific circumstances of inequality. Persistent social inequalities and extreme poverty, coupled with deep conflicts with a majority culture that can overwhelm the minority economically, produce a situation of public deliberation in which the concerns of the Native American minority culture count for little in larger political institutions. These inequalities in deliberation make it such that this group becomes a permanent minority, consistently disadvantaged in

civic deliberation. Its concerns do not receive reasonable consideration from other citizens, and its members cannot reasonably expect to
influence deliberative outcomes. This extreme poverty, the large cultural distance from European collective goals and assumptions, and
other deliberative disadvantages in the Native American case make
the restrictions on property rights and mobility a fair moral compromise in this case. The restriction of voting rights is more problematic.

Before proliferating rights claims can be discussed, a number of
different cases must be distinguished. Without the presence of persistent inequalities, neither the Afrikaner minority nor the Quebecois
majority can legitimate its calls for distinct jurisdictions and for restriction of the rights of other groups. The principles guiding less
extreme cases should be the following: Do such measures promote
public deliberation? Do they make possible the continued cooperation of minority groups in the larger public sphere? Local jurisdictions in the United States often fulfill the latter standard by
promoting a coherent voice for Native Americans in the larger, civic
public sphere. Representational voting schemes are one way to ensure
that unequal minorities can reasonably expect to affect the outcome
of deliberation.[43] However, they do not always promote the use of
plural public reason; rather, they often bring about a separation of
the disadvantaged group from the larger public sphere. Such solutions for modifying voting rights fall on the horns of the liberal
dilemma outlined above, as do theories that stop with the plurality of
civil society alone. Moral compromises are fair if they meet two main
criteria: that they take into account political inequality and that they
make possible continued participation of all groups in a common
deliberative framework.

More appropriate are forms of voting that are still consistent with
the framework of the political equality and common citizenship implied by both majority rule and "one person, one vote." These standards need not be interpreted so narrowly in a fair moral
compromise, particularly when they are applied to a system of winner-
take-all elections for every office. Here proposals of "cumulative voting systems" are better than "group representation systems" as ways to
overcome persistent inequality and permanent minority status. Put
simply, cumulative voting gives each voter multiple votes (say, seven

votes for a seven-seat city council); in contrast, group representation apportions the council seats proportionately among groups, granting special status and voice to cultural minorities or other groups in need of protection.[44] Both group representation and cumulative voting compensate for the disadvantages of under-representation in deliberative institutions. But cumulative voting does so in a way that incorporates the principles of "one person, one vote" and majority rule even while compensating for the particular circumstances of many inequalities. More important, it encourages continued active cooperation and participation in a common public sphere, fostering cooperation and the forming of coalitions among diverse groups in ways that proportional representation schemes do not.

In this way, cumulative voting fits the two main criteria for successful moral compromises: it takes into account persistent inequalities and it promotes the ideals of common citizenship. By overcoming disadvantages, such strategies help make the public reasons of all groups count and thus encourage their continued cooperation in deliberation with the reasonable expectation that they will be able to affect the outcome. Cultural pluralism should change how we think of representation, but in such a way that we maximize the participation of diverse groups in the same political process and in the same civic public sphere. It should also change how we think of the formation of groups themselves. Groups should not be culturally fixed categories; rather, group formation should be open, pluralistic, and dynamic. The plurality of groups in civil society promotes deliberation only if group associations can form and re-form themselves in the public sphere, thereby promoting the social conditions for overcoming persistent inequalities of culturally fixed and disadvantaged groups.

In the last three sections, I have shown how the plural use of public reason can solve problems of deep conflict that emerge in culturally pluralistic settings for deliberation. The thrust of my argument is that a certain type of solution to such problems is possible and can emerge in public deliberation, properly understood and structured. I have called this possibility moral compromise, and I have given a diverse set of examples of such compromises, some more substantive and others more procedural. Substantive moral compromises that

arise from deliberation have the general form of the solution to conflicts over abortion as outlined by Dworkin: they involve recognizing
the reasons of others and taking them up as parts of the overall solution—in this case, both the autonomy of the woman and the value of
life are recognized as public reasons. In procedural solutions, such as
the cumulative voting system offered by Lani Guinier,[45] the terms of
cooperation are modified so as to make deliberation more inclusive,
to make it possible for even disadvantaged minorities to have the reasonable expectation of affecting outcomes in the sphere of common
citizenship. Procedural compromises are based on the ongoing recognition of the need at times to modify the decision-making processes
that structure deliberation in order to make minority opinions more
effective in securing public uptake. When such efforts fail, in some
cases it may be necessary to grant to certain communities powers of
self-government—particularly in cases, such as those of Native
Americans in the United States and Canada, where a persistent minority is the result of a history of conquest.

Most substantive compromises reached in public deliberation will
be part of ongoing self-governance by citizens. It is only in the case of
deep conflicts that the framework of deliberation itself must be modified. If that framework is already pluralistic enough, it is often sufficient to recognize the public reasons of groups by granting them
exemptions from particular laws or policies. Such exemptions might
include laws that disadvantage certain ethnic groups—for example,
Sunday business closing and restrictions on animal slaughtering for
Muslims and Jews, motorcycle helmet laws for Sikh men, or official
dress codes in public institutions such as schools or the military for
many different groups. In deliberative democracy, it would be misleading to call these exemptions "polyethnic rights" or "differentiated citizenship."[46] Rather, they are part of the ongoing process of
public deliberation by which general norms are applied to specific situations. In cases of compromise, such exemptions are best regarded
as outcomes of public deliberation that recognizes the equal value of
cultural expression and public safety as public reasons. The dialogical
mechanism of moving back and forth between the demands of general rules and the exigencies of the particular situation make deliberative arrangements ideally suited for the ongoing problems of

potential inter-group conflicts about applying particular decisions or rules in specific situations. Such applications are often highly contested and demand much public deliberation on the reasons for applying laws to particular cases, making differentiation in the reasons for such decisions the rule and not the exception.

There may be many other instances of moral compromise that involve quite different forms of both substantive accommodation and procedural inclusion. I have only sought to sketch out the general form of possible resolutions to deep conflicts. What all of these solutions have in common is that they avoid the dilemmas of singular public reason: on the one hand, they avoid the overly strong assumptions of convergence typical of impartialist accounts of public reason, even dynamic ones such as Habermas's; on the other hand, they avoid the overly weak assumptions of the mere fact of reasonable pluralism, typical of Rawls. While the former make the standard of agreement too high in pluralist settings in which public reason is itself contested, the former do not get us any closer to specifying how it is that deliberation is possible in pluralist settings, except by avoiding conflict altogether. Of course, in many instances, the solutions that either avoidance or singular public reason suggest may be what citizens ultimately adopt in actual deliberation. Citizens may sometimes be able to recognize in one another's claims that some such conflicts are strictly matters of justice whereas others may be left to the freedom of conscience and thought. But those very solutions, like the common use of the mechanism of voting, are on my view themselves best seen as moral compromises reached in processes of deliberation. Otherwise, we too easily fall into the temptation of equating these very particular solutions and mechanisms with democracy itself, and thus too quickly condemn as undemocratic and unreasonable anyone who disagrees with their use. Such rhetorical claims about particular pragmatic devices and mechanisms typically articulate only one side of a deep conflict, rather than offer a possible cooperative solution. Settling a particular conflict by leaving it a matter for the liberty of private conscience remains a possibility, but it, too, is only one compromise that may emerge in the dialogical mechanisms of actual public deliberation. My argument for moral compromise has shown not only that solutions to cultural conflicts are possible, but also that deliberating about such conflicts has a political point even when citizens may rightly be said to disagree reasonably. Such deliberative possibilities should caution theorists from drawing the limits of public reason too quickly, either to settle such conflicts *a priori* in terms of some univocal structure of public reason or to make such solutions empirically impossible in light of the mere fact of pluralism. Both such claims ignore the plurality and contestability inherent in public reason.

The key to accommodating pluralism in public deliberation is this: to consider a political decision legitimate, citizen-deliberators need not make the strong assumption that their deliberative process makes it more likely that the outcome is one on which all would ultimately and ideally *converge*. Rather, it is enough for them to assume that, given the conditions of deliberation, outcomes and decisions allow an *ongoing cooperation with others* of different minds that is at least *not unreasonable*. Citizens are justified in making this corrigible supposition, for all practical purposes, if the deliberative process satisfies at least three closely related conditions: First, the discursive structures of informal and formal deliberation make it less likely that irrational and untenable arguments will decide outcomes. Second, decision-making procedures are structured so as to allow revisions—of arguments, decisions, and even procedures—that either take up features of defeated positions or better their chances of being heard. Third, deliberative decision-making procedures are broadly inclusive, so that minorities may reasonably expect that they will be able to affect future outcomes in ways that they have not been able to so far. This is not, to be sure, a full account of rational cooperation—for that, one would have to bring in the costs of non-cooperation and the presence of guarantees of basic rights. But it does broaden the normative account of legitimacy to recognize forms of compromise that are public and not simply based on strategic calculations.

In any case, the first condition implies that the various institutions and publics outlined in the second section of this chapter have, at the very least, a negative and hence critical function. That is, they are meant to elevate debate to a civil and public level by ensuring that simple and crude appeals to prejudice can be publicly challenged and undermined, that subtle and not-so-subtle coercion will be exposed and contested, and that unjustifiable exclusionary mechanisms will be eliminated and corrected. On many issues, vigorous pursuit of these measures may suffice to produce a positive consensus. But this need not be the case, and reasonable disagreements may still persist. That, however, is just the point: that all *un*reasonable disagreements, as well as all unreasonable *agreements*, be eliminated.

With the elimination of unreasonable appeals to fear, prejudice, and ignorance, many citizens may transform their preferences and beliefs and adopt substantively different positions. But this depends on many empirical factors and is not always the case. On the contrary, it may be that people retain their original views, only now supported by even better and hence more reasonable arguments which only sharpen existing conflicts. In other words, a deliberative framework functions primarily to raise the level of debate, even when it does not produce agreement. Insofar as a vibrant public sphere contains a variety of arenas and publics that submit unreflective views to criticism, insofar as institutional checks screen arguments against careful and public scrutiny of the facts and against a representative inclusion of different constituencies, and insofar as the mass media are not myopic, it should be more difficult for proposals and candidates to carry the day on the basis of empty rhetoric. Making reasons public may "launder" them, "filtering the inputs" of public deliberation about conflicts through public testing.[47]

The second condition, revisability, appears in a number of forms, one of which is already implicit in the first condition. Precisely because the public testing of reasons and outcomes in effect "launders" majority views, it enables minorities to influence the set of reasons that justify outcomes. Thus, the fact that rational deliberation is guided by publicity can engender a revision of *substantive arguments* that, even if it does not terminate in consensus, can bring positions closer together so that a kind of moral compromise becomes possible. Often, however, one associates revisability simply with the changing of earlier outcomes through the repetition of the procedure (or through the use of an alternative procedural route). Democratic procedures typically allow for this in many different ways, including periodic elections, the repeal of laws, judicial and other forms of review, and amendment of the constitution. As I shall argue below, such a

process is central to popular sovereignty. Finally, revisability can reach
to the procedures themselves: democratic procedures may be revised
in order to reestablish the equal power of minorities to influence deliberative outcomes in the face of contingent social and demographic
facts that may undermine cooperation. If such facts make minorities
permanent, democratic institutions will not be "well ordered" in
Rawls's sense; they will not ensure the political equality necessary for
mutual cooperation. In each of these forms, revisability has the effect
of "compelling the majority to take the minority into account, at least
to a certain extent."[48] For example, beginning in 1937 the extension
of the Equal Protection Clause to include government activism in
the economic sphere helped redress social imbalances that undermined equal participation in political procedures.[49]

The possibility of having one's defeated position taken into account, as well as other forms of revisability, points to the third condition: inclusiveness. With substantive revisions, for example, minority
positions have a role in shaping majority outcomes. The future possibility of reversing majorities means that minorities are not perma-
nently excluded from decision making, and procedural revisions are
introduced precisely to safeguard this possibility by increasing voting
equality. In general, more inclusive deliberative and decision-making
procedures make it more likely that citizens will overcome their myopia and their ethnocentrism. For example, knowing that their decisions may have to be revised to maintain publicity and equality,
citizens will think of their democratic practices in an inclusive and future-oriented way. Most important, they will come to realize that they,
too, may occupy the minority position.

This pluralistic conception of publicity opens up a space for forms
of compromise that go beyond the balance of interests envisioned by
Habermas. Here I will simply illustrate how a kind of moral compromise becomes possible insofar as deliberation allows citizens to see
that an opposing view is not simply based, at least in any obvious way,
on self-deception or prejudice. This makes it easier to search for a
common framework that is accepted by each group for *different* reasons but allows opposing groups to maintain social cooperation.
Moral compromises seek to change the framework for ongoing deliberation in such a way that each party can continue to cooperate

from within his or her own perspective. Here the idea of a framework includes both the pool of available reasons and the procedures of deliberation—two elements that are often distinguishable only analytically. Hence, successful moral compromise must expand the pool of available reasons in order to get beyond the incompatibility of current interpretations, and it must be procedurally fair.

In sum, one would expect such mechanisms for cooperation and compromise to become particularly important when political decisions concern difficult issues of justice that, for some, do not allow for compromise. Suppose, for example, that I vote in the minority on an issue that I consider a question of justice or even of fundamental political rights. If the lack of open discussion leads me to believe that the majority will be influenced by passion, prejudice, or ignorance, or perhaps manipulated by powerful interests that control access to the mass media, then on either the strong or the weak interpretation of rational deliberation I have good reason to question the legitimacy of the outcome, and my compliance with the decision should be grudging at best. But if there has been open and honest treatment of the issue prior to the vote, I will be less justified in doubting the legitimacy of the outcome. Even if I still disagree with the majority, I can at least see that their position can be argued in public. Moreover, procedures used to construct compromises can allow minorities to accept decisions based on future-oriented considerations, such as the revision of laws or the building of new coalitions. If I take the unanimity requirement in Habermas's democratic principle at face value, however, I will seemingly always be justified in questioning the very legitimacy of all majoritarian outcomes, no matter how well-debated and revisable. By contrast, if I accept a weaker reading of legitimacy, I can dispute the ultimate correctness of the outcome (which seems open to reasonable dispute in this case) and still acknowledge that the outcome has legitimacy insofar as it is not obviously unreasonable. I can therefore reasonably expect that the outcomes may be revised in the future and thus that my continued cooperation and participation may bring the change about if my reasons are publicly convincing enough to shape the course of future deliberation. I may also reasonably expect that my reasons will receive consideration in such a process, even if they have not been accepted by others thus far. Above all, because the framework of deliberation itself can be publicly contested, I need not abandon my common citizenship and participation in the civic public sphere with those with whom I disagree. Of course, this expectation is reasonable only if minorities actually participate in this civic public sphere on equal footing.

Conclusion

Democratic decision making places high demands on the self-reflective and public uses of reason, particularly under the conditions of plurality. Liberals have long pointed out that democratic institutions cannot be based on the assumption of shared, substantive moral agreement. Rawls's *Political Liberalism* gives a powerful defense of this view, but one that does not provide an account of how to deal with the increasing challenge to the institutions of public reason posed by deep cultural conflicts. Democratic deliberation can be reasonable under these conditions if it is characterized by the dynamic exercise of plural public reason guided by the ideal of democratic citizenship. Various solutions to the moral conflicts of pluralism emerge from such deliberation, including cooperation, institutional differentiation, and moral compromise.

Good democratic arrangements and their normative constraints promote such solutions by ensuring deliberative liberties and the conditions of mutuality in dialogue. The former are related to achieving equality among citizens who possess political and human rights, now understood procedurally in terms of the conditions under which citizens publicly reason and deliberate. This may include compromises in which these rights are distributed differentially or in which voting procedures broaden majority rule to take into account the position of unequal minorities. The latter expand the framework of common citizenship by incorporating differences. Only by going beyond the restrictions of impartiality and singularity can public reason be made a workable norm for resolving conflicts of principle in pluralist democracies. If deliberative democracies do not resolve such moral conflicts, cultural pluralism is indeed a limit upon the public use of reason. For democracies that do resolve such conflicts in fair moral compromises, however, vibrant pluralism only increases the potential for reasonable and inclusive public deliberation. In a time when deep conflicts can ignite virulent nationalism and religious fanaticism, political liberalism cannot ignore the new challenges of cultural pluralism to social peace and stability.

Pluralism is not, then, an insurmountable epistemic or moral obstacle for public deliberation that abandons unanimity and seeks plural public agreement. The underlying difficulty is that cultural differences are more often than not associated with social inequalities, which ramify the difficulties of pluralist agreements. The broader the public sphere, the more difficult it is for certain groups to participate effectively in a framework they have neither defined nor greatly influenced. Minorities in particular have difficulty receiving uptake in deliberation, because they also suffer from persistent social inequalities. Persistent inequalities may lead to difficulties in participation in public deliberation, particularly for those minority viewpoints that need to struggle to gain public recognition. Thus, the common empirical correlation between minority cultural status and social inequalities could undermine a free and open public sphere. Without correcting for inequalities, deliberative arrangements under these conditions could even lead to elitist consequences. If deliberative democracy does not solve the problems of pluralism, it may simply become rule by "mere" majority group; if it does not find a way to compensate for the effects of inequalities, those who are the most successful and competent in deliberation could well be those who are already the most well off. The challenge for democracy is to correct for such inequalities in such a way as to promote public deliberation.

3

Deliberative Inequalities

Acceptable solutions to cultural conflicts may emerge in deliberation governed by two interrelated democratic norms. The first norm is political equality. The deeper the conflict, the more important it is that the parties have equal standing in deliberation about it. The second norm (a related one) concerns the presumption that the conditions for effective participation have been met. In situations of conflict, it is important that all parties believe that their concerns have been adequately voiced and that their reasons have been considered, even when they ultimately do not carry the day. Cultural pluralism heightens the uncertainty of achieving deliberative uptake, as well as the problems of gaining mutual recognition and respect. The mere rejection of one group's public reasons by others does not in itself indicate a lack of respect for one another, but some groups can make the case that such failure to convince others with their public reasons is part of a larger pattern. If members of a minority believe that their views are never a recognizable part of the outcome of deliberation, eventually they no longer may be willing to cooperate in political problem solving—and rightly so, since such a deliberative process cannot be a public activity for them. Every deliberator must have the confidence that he or she will, at least on some occasions and on some issues, favorably influence deliberation. Such a capacity requires at least a minimal threshold of public effectiveness, the measure of political equality in the deliberative process.

The lack of such efficacious participation, or adequate public functioning, by the socially less well situated is the primary problem of inequality in democracies, and deliberation is no exception. Social inequalities tend to reduce the efficacy and influence of less well off deliberators: their lack of cultural resources and of opportunities to develop various public capacities as they are currently defined make it more difficult for them to make their reasons publicly convincing; they do not easily convert their needs and convictions into effective contributions to decisions. Proportional representation is often proposed as a solution to this problem of public voice. The more foolproof it is, however, the less it promotes deliberation among various groups in the public sphere. Other measures must be taken to promote a wider spectrum of opinions and participants within deliberative institutions. As I argued in chapter 2, some decision-making mechanisms, such as cumulative voting, might achieve the desired effect without inhibiting deliberation. The same goal of equality guides such legal measures as the Fairness Doctrine applied to the expensive broadcast media and recent attempts at campaign finance reform.

In order to promote deliberation, such corrective mechanisms work best when they push minorities or disadvantaged groups over the threshold of being ignored and of having their reasons excluded from the public sphere. Mechanisms that ensure certain (minimum) outcomes may promote egalitarian purposes in certain circumstances, but they do not necessarily expand the universe of public discourse. They are based on an inadequate, outcome-based conception of political equality that would require non-deliberative mechanisms to achieve the proper threshold of effective participation. Without achieving such a threshold of equality, corrective measures may become publicly ineffective and democratically capricious. In this chapter I shall develop a conception of deliberative inequalities that could guide such radical democratic reforms and help them avoid unintended, anti-deliberative consequences.

It is easy to overemphasize the cultural basis of political conflict, which allows the persistent inequality of various cultural or social groups to remain entrenched. Economic conflict also can become entrenched, especially when it produces directly opposing interests and zero-sum situations. When a functioning public sphere exists, the problem of reform is to find ways to give politically unequal minority groups effective voices. Ensuring the access of all to the public sphere places high demands on the practices that ensure political equality. Large inequalities demand more constraints on the political process for the sake of fairness, and these constraints often seem to limit the potential for deliberation. But not to correct them limits the themes and topics made publicly available in deliberation. In this chapter I will show how deliberative democracy can avoid the horns of this dilemma and take corrective measures that promote, rather than limit, deliberation. In order to solve this problem, a new capacity-based conception of deliberative inequality is necessary. Even if both material and cultural goods are included, equality of resources and equality of opportunity are not sufficient for this task. Only equality of political capacities makes deliberation fully democratic. Only on this condition does the epistemic quality of reasons improve as a result of the deliberative process; only then do deliberators benefit from the diversity of opinions and prospects.

In view of the strains that differences place on deliberative activity, it is not surprising that Aristotle believed deliberation to require strict equality. For Aristotle, not only must citizens be roughly equal economically, as propertied male heads of households; they must also be the *same* in their general capacities, education, and cultural values (especially those that count as requirements for excellence or virtue).[1] As equals, citizens can be both rulers and ruled; as the same, they can all strive for the same goals and excellences, and can all hold the same standards of practical judgment. Aristotle held that both sameness and equality were necessary conditions for the self-rule of citizens in well-ordered constitutional polities. In situations of inequality and difference, Aristotle held that deliberation cannot order political ends and that it results in instability.

In chapter 2 I indicated why *difference* not only is possible in democratic deliberation but also promotes a more dynamic and inclusive form of public deliberation. In the present chapter I want to show how deliberation is possible even with preexisting, large, and relatively persistent *inequalities*. Of course, public deliberation does not leave them in place. Rather, the point is to correct for their effects both in the deliberative process itself and in the unequal outcomes that such asymmetries consistently produce. By limiting the public scope of deliberation, inequalities can create a vicious circle; in deliberation limited in this way, citizens who are influential are not aware of the limited scope of their deliberation and will not be concerned with inequalities. A public sphere can function well and improve public reasons only if all citizens can effectively exercise their freedom within it.

I call the asymmetries of public capabilities and functioning that persist in most public spheres "deliberative inequalities." Such group-related asymmetries are usually classified as inequalities of opportunity, of resources, and of capability. Put in political terms, there are three basic types of deliberative inequalities: power asymmetries (which affect access to the public sphere), communicative inequalities (which affect the ability to participate and to make effective use of available opportunities to deliberate in the public sphere), and "political poverty," or the lack of developed public capacities (which makes it less likely that politically impoverished citizens can participate in the public sphere at all).

Political poverty designates a failure of capacity in public deliberation: a group-related inability to make effective use of opportunities to influence the deliberative process in favor of concerns of the group's members.[2] This conception of equality emphasizes the fact that agents begin with initial social differences in the capacity to have their concerns receive public consideration by others. Given that political agency requires that citizens engage in the joint social activity of deliberation, I favor the use of the term *capacities* over Sen's favored term, *capabilities*. It better captures the sorts of abilities that citizens need to participate effectively as equals in public dialogue. In order to be minimally effective in deliberation, a deliberator must be able to initiate public dialogue about an issue or a theme, in which his or her reasons may receive deliberative uptake. Just as economic agents must have the capacity to avoid acute hunger and severe malnourishment, so too public actors must have the ability to avoid being excluded from public life and to avoid having their concerns consistently ignored. Of course, being impoverished or wealthy in this political sense admits of degrees. Citizens have the capacity to avoid such persistent disadvantages only if political equality establishes a threshold of access to deliberative resources and to the conditions necessary for the development of public capacities. To the extent that inequalities exclude groups from political life, they violate one of the main conditions of publicity: citizens' general expectation that they have the opportunity to contribute to public deliberation. Such poverty makes groups of citizens particularly vulnerable in deliberative decision making.

Because public deliberation is not compatible with persistent social inequalities, political equality in deliberation can serve as a critical standard of democratic legitimacy. Such a standard is at the very least useful as a counterfactual norm, since it entails a set of social and cultural conditions necessary for successful public deliberation. These conditions specify how equality can be realized in deliberation: all participants must develop their public capacities, have access to the public sphere, and have the opportunity to influence the course of deliberation in a favorable direction. Untouchables in India, for example, may have formal opportunities for input, but their mere support for a policy may lead to its defeat. Deliberative inequalities are thus best seen not as violations of procedural norms that define opportunities for input but as the violations of certain thresholds of political equality. Below a threshold of access to public resources and opportunities, it is less likely that all citizens will develop their public capacities or have their public reasons heard and respected. The fair distribution of the moral and political costs of decisions is a good indicator of such deliberative justice.

The analysis of deliberative inequalities is also important for another reason: it resists a potentially elitist tendency in deliberative theories, one that is certainly present in Aristotle and in some early Enlightenment thinkers. Aristotle restricted deliberation to those who were already virtuous, wise, and well off. Some Enlightenment thinkers held that only those who were capable of being impartial and detached could be entrusted with crucial decision-making powers, which required not having urgent needs or pressing interests. These are not the elitist dangers that deliberative democracy faces today. Under modern conditions of diverse interests and a lack of consensus about impartial standards, deliberation could become elitist: the rule of those able to achieve their private goals by public means. Deliberation without corrections for inequalities will always have such elitist tendencies in practice, favoring those who have greater cultural resources (such as knowledge and information) and who are more capable of imposing their own interests and values on others in the public arena.

In this chapter I offer a solution to the problems that a fundamental fact of modern society presents for democratic deliberation: like the fact of pluralism, the fact of large inequalities of social and cultural resources seems to make deliberation an impossible ideal for modern societies. These inequalities are now large enough to produce political poverty among many groups of citizens. I will show that such poverty in deliberation results in public exclusion coupled with political inclusion. On the one hand, politically impoverished groups cannot avoid public exclusion; on the other hand, they avoid cannot political inclusion. Since contestation requires the resources and capacities that impoverished citizens lack, political poverty creates a vicious cycle analogous to those of economic poverty. Thus, political poverty reproduces itself in deliberation.

As these remarks indicate, my capacity-based analysis takes public exclusion and non-voluntary inclusion to be operational measures of political inequality. A capacity-based account also provides the best explanation of such political consequences of social inequalities. It is not that inequalities of resources and opportunity are irrelevant. Rather, a capacity conception has three main advantages for deliberative theories of democracy. First, successful deliberation is directly related to highly developed capacities for communication. Second, such a notion of political equality admits of degrees and is not an all-or-nothing concept. Third, by virtue of political inclusion without effective participation or voice, impoverished citizens often have no real alternative but to comply with political decisions. After developing each of these aspects, I turn to proposals for correcting such inequalities democratically and to the alternative forms of power generated by communication and solidarity in the public sphere. The challenge here is to avoid repeating the dilemmas of inclusion and exclusion through corrective measures.

Communicative Inequalities and Distorted Communication

Although public deliberation presupposes political equality, it cannot entirely filter out the consequences of large differences in wealth and power. In the *Social Contract* Rousseau seems to demand only enough equality to maintain civil liberty. According to Rousseau, some inequalities (e.g., in wealth) can be quite wide, even in some politically relevant respects (such as capacities). With regard to wealth, problems emerge only with extreme differences: "No citizen should be rich enough to be able to buy another, and no poor enough to have to sell himself."[3] Even when the poor cannot be bought, their resentments lend support to demagogues and lead to rapid and cyclical changes in regimes. Relative equality is thus primarily a condition for social stability for Rousseau, just as it is for Rawls and for many proponents of economic democracy today.[4]

By this measure, political power can be unequal to a certain extent. Here Rousseau uses an intrinsic rather than a relative standard: political inequalities must fall short of all forms of violence and be consistent with the limits of the rule of law.[5] For Rousseau both wealth and power are conditions for *public* autonomy, a form of freedom that tolerates only so much violence and inequality. Although Rousseau is correct that large inequalities undermine publicity, his broad thresholds are too poorly defined to suffice for deliberative equality. The absence of tyranny falls well short of deliberative equality, which requires distributive conditions that ensure the effective participation of the entire public in deliberative dialogue. The problem here is to develop some way of distinguishing apparent from actual publicity and to give an account of the ways in which the lack of communicative equality limits the give and take of dialogue.

Here the social-scientific analysis of inequalities of resources and power can be helpful, particularly concerning the way inequalities structure social interaction. It may be able to make manifest how asymmetries of power continue to operate within the public sphere and in the very dialogical mechanisms that produce agreements. Powerlessness and poverty have a political meaning in this context and can be given a well-defined threshold. There is a good empirical indicator for unequal deliberative capacity: whether or not citizens or groups of citizens are able to initiate public deliberation about their concerns. This ability to initiate acts of deliberation represents the basic threshold for political equality. Above it, continued cooperation indicates democratic legitimacy, even when particular groups of citizens continue to disagree with existing decisions and policies. Below it, the appearance of continued cooperation is only behavioral compliance for non-public reasons. Compliance is then not a public or political choice based on the recognition of legitimacy. Persistently disadvantaged groups have no public reason to recognize the legitimacy of a regime with which they disagree but whose power over them makes them subject to decisions they cannot afford to ignore.

Such inability to initiate public deliberation is a widespread phenomenon of asymmetrical face-to-face interaction and dialogue. This communicative inequality often takes the form of failure to be able to take turns without being interrupted or to shift the topic of conversation successfully, as in the male-female interactions analyzed by Don Zimmerman, Candace West, and Angela Garcia.[6] Similar restrictions emerge in asymmetrical doctor-patient relations: patients suffer from an inability to initiate discourse and to shift topics with doctors and staff in clinical settings.[7] Some explicit asymmetries are the most extreme manifestations of power: in an interrogation, a prisoner can only answer the question put by the interrogator, who begins the interrogation by imposing the rules of an intentionally restricted system of communication roles upon the prisoner and by demanding acquiescence to them.[8] Apart from extreme cases, more often than not implicit restrictions operate in the ordinary dialogue necessary for public deliberation.

The historical emergence of the public sphere may be thought to eliminate the most pernicious influences of power and wealth on public dialogue, at least with regard to social status. Indeed, all members of the public are supposed to have equal status. In the literary public sphere of the salons and the coffeehouses of the eighteenth century, according to Habermas's historical analysis, social status was left at the door, at least in principle: ". . . in the salons the nobility and the grande bourgeoisie met with the intellectuals on an equal footing"; in the American literary public sphere of the same period, participants were equal citizens of a "republic of letters."[9] Only when the sons of the aristocracy joined with the sons (and in rare cases the daughters) of craftsmen and shopkeepers could they compel political authority to legitimate itself before the tribunal of public opinion. For this to be possible, the limiting influences of wealth and power had to be suspended, creating the forms of civility, tact, and conversation necessary for relations and interaction among equals. The force of public reasons could then replace the influence of social hierarchies. The public of "private persons" emerges not only when "the power and prestige of public office were held in suspense" but also when "economic dependencies in principle have no influence."[10]

The distorting and restricting influences on publicity are varied: they include not just wealth and power, but also the institutional mechanisms through which market forces and state violence operate. By eliminating them, the new public sphere became more inclusive: it suspended precisely those inequalities and hierarchies that operate by exclusion and limit the scope of public judgment to "exemplary" or "representative" figures. Besides eliminating forms of speech that required such authority, the emergent public sphere inaugurated new forms related to the expression of needs and desires, viz., the discourses of aesthetic sensibility and ethical authenticity.[11] Nonetheless, the public sphere did not, and indeed could not, suspend all such deliberative and communicative effects of social inequalities of power and wealth. Such effects cannot be eliminated so readily from public discourse as can the limitations of state and religious authority. Censorship in the form of explicit prohibitions is not the issue in constitutional states, but rather more subtle forms of self-censorship that operate publicly through the imposition of cultural forms or styles of political communication.[12] Moreover, the public sphere could not eliminate appeals to power or privilege; it could only change conditions so as to make it more difficult for them to succeed.

The constraints of publicity do not eliminate verbal forms of power and their effects. Consider an act of verbal intimidation. Claims to expertise based on accumulated cultural resources and capacities can be intimidating if accompanied by a widespread social belief in their privileged epistemic position. They become acts of intimidation when their purpose is to bring discussion to a halt and to settle on one of many possible acceptable interpretations. Right-wing talk-show hosts in the United States use more direct intimidation as a double bind to poison public discourse: unpopular or liberal guests or callers are intimidated if they do not respond; if they do respond, accusations made against them are given public credibility. Other forms of intimidation are neither always explicit nor always intentional. The distinctiveness of intimidation is that it works only on a person "predisposed to feel it, whereas others will ignore it."[13] Intimidation in this sense is an effect of being part of a network of social relationships that cannot be easily suspended in public deliberation. It can, however, be made a theme for deliberation and public scrutiny.

Such examples illustrate the implicit forms of unequal power, influence, and resources that can continue to operate in the public sphere. Cases in which overt power automatically gives a speaker communicative success are not, however, paradigm cases of social power as manifested in public use of language. They are simply non-public forms of communication in Kant's sense: directed to a restricted audience. Power operates publicly by undermining the successful operation of the dialogical mechanisms on which deliberation depends. Deliberation becomes non-public in two senses: non-public reasons can guide deliberation, even without becoming themes for dialogue; and the dialogue in which deliberation takes place is no longer public, losing the public character of the back-and-forth movement of exchanging and criticizing reasons. In the case of intimidation, such exchange may not occur. More often, it takes place but the reasons of some speakers are ignored. This is often the case in legal interpretation of the scopes of various rights claims. Rights of privacy might then be applied selectively to persons: whereas the rights of culturally "unmarked" persons (white, male, heterosexual) to privacy have long been guaranteed, "marked" persons do not share these protections (sexual privacy, protection from illegal search, guarantees of bodily integrity).[14]

When publicly available reasons are ignored, deliberation adopts the perspective of the dominant group rather than shifting among the richer set of perspectives of all those concerned. Other mechanisms of deliberative uptake similarly become limited, as when a norm is interpreted through the particular application favored by a powerful group. Such norms may include the official language of political deliberation, which may favor particular ethnic groups; the formal style of public discourse, which may favor a particular class; or the styles of political communication, which may reinforce a particular gender-based interpretation of the public/private distinction.[15]

These communicatively structured political inequalities also operate through the ideologies that support and justify them; they are built into the interpretive frameworks and institutions that organize deliberation. In these cases persons with grievances cannot participate effectively, since they cannot alter the common framework for deliberation. Once dialogical mechanisms are so inhibited by asymmetries, deliberation ceases to be pluralistic and dynamic. Rather, it becomes the public reason of a single group or class, with its historically limited interpretations of the results of past deliberation.

Let me illustrate the influence of pervasive inequalities and asymmetries on deliberative mechanisms. Racism has historically been a direct manifestation of power. American Constitutional law abounds with statements about political equality, yet these statements were for decades interpreted as consistent with both slavery and the restricted political status of women. Abolitionists ultimately succeeded in bringing new interpretations into public debate, often by insisting that religious and philosophical doctrines invoked in the Constitution did not sanction slavery. By mobilizing themselves into a public movement, abolitionists challenged the prevailing interpretive framework sufficiently to bring new moral intuitions into the public debate; the public reinterpretation of norms brought into play the dialogical mechanism of reflective equilibrium. Such a hermeneutic process of retrieving aspects of America's political traditions and democratic culture eventually became even deeper as other excluded groups entered the public sphere and advanced their own interpretations of shared moral intuitions. The Fourteenth Amendment provided a new framework for political judgment and later provided a basis for new contestations of many other exclusions from public life.

Such examples can be generalized further. Inequalities of power enter into the very definition of the problematic situation to be deliberated upon, and such definitions themselves may promote or inhibit deliberation. Power can be expressed in the way in which problems are defined and thus "framed," often in such a way that the participatory success of powerful groups is ensured.[16] For example, technological and industrial accidents, such as those at nuclear power facilities, were for several decades framed as "engineering problems" to be settled by experts. This frame for the risks of nuclear power effectively removed the issue from public debate, excluding public deliberation about the advantages and disadvantages of such technologies and about the distribution of the risks posed by their development and their use. In this case, critics and social movement activists have worked less to plumb the depths of our moral intuitions than to change the frame in which the problem is defined and in which events are interpreted. Similarly, activists in the battered-women's movement have successfully transformed the definition of wife beating from a problem to be treated within a framework of individual pathology and "clinical expertise" into a political question about gender inequality in the application of social and legal norms.[17] These same gender inequalities, coupled with the power of medical institutions in the twentieth century, served to make this a non-politically-defined problem until activists defined it as one governed by public norms and relationships. Here the activists' shift in interpretation produced what Benjamin Barber calls "strong democratic talk"—talk with substantive deliberative uptake that affects actual decisions.[18]

These examples illustrate the ways in which power asymmetries are sustained in the public sphere. Power does not work by simply ensuring success for advantaged speakers and failure for disadvantaged ones, as it does in non-public settings. It works by undermining and fixing the various back-and-forth mechanisms of dialogue through which public deliberation works. Since such effects violate the legitimate expectation of deliberative uptake of less powerful speakers (whether through non-public inclusion or through exclusion), any decision made under these conditions may be criticized as violating standards of political equality in deliberation. The standard here is equality of deliberative opportunity, used to analyze inequalities manifested in political communication.

Following Habermas, we might call such violations of communicative quality and restrictions on public communication "systematically distorted communication."[19] According to Habermas, distorted communication involves latent strategic action and "is the result of the confusion of action oriented to understanding and action oriented to success, of strategic and communicative action."[20] Here power is dyadic: it is the ability to impose one's plans and goals upon others.

For all its insights, such an analysis operates with too limited a conception of inequality. Unavowed intentions need not be present in cases in which power is maintained through unequal capacities, as in the communicative inability of dominated groups to express their needs or the inability of dominating groups to listen. For example, family-planning programs in the Third World in the 1950s did not consider the reasons why destitute parents needed to have more children; instead, they began to promote sterilization when other birth-control measures failed. Similarly, child care is still not on the agenda of economic needs in most North American workplaces; it is only recently that any effort was needed to keep it off the agenda. But rather than describe such consequences in terms of actors' intentions, it is better to describe them in terms of their effects—in terms of how inequalities restrict communication in the public sphere.

When "structural restrictions in communication" are present in interaction,[21] reasons can produce agreement that would not be accepted under the conditions of publicity. In this way, distorted communication can still make possible the consensus necessary for further cooperation and participation, without coercion and fraud. Communicative restrictions can limit *how* people participate and how effective they are in the public sphere, as well as what emerges as possible solutions to problematic situations. It is important, then, to analyze the variety of ways in which communication can be restricted so as to disadvantage some speakers and benefit others. In deliberative democracy, the consequences of distortions of public communication may produce "communicative inequality." This form of inequality emerges in the public sphere, in which successful speakers at least claim to be able to address an unrestricted audience about common concerns and universally accessible themes.

Through inequalities of this sort, distorted communication can enter into public discourse. I have shown how informal norms of interruption can become unnoticed and be taken for granted in many persistent forms of asymmetrical interaction. Although there have been no avowed norms of deference in communication between men and women for some time, informal norms enable men to assume wide powers as speakers. Similar restrictions may operate in formal organizations and institutions where agenda-setting power is delegated but there are no real opportunities for addition or revision. In order to be democratic and publicly convincing, agenda setting itself must be deliberative. Bureaucratic organizations often filter and select out issues and alternatives from the decision-making process. Rather than always promote efficiency, it can also be a "mobilization of bias" that frames decisions in such a way as to produce a "non-decision" in Bachrach and Baratz's sense.[22] If an issue or a demand has been prevented by such bias from reaching the forum of public deliberation, then the organizational structure has produced a non-decision, which eventually distorts and skews deliberation. Typically, such non-decisions filter out legitimate conflicts and challenges to the prevailing institutional structure or mode of problem solving, such as democratic challenges to bureaucratic interventions and planning.

In light of such examples, we can characterize distorted communication in the following ways. First, and most generally, communication is distorted when the social distribution of power and resources undermine the conditions for communicative success. Under such conditions, communicative acts that might otherwise succeed fail and ones that might otherwise fail succeed. Distorted communication produces deliberative outcomes in the form of decisions that fail to take into account the concerns and the reasoning of entire groups of citizens. These sorts of outcomes show the second general feature of distorted communication: it produces outcomes that violate the publicity conditions of deliberation. How can such counterfactual standards be applied in a fruitful way to actual deliberative situations? Habermas provided one form of such an analysis of asymmetries in communication in his much-disputed and often-misinterpreted conception of the "ideal speech situation."[23] Habermas analyzes these ideal conditions primarily in terms of "opportunities" to speak: in an ideal situation of communicative equality, all speakers must have equal chances to speak—to initiate any type of utterance or interaction, to adopt any role in communication or dialogue, and so on. Without equal opportunities to employ all forms of speech, any agreement reached could be considered to have been coerced.

In order to be applicable to actual public deliberation, Habermas's ideal conditions must be recast. This is the task of a theory of deliberative equality, and the best definition for the purposes of deliberative arrangements is related to requisite capacities. Perhaps the most important form of communicative equality of opportunity is the capacity to initiate public debate and discussion on a theme or a topic. Such acts represent a threshold of political inclusion, and the capacity to perform them is the best operational definition of "adequate" public functioning. More than just opportunity, these acts require great communicative capacity, great cultural resources, and great access to political power and institutions. On this opportunity model, communicative equality is primarily cashed out in procedural terms. Such proceduralist criticisms prove quite fruitful in discovering implicit asymmetries in existing practices (as in the case of agenda setting) and point in the direction of deliberative procedures that go beyond simple majority rule. But the model does not go far enough to be useful for the analysis of political inequality: Habermas's ideal is too specific and too limited to deliberative opportunity. With this communicative equality in place, the public sphere is supposed to do the rest. Institutional examples abound: criminal procedures often correct for the enormous disadvantages of the accused over and against the power of the state. The Equal Protection Clause of the U.S. Constitution provides a framework for rectifying many inequalities in public institutions. Even so, such corrections are often difficult to achieve— even for simple formal rules, as evidenced in the many debates about what counts as a voting scheme that does not disadvantage minority groups.

Formal procedures, however, cannot correct for every form of inequality, especially if the reflexive aspects of formal institutions (that is, their corrective mechanisms for revising their own rules) are distorted by power or by culturally specific exclusions. Equality of opportunity deals with only a small subset of communicative inequalities, related to violations of basic rights of expression, communication, and association. The opportunity to speak does not lend any convincing force or effectiveness to what one says. More often, ineffective and disadvantaged participants lack public voice rather than procedural opportunities; that is, they lack a vocabulary in which to express their needs and perspectives publicly.

Strong institutional measures are often necessary to rectify past injustices and to break out of the vicious circle of public exclusion: a

group needs access to the public sphere in order to remedy such injustices, yet at the same time existing inequalities make them unable
to avoid exclusion. As I mentioned in chapter 2, there is a long history in various democracies of experimenting with different voting
and representational schemes to overcome problems of persistent
minorities. While many schemes use proportional representation to
ensure relative equality and minimum effectiveness, they employ sta-
tistical rather than deliberative criteria for what they might entail.
Most important, these and other similar schemes inhibit rather than
promote deliberation. Creating a system that ensures the minimal
efficacy of a group through voting or representation may decrease the
group's opportunities for deliberation: the group's public reasons do
not have to be generally convincing, nor do they have to be addressed
to the gallery of citizens at large. But once stabilized, such devices may
inhibit deliberation (as in Israel, where parties on the religious right
have succeeded in removing problems from the public agenda, including the issue of who has the right of return). Other measures,
such as granting automatic veto power to representatives of minority
groups, may similarly inhibit deliberation, even if they may also protect basic rights in some extreme situations. On a deliberative account, corrective measures ought to promote full participation in the
public process, rather than causally affect outcomes.

In order to supplement procedural equality without granting dis-
proportionate efficacy to certain deliberators, a more extensive form
of equality is needed to promote strong democratic talk. Without effective participation, the conflicts and dissent that large inequalities
produce will be kept off the agenda. Not only did changes in the
concept of political equality in Reconstruction and the New Deal give
minorities new opportunities for participation; they also put new,
economic themes on the public agenda. Political equality cannot simply be a matter of exercising the same liberties in deliberation; it
must also be a matter of being able to make use of them. As in Rawls's
rights-based distinction between equal liberties and the "fair value of
political liberty,"[24] deliberative theorists must distinguish between
merely formal "opportunities" to deliberate and the capacity to make
"fair use" of citizens' public reason. "Fair use" must mean effective
functioning in deliberative arrangements, despite differences in social
position and cultural resources.

Strong democratic talk requires access to deliberative resources and capabilities, along with basic equality of opportunity. The stronger the deliberative talk, the broader the notion of political equality that is needed: it is clear that inequalities of resources and capacities translate into the public sphere in the form of deliberative disadvantages. If communicative inequalities refer to cultural conditions of unequal power and unequal opportunity, social and economic disadvantages result from "political poverty." Poverty in this sense is a measure of minimal political equality: it sets the threshold requirement of being able to initiate public deliberation and to participate effectively. The development of such abilities is the "floor" of deliberative equality.

In the next section I shall adapt Amartya Sen's analysis of economic inequality to the political sphere and develop a "capability," as opposed to a "resourcist," account of political poverty. I shall develop a specifically deliberative conception of inequality that is useful for the analysis of political exclusion and ineffectiveness in deliberation. I shall then turn to the analysis of the informal and non-institutional means by which public actors can overcome such inequalities, including building upon existing informal networks of communication and existing solidarities for collective action. Collective actors may influence public deliberation through non-compliance and resistance. More typically, collective actors, usually in social movements, gain access to the public sphere by altering some of its constitutive presuppositions. Once the public changes itself, in a democracy it may be able to transform those social and institutional conditions that are dependent on the cooperation of free and equal citizens.

Political Poverty: Deliberation and Distributive Inequalities

The analysis of communicative inequalities in the last section shows how latent forms of power and coercion persist even in deliberative arrangements, despite institutionally secured liberties and procedurally guaranteed opportunities. Such inequalities take various forms and persist through diverse mechanisms, the close analysis of which suggests that a variety of institutional designs and procedures are needed to rectify them. In this section I would like to consider other forms of deliberative disadvantage—particularly those related to distributive issues, such as the unequal distribution of resources and capacities.

Theories of economic inequality have traditionally attempted to measure well-being or its absence, poverty. Inequalities are measured in a number of different ways: in terms of well-being, resources, and, more recently, capacities. Whereas political equality does not directly concern well-being, the latter two forms of inequality have profound effects on the capacities of citizens to participate in political life—so much so that we may say that some citizens are not only economically but also politically impoverished. Disadvantages that result from the unequal distribution of many resources and capabilities may produce consistent failures in deliberation. As in the case of market failure, disadvantaged groups may not be able to participate in appropriate public forums at all. But differences in resources become significant to the extent that they prevent groups from adequately functioning in public life. Because of the way in which resource and other inequalities become relevant in democratic politics, I argue that a capacity-based account is therefore best for political equality, especially in view of the demands made on citizens' autonomous capacities in deliberation and in view of the diversity of citizens' goals and values to be achieved in public functioning. Most of all, such an account demonstrates the relationship between these capacities and differences in having one's public reasons considered or ignored in deliberation. Procedural notions of political equality in particular fail to account for the effects of antecedent differences in social and cultural position related to public functioning.

I will use the term *adequate functioning* to mean the capacities for full and effective use of political rights and liberties in deliberation—capacities that are evident when citizens successfully initiate deliberation, introduce new themes into public debate, and influence the outcome. Lacking these capacities, politically impoverished citizens may be left out of democratic majorities formed in decision-making processes. In cases of deliberative failure, non-compliance is a possibility, but that may not be a desirable option for those who are worst off in terms of resources and capabilities. Thus, a vicious circle of public exclusion may begin: an excluded group can overcome its exclusion only by initiating public deliberation, precisely what exclusion makes more and more difficult. Political poverty is, therefore, typically a group-related inability to make effective use of opportunities to influence the deliberative process.[25] In order to be effective in deliberation, a deliberator must be able initiate a public dialogue about an issue or a theme—a dialogue in which the deliberator's reasons may receive deliberative uptake. Similar self-perpetuating cycles result from economic destitution, including the need for large families and the effects of lack of nourishment on productivity.[26] Capacity failures of both kinds are often consequences of the control of better-situated deliberators over the conditions of social activity and the distribution of the burdens and benefits produced by cooperation.

As I have noted, relative poverty violates one of the main conditions for successful deliberation: citizens' general expectation that they have the opportunity to contribute to public deliberation and receive deliberative uptake from others. In order to recognize the legitimacy of decisions and to be motivated to cooperate, citizens must know that their contributions will be respected in a very minimal sense. At the very least, they must not be ignored in the deliberative process. They must also be able to initiate public acts of deliberation about themes and topics which affect their lives and are most important to them. While ignoring their claims, powerful groups can make presumptive claims about the "we" that has deliberated publicly or come to an agreement, a "we" that does not pass the counterfactual tests of the norms of strong publicity and political equality. The problem is "tacit consent" in deliberative democracy. In order not to comply, it takes a considerable degree of political power and capacity to contest such an inclusion in a non-public we. Yet it is the only means available in democracies. This problem of ineffective public contestation creates the vicious circle of political poverty.

Given the incompatibility of democratic deliberation with persistent inequality, the norm of political equality in deliberation serves as a critical standard of democratic legitimacy. *Political poverty* consists of the inability of groups of citizens to participate effectively in the democratic process and their consequent vulnerability to the intended and unintended consequences of decisions. The consequences of such poverty are public exclusion and political inclusion. On the one hand, politically impoverished groups cannot avoid public exclusion;

they could do so only if they could successfully initiate the joint activity of public deliberation. On the other hand, such groups cannot avoid political inclusion, since they are the legal addressees of the deliberative agreements over which they have no real influence or public input. Because they cannot initiate deliberation, their silence is turned into consent by the more powerful deliberators, who are able to ignore them. This asymmetrical inclusion succeeds by constantly shifting the considerable political burdens of contestation onto the worst off, who lack the resources, capacities, and social recognition to challenge presumptively democratic agreements. Such challenges are made more difficult if a group's values are not recognized by other citizens as plausible reasons in public deliberation.

Below this poverty line, politically unequal citizens do not have the reasonable expectation of being able to affect decisions. Citizens who have developed the capacity for effective deliberation can avoid both exclusion and inclusion: they are neither excluded from deliberation nor included in the constraints of plans devised by others. A good empirical indicator of such a deliberative capacity is whether or not citizens or groups of citizens are able to initiate public deliberation about their concerns. This ability to initiate acts of deliberation thus provides a measurable threshold for political equality and reasonable cooperation. Above it, continued cooperation indicates democratic legitimacy, even when particular groups of citizens continue to disagree with existing decisions and policies. Persistently disadvantaged groups have no reason to recognize the legitimacy of the regime with which they disagree but whose power over them makes them subject to decisions which they cannot afford to ignore. Poverty in this sense is a measure of minimal political equality in a democracy: it sets the threshold requirement of publicity in deliberation in terms of the equal capacities to participate effectively. The development of such abilities is the "floor" of civil equality, since they offer citizens greater possibilities of deliberative uptake for their differing reasons, some of which may not yet be publicly recognized as worthy of consideration.

Before developing the implications of political poverty for public deliberation, let me mention several limitations to the analogies between economic and deliberative inequalities. There are large differences between political and economic functioning, as well as greater uncertainty in the exercise of social freedom in attaining political goals. In achieving adequate functioning in the public sphere, cultural resources and their specific definitions are more significant. Often the effectiveness of some deliberators is limited by their inability to formulate publicly convincing reasons appropriate to the frameworks of other deliberators. Moreover, even the most effective participants in the public sphere cannot causally determine outcomes in the way that economic agents with sufficient means may achieve their ends. By contrast, if I have the proper combination of resources and capabilities in the economic sphere, I should (all things being equal) be able to achieve the goals that I consider important to my well-being. In the public sphere, this same combination ensures only that I can avoid being excluded. Creating the conditions for uptake and continued cooperation is the aim of my deliberative contribution; my well-being is only a by-product of this goal. Besides differences in the need for cooperation to fulfill goals, the difference between economic and political equality concerns the "fact" of "natural" differences in abilities relevant to the political arena. Political equality certainly does not eliminate the possibility of wide differences in publicly relevant capacities. It does, however, establish a threshold for the entry of all citizens into public life: the presumption of a set of minimum, shared public capacities.

In *Inequality Reconsidered* and other writings, Amartya Sen challenges the dominant welfarist (or utility) and resourcist (income or commodity) metrics of economic inequalities. Both metrics founder on the lack of a reliable basis for interpersonal comparisons, including differences in health and differences in gender. Consider a pregnant woman. She requires more nutrition to achieve proper bodily functioning, and thus her well-being cannot be measured simply with regard to her access to a certain commodity packet (say, a certain amount of food relative to her size). According to Sen, the proper measure takes into account the capability of the agent to convert resources into the means to achieve her goals. Such a capability measure of agency is sufficient for the economic case: given capability and resources, one can, all things being equal, achieve adequate functioning. Nothing then stands in the way of such an agent's achieving her particular goals. But this is not the case for political or public functioning.

Even if one has the capabilities and the resources, one may fail to achieve one's public goals, which depend in crucial ways on the uncertain cooperation of others. Still, given that people need the capability to act publicly as well as to achieve well-being, democracies must work to eliminate inadequate functioning among their citizens.

Typically, philosophers who link political and economic equality in democracies have focused on the effects of resource inequalities. But agents may fail in their public functioning not because of a lack of resources but rather because of inadequately developed capacities, especially relative to other agents. In those cases we may speak of "capacity failure," and thus of political poverty in a non-metaphorical sense. Cultural capacities and resources are crucial here, since they specify the *type* of functioning that typically produces success in a given context. In deliberation, only a particular sort of exercise of abilities may effectively convince other agents to cooperate. Public contestation concerning one's effectiveness in public functioning leaves the impoverished in a double bind by requiring what political poverty makes difficult: the capacity to be effective in public debate and discussion.

But why consider capacities and functioning as parts of a critical standard by which to judge actual political outcomes? If there are "inherent" differences in ability and in the social distribution of knowledge, distributive political equality seems an unrealistic ideal. This objection, which is especially plausible for complex societies, once again suggests why weak notions of procedural equality and equality of opportunity have their appeal. Stronger requirements of equality may also conflict with political liberty and imply some perfectionist doctrine of the good. Outcomes that reflect such stronger norms of equality, it is claimed, cannot be consistent with the priority afforded to the liberty to pursue one's own conception of the good life. Consider two versions of this objection put forth by the egalitarian philosophers John Rawls and Jürgen Habermas.

In *A Theory of Justice*, Rawls argues that differences in primary goods are the proper concern of a norm of distributive justice; differences in ability are, by contrast, a matter of good fortune and thus are unavoidable. Moreover, the conception of equality required by justice as fairness cannot avoid being sensitive to endowment and ambition.

Rawls thinks that the evidence of "psychological facts" shows a strong relationship between a person's effort and "natural abilities and skills and the alternatives open to him."[27] The better endowed, he argues, are not only more likely to achieve more; they are also more likely, other things being equal, "to strive conscientiously." From these "facts" about endowment and ambition, Rawls concludes that meritocracy ignores that there is "no way to discount for their greater good fortune."[28] Such good fortune includes better luck in political competition, which among the many human abilities and skills is relevant to political success as a contingent historical fact. The more numerous and complex the relevant abilities, the less likely it is that they will be had by a few. Although Rawls admits that the psychological facts about effort and reward can be exacerbated by social facts, we would not normally regard meager capacities as detracting from opportunities.[29] This claim, however, cannot be true for political opportunities and public capacities; their lack undermines the legitimacy of decisions once citizens fall below a certain threshold with regard to their public functioning and the extent of their social freedom.

Rawls's primary-goods conception of equal political opportunity is too narrow: not only is it difficult to determine which capacities are "natural"; in addition, incapacities, natural or otherwise, still may determine how many social burdens are distributed in violation of the difference principle. It is hard to see how inequalities in political capabilities could ever work to the benefit of the disadvantaged in a democracy. It is also the case that it is more difficult to develop public capacities when one is overworked or burdened with necessary domestic tasks rather than basic resources distributed by social roles.

As opposed to Rawls, Habermas bases his argument against requiring stronger norms of political equality in contemporary democracies on social facts.[30] Some of these facts concern unavoidable costs and resources necessary for the deliberative process itself; these include the costs of information and, particularly, of that scarce resource, time. The fact that the deliberative process itself requires resources in order to function could lead to "inevitable inequalities."[31] The list of scarce resources and inevitable inequalities relevant to deliberation is potentially quite long: besides differences in natural abilities and the scarcity of time, one might include the unequal distribution of cognitive and moral information and expertise due to the division of labor and the selectivity in the distribution of information. Habermas lists a series of such "facts": ". . . the structure of the public sphere reflects unavoidable asymmetries in the availability of information, i.e., in the equal chances to have access to the production, validation, steering and the presentation of images."[32] Such distribution of resources would lead to a situation with regard to information much like Rousseau's description of large discrepancies in wealth: some citizens are so poor in the politically necessary resource of information that they cannot effectively participate and must defer to those who possess more information. The epistemic advantages that accrue to those with resources permit the following formulation of the threshold of resource equality necessary for public deliberation: inequalities of resources, including information, cannot be so great that others can exploit the openness of democratic institutions. When citizens are unequal with respect to capacities to acquire and use information, exclusion is a by-product of the resultant inadequacies in public functioning.

The capacity-based notion of political equality in deliberation permits us to discuss political rights and liberties in a different way than either Rawls's procedural opportunities or Habermas's emphasis on aggregate resources. Freedom is, on this account, the capacity to live as one would choose; it is the capacity for *social* agency, the ability to participate in joint activities and achieve one's goals in them.[33] For political liberties, the issue is effective use of public freedoms, which may be absent even in the absence of coercion or prohibitions. Indeed, "disease, hunger and early mortality tell us a great deal about the presence or absence of certain central basic freedoms,"[34] and this may be true even in democracies with well-functioning public spheres. Persistent inequalities of race, class, and gender are not merely the results of the unequal distribution of resources; they are also due to the lack of social agency by these groups in relation to the goals and interests of others. The interests and needs of those who are not effectively functioning agents in this sense do not figure in political deliberation and decisions. Without what Sen calls "effective freedom" for all, cooperative arrangements promote the goals and plans of others, who are able to convert their opportunities and information into effective action. Political poverty is thus primarily comparative, in that the choices of others may make it difficult for worseoff groups to exercise their agency and to live as they would if their public reasons could not be ignored in the democratic process.

The solution to such culturally reinforced political poverty is strikingly similar to Sen's solution to the problem of recurring famine. According to Sen, famines are due not to shortages in supply but rather to breakdowns of social relations of entitlement. He argues that the best way to avoid such breakdowns is sufficient democratic self-governance to avoid the loss of public control over existing distributive networks.[35] Here, too, the best way to avoid political poverty is through democratic institutions and an open public sphere. Such a public sphere can create the conditions for political expectations of effectiveness. So long as groups have some foothold in the public sphere (that is, the ability to initiate democratic deliberation), they can begin to be included in decision making. Either certain capacities are developed in all citizens or else democratic institutions will exclude their politically impoverished citizens. Different institutions may have different political economies and thus different thresholds of poverty: if participants all have highly developed public capacities and are well informed, the division of labor is not only less likely to cause breakdowns in cooperation but also less likely to have inegalitarian consequences.

Under the constraints of well-ordered democratic institutions and a well-functioning public sphere, the development of public capacities, and not power or resources *per se*, provides the primary measure of effective political freedom. Just as power can be delegated to representatives without the loss of equality, resources can be made more nearly equal without necessarily increasing the effectiveness of the groups suffering most from persistent inequalities. If threshold requirements of resources and capacities are met, then such public use of reason can overcome the inequalities generated by other, nonpolitical social and psychological facts. The threshold ensures the capacity of citizens to make effective use of their freedom: not to be ignored and to make their public reasons convincing to others. With such thresholds in place, public decisions may still be unfair or uninformed but they do not produce the persistent forms of inequality that exist below the threshold of political poverty. This is not to say that overcoming inequalities is an easy task. Indeed, such public corrections for exclusions and such rectifications of past inequalities cannot be accomplished by individuals in isolation, even in their role as citizens exercising their public capacities.

Once common convictions about public reasons emerge, citizens can act in concert and form groups or associations, in which they may pool their resources, capabilities, and power and remove more entrenched barriers. The corrective capacity of such associations is a crucial part of the recursive character of the public sphere when groups make their political inequality an issue for democratic deliberation.[36] If they cannot do so they are, *de facto*, politically impoverished. However, by generating political power through their associations and through their capacity for collective action, such groups build up their social networks and gain entry into the public sphere. They succeed by capturing the public's attention enough to change the public itself, and in so doing they eliminate the effects of certain inequalities. Once the public character of their concerns is acknowledged in deliberation, previously excluded groups achieve public respect and with it equal standing in deliberation.

Remedies for Deliberative Inequalities: Institutional Reform and Collective Action

Correcting many forms of inequality requires public policies that promote participation in social life generally, such as resource thresholds ensured by public education, social security, and welfare programs. Political inequalities present particular difficulties, since the terms of debate about them are formed in the same political process that produced them. Inequalities limit the possibilities of dialogue, exclude many forms and styles of expression, and permit better-endowed groups to use the public sphere strategically to further their own ends. Many different forms of inequality can be interconnected in the public sphere, making the public sphere less accessible to oppressed groups and requiring of them much greater effort to secure public attention and uptake. If time and attention are admittedly relatively scarce public resources, then the effects of deliberative inequalities can be persistent in the public sphere. They are difficult to overcome if the vicious circle of public exclusion makes it less likely that inequalities become problematic to many and that solutions reflect the needs of those affected by them. In a deliberative democracy, rectifying inequalities requires restoration of the features that make deliberation cooperative and public reasons more convincing. In the rest of this section, I want to show how inequalities can be corrected in ways that promote more public deliberation and are consistent with a capacity-based conception of political equality.

In societies that are already at least minimally democratic in their institutions, there are two basic strategies for restoring the conditions of a free and open public sphere. The first has to do with creating new public spaces for deliberation: participants can use them not only to express new public reasons but also to try to restore the wider public sphere and make it more inclusive. To do this, challengers need to form themselves into collective actors by mobilizing already-existing informal networks of communication among groups to create social movements, as African-Americans did with the civil rights movement in the South. The second strategy is institutional: groups employ the power invested in institutions to create and enforce the conditions necessary for public deliberation and make them relatively permanent. These more formal means may include employing the problem-solving capacities of institutions, backed by law and political power, to alleviate the causes and conditions of inequality. In particular, institutions can guarantee that certain procedural and distributive conditions are met in order to ensure greater political equality, as in voting-rights legislation, campaign-finance reform, and the regulation of public-affairs discourse. (I shall discuss another cultural resource—the role of social critics in the democratic public sphere—in chapter 5.)

Public deliberation about weaknesses and consequences of existing institutions and decision-making processes can correct some of the limitations that result in political inequality. However, such formal means seem ill suited to overcoming many forms of political poverty. They share the weaknesses of the proceduralist conceptions of deliberation and the resourcist conceptions of equality that provide their intellectual backing. As Sen has argued in the case of economic inequalities, capacity-based inequalities are not correctable in this manner. As important as they are in reforming certain practices, such solutions tend to try to redistribute political resources and to limit the use of them by those who already possess them. Piecemeal campaign finance reform typically tries to cap the amount wealthy individuals, corporations, or political action committees can contribute. The Fairness Doctrine also considers the quantity of public affairs communication. In both cases, setting limits does not necessarily enable more impoverished citizens to participate. Similarly, other reforms offer candidates a particular, publicly financed sum, thus equalizing various opportunities. But this sum is like the commodity packet of traditional welfare economics; it does not consider the difficulty of effectively converting resources into activities that would fulfill one's goals. Nor do such quantitative measures consider the vulnerability of agents to the political decisions of others.

In contrast, reform based on promoting the public capacities necessary for effective agency would set neither limits nor some common quantity of time or money. Rather, it would consider how such resources, procedures, and opportunities can be effectively used in building up associations and other communicative networks. Similarly, in the case of minorities' voting rights such an account endorses solutions which I proposed in discussing problems of pluralism. As opposed to distributing representation as a proportional resource, a cumulative voting scheme enables a minority to build up coalitions and public associations cutting across the barriers that made a particular group's inequalities persistent. In such schemes, the development of capacities is encouraged by changes in the political economy of how minorities achieve representation; these changes in incentives make it more difficult for the majority to ignore their views and interests. In any case, many *political* redistribution reforms are limited by resourcist and utilitarian assumptions that are not directly applicable in the political realm or to the problems of poverty and vulnerability. But such redistributions of resources and limitations on political power are the ones available through institutional reform of the political process.

But not all forms of poverty can be corrected by such institutional and procedural reforms, particularly if they require the development of new contexts and vocabularies for deliberation. Such deliberative spaces, associations, and forms of expression emerge out of civil society in the practices of impoverished groups. Most of all, they are results of attempts at collective action within deliberative political arrangements. Such emerging publics must transform themselves and their forms of association, often in spite of the political culture of the public sphere.[37] Contestation should not be overestimated: social networks are often reproduced through agreement and consensus. James Scott calls these refusals to carry out the terms of disadvantageous cooperative relationships "the weapons of the weak." On this view, dominated groups contest these values in institutions of direct cultural reproduction. For example, some educational institutions attempt to reproduce a particular version of the prevalent culture. In France use of the French language is forced on linguistic minorities.[38] In England, existing class relations are reproduced through educational institutions in which teachers discipline students who engage in unorganized acts of class resistance and non-cooperation.[39] The last example shows a strong dialectic at work in cultural contestation: resistance, too, can serve a functional role in reproducing inequalities, precisely in continuing institutional failures. Even as a cultural basis for deliberation in civil society, everyday contestation is pre-public. It can become public by creating the basis for an alternative public sphere in which new forms of expression and interaction can flourish. Out of resistance in schools and factories may emerge a "proletarian public sphere"[40] with its own networks of interaction, solidarities, and forms of association. Such sub-publics may exist for long periods, developing alternative institutions and forums for public expression, such as their own presses (as has been the case in both African-American and gay sub-publics).

In the absence of persistent and cyclic political poverty, sub-cultural forms of expression enrich the public reasons available in the civic public sphere. By infiltrating into this larger public, such expressions can have indirect effects on forms of political expression. But sub-publics can also become minority cultures, with their own public reasons and with the eventual deep conflicts that such segregated pluralism inevitably produces. Public deliberation can overcome the effects of inequality only when a dialogue between sub-publics in the civic public sphere begins. In this way, it can undercut the self-defeating and self-reproducing dialectic that too often turns daily resistance into a mechanism for reproduction of the very inequality being contested in civil society.

The idea of a sub-public does not simply denote a voluntary association in civil society. It also denotes a network of social relationships and communicative interactions that can develop as a collective actor that enables its members to contest a shared grievance effectively and publicly. Social movements do not simply emerge as individuals come to realize their common concerns or interests. Rather, as studies of various movements have shown, it is out of "a pre-existing communication network or infrastructure within civil society that a movement forms; it is through already-established networks that social movements and groups develop."[41] Previously isolated and unorganized individuals may form small, highly local associations, but they become movements and thus effective actors in the public sphere when they are already linked in a communicative network through which their protest can spread and be generalized into other communication networks.[42] Such organization of public protest permits the pooling of resources and capacities necessary for the group to gain public attention and to identify its protest as addressing a "social problem."[43]

Such solidarities and communicative networks may be called "civil society," but not in the usual sense of the term. Civil society usually refers to a plurality of voluntary associations and autonomous groups. It is another step for such groups to interact with one another and to build organizations large enough to pool their resources and capacities, thus enabling them to participate in the public sphere along with other organized groups and institutional actors. Civil society, as the aggregate of all such networks and informal groups, does not yet constitute a public sphere. In civil society groups need not deliberate together, nor need they organize themselves around the goal of publicly expressing their grievance or of convincing and answering others with public reasons.[44] This sort of orientation to the "gallery" of citizens in the public sphere distinguishes the civil rights and feminist movements from other organized groups in civil society; these movements pushed beyond the civil society of informal networks and

associations and became organized collective actors in the civic public sphere.

The emergence of a movement as a collective actor has two effects
on persistent inequalities. First, it is a mechanism for pooling the resources, capacities and experiences of various persons and groups,
and it gives coherent expression and unified voice to their shared
problems and grievances. Second, solidarity within these informal
networks permits pooling of resources and information and thus the
creation of public goods within the movement as a way to compensate
for resource inequalities and political poverty. The organization of
the movement itself also gives it a voice, putting it in dialogue with
other actors and institutions who recognize their grievances as public
problems or expand the pool of their public reasons. Small acts of
contestation can then be generalized into protests and become a
public challenge to the existing distribution of deliberative resources
in institutions. Once given powerful public expression, the movement's grievances can be publicly recognized as legitimate and made
part of the public agenda of decision-making institutions. Of course,
this may be a long process, sometimes requiring more resources than
other movements require and sometimes failing altogether. The pro-
life movement resembles in some respects the civil rights movement
to which it often symbolically appeals. However, as opposed to the
civil rights movement, it has not found public resonance and forms of
expression outside of the churches from which it originated. It has
not succeeded in translating the movement's reasons into the public
sphere; they remain non-public, however widely convincing and
widely shared among citizens.

The task facing citizens who form a movement is to become a collective actor in the public sphere and thus to gain more stability and
unity than the episodic and informal social networks from which they
emerge. Groups may fail to achieve even minimal stability when they
lack sufficient power to resist coercive measures taken against them by
authorities in the institutions they wish to change. Democratic limitations on such violence in the rule of law are crucial if the public sphere
is to expand. Sometimes the failure to gain public attention can im-
pede a movement's growth. For example, black churches in Baton
Rouge staged a bus boycott before Montgomery, but attention to the

Baton Rouge boycott was limited to the communication networks of Southern black churches. With the success of Montgomery in achieving both institutional and public attention, a more permanent, broader, and more effective civil rights movement was formed.[45]

The problem for movements of the politically poor is that political poverty produces public isolation. Although local organizations are successful in creating networks of solidarity and mutual support among members, by themselves they do not have much success in constructing and defining social problems for public attention. Other problems may be organizational; even with pre-existing solidarity, organizational structures may not be sufficient to aggregate and deploy resources.[46] Such resources are necessary to meet the costs of political conflict and to achieve specific collective goals, such as ending the racial segregation of public facilities.[47] The construction of ongoing organizations preserves networks of solidarity and extends them into new contexts; such means "make it easier to aggregate resources and to use them in collective action."[48] But resource aggregation is best seen as a means to the end of public communication. Organization is especially necessary for a previously ineffective group to communicate its grievances adequately to the public sphere.

The primary role of social movements in deliberation is to make grievances public and to provide an arena in which citizens can exercise their capacities and freedoms in order to gain entry to the larger public sphere of all citizens. A truly democratic society fosters and protects such associative bonds as a requirement for a vibrant public sphere capable of correcting its own inadequacies. However, as I noted in the preceding section, there are less dramatic ways in which inequalities can be remedied by more directly institutional means. When decision-making processes become relatively permanent and routinized in institutions, inequalities can be corrected through procedural reforms and changes in institutional design alone. Institutional changes, such as campaign finance reform or government support for discourse on public affairs (inadequately represented in market-oriented media) should always maximize the benefit to those most disadvantaged in deliberation. Such a maximin compensatory strategy serves two purposes: besides being an appropriate principle of deliberative justice, it restores the open and inclusive character of communication in the public sphere. Changes in voting procedures must benefit those who have been disadvantaged by the current scheme, but they must do so by increasing opportunities to be included in the public sphere rather than by guaranteeing success.[49]

Once impoverished groups can participate directly in the public process of defining a problematic situation, procedural changes promote equality of opportunity among citizens by giving them equal standing. The same can be said for other deliberative rules, including ones that aim at generating greater inclusiveness in agenda setting and more reasonable judgments of possible alternatives. Such inclusiveness is particularly important in institutions that require the election of representatives; with a more inclusive set of alternative candidates, representatives will be more accountable to citizens who choose them on the basis of a broad set of public issues. With procedures that promote opportunities for alternative proposals or candidates, it will be more likely that the urgent needs of disadvantaged groups will be considered. Charles Beitz suggests that the need for considering alternatives in reasonable judgments implies a criterion for agenda setting: in any electoral competition, procedures must ensure the representation of every salient position—that is, every position whose representation in an election "would increase the chances that urgent interests of some significant portion of the population will be adequately attended to."[50] Such procedures still presuppose that no group is so excluded and impoverished that it is unable to establish the urgency and the salience of its position so long as the agenda is neither too long nor too short.

This criterion of salience does not imply that institutions must consider *all* alternatives; they will remain selective in order to be able to reach some decisions under time constraints. But such opportunity costs are not the sole reason for agenda constraints. The primary reason is cognitive. Too large an agenda with too many different positions makes for fewer well-informed judgments. Representation requires devices for filtering out some alternatives; completeness is undesirable since it undermines the quality of deliberation through consideration of irrelevant or unacceptable positions.[51] But the most important feature for agenda setting is that the procedure be democratic, so that the procedure for closing the agenda becomes an occasion for (and sometimes the focus of) deliberation. Salience, too, has a practical side: coherence with other decision-making procedures, such as majority rule or parliamentary thresholds, enters into deliberation about agendas. Thus, salience must be supplemented by a public process for discovering what is salient: which positions are salient and who may represent them are questions for public deliberation, which (given the democratic nature of the decision-making procedures) can be answered only if the broadest spectrum of political interpretations are on the agenda. Democratic institutions remain legitimate only if they can remain open to the larger public sphere in which they are embedded.

Deliberative arrangements require that institutions have mechanisms for opening their agendas to public input; they must be open to revision as new groups begin to capture public attention and receive recognition for their definitions of the problematic situation. Considerations of legitimacy and popular sovereignty require that public agendas be narrowed gradually and publicly through deliberation, so that no generalizable interests are excluded without due consideration and respect. In the case of complex and conflictual issues, such narrowing of alternatives is itself part of the deliberative process, and it also promotes greater accountability of representatives when such matters are open for debate rather than determined by organizational non-decisions.

Because inequalities of resources permit differential access to the public sphere, deliberative democracies are faced with regulating many forms of political speech. Large corporations have the capacity to take out space on the Op-Ed page of the *New York Times* or to initiate large television campaigns to promote their political agendas. Commercial speech of this kind represents an unfair advantage in the quest for public attention; it gives advantages to corporations and established political parties over individuals and nascent organizations as collective actors in the public sphere. The issues here are similar to those associated with campaign finance reform: most measures of equality require limiting the speech of advantaged actors, or redistributing resources up to a minimum of time or money for all salient positions. In view of the commercial, market-driven, and therefore non-neutral nature of many avenues of political speech, many forms of political dialogue are underrepresented in, if not excluded from, mass communications. Because of the market structure of media institutions, regulation and restriction of some types of commercially produced political messages are more appropriate than making certain resources more nearly equal through campaign finance reform. Like agenda narrowing at appropriate times, such restrictions promote rather than inhibit deliberation, since more speech under such unequal conditions only further disadvantages the worst-off. Not only the Federal Communications Commission's power to regulate "free and fair competition" but also the standards of salience and urgency require assistance for groups with resource disadvantages. Owing to the importance of gaining public attention in deliberative democracies, commercially funded and manipulative forms of disinformation may subvert epistemic judgments about the facts and implications of policies. False analogies to the "marketplace of ideas" have made any regulation of public discourse seem to be restrictive, inherently limiting, rather than promoting, the conditions for democratic self-governance.[52]

The same justification also suggests not merely regulation but also compensation for resource disadvantages through taxation or some other mechanism, especially if there is organized opposition to social movements in the form of large organizations such as bureaucracies and corporations. Whatever constraints or compensations are introduced through various legal means, the redistribution of politically relevant resources must actually promote wider political deliberation. The advantages of organizations with large economic resources are still a potential obstacle to public deliberation, but a less insuperable one if threshold requirements of political equality are extended beyond individual citizens to collective actors such as voluntary associations and movements. Such compensations restore conditions of publicity to political communication, promoting access to minority views. As for positive steps to promote a broader spectrum of opinion, it is more likely that multiplying non-market avenues of mass public communication will be more effective in building up a vibrant political public sphere.[53] In the age of sound-bite democracy, public broadcasting corporations supported by taxation should make the quality and civility of public affairs discourse and informed public opinion their main responsibilities.

In deliberative democracy, First Amendment protections could be interpreted in a new way: as promoting deliberative self-government through a vibrant and open public sphere. One such protection is the distorting effect of lack of access to relevant opinions and information, which limits citizens' use of public reason and their capacities for autonomy. Citizens can deliberate well only when there is the back-and-forth exchange of many different viewpoints and opinions. As Meiklejohn puts it, ignoring opinions of some citizens distorts decisions; it is "that mutilation of the thinking process of the community against which the First Amendment of the Constitution is directed."[54] Rather than thinking of legal remedies as protecting only negative liberties, it would be better for public opinion if the courts were also to aim at enhancing public dialogue through overcoming deliberative inequalities. Not more speech (which tends to benefit those who are already functioning effectively), but more deliberative exchange and dialogue are desirable. Only then would corrective reforms and legal protections enhance the exercise of the self-governing capacities of impoverished citizens and break the cycle of political poverty. Just as it did in development economics, the capacity-based account of political inequality shows that poverty can be reproduced despite resources and opportunities if resources and opportunities cannot be converted into influence in the deliberative process. Effective participants are able to convert their convincing public reasons into favorable influence. On my account, political equality requires more than Rawls's difference principle, which applies to the distribution of benefits in various outcomes. In deliberative democracy, all citizens must exercise their autonomous capacities in the *process* of decision making. If inequalities are so large that some citizens cannot do so, then deliberation fails to meet the basic conditions of non-tyranny and publicity. For those citizens, the decisions made are democratically illegitimate, even if they pass the test of the difference principle.

Inequalities in Pluralistic Societies: Some Examples

My aim in the preceding section was to formulate an ideal of political equality that could serve as a useful critical standard for judging the effects of inequalities of opportunity, resources, and capability in public deliberation. It also established threshold requirements for effective participation in actual deliberation. My examples were drawn from the North American experience of democracy and free speech. In conclusion, let me show the fruitfulness of these conceptions of political equality and poverty in judging problems of deliberation in other societies. First, I shall show that such inequalities play a crucial role in exacerbating deep conflicts in pluralistic societies. I shall then consider the applicability of the critical standard of deliberative equality to problems of complexity, which raise new problems for effective participation in decision-making processes.

In order to consider the effects of inequalities in pluralistic societies, it is useful to adopt Will Kymlicka's distinction between two different sites for cultural pluralism: multi-nation states and polyethnic, immigrant societies.[55] Whereas multi-nation states typically consist of geographically distinct ethnic groups, polyethnic societies have no geographical divisions among groups. Even without such divisions, the various ethnic groups often do not have equal access to political power or to the public media, since both may be controlled by minority or majority groups. The difficulties of entering the public sphere in most immigrant societies are somewhat different from those in multi-nation states. Immigrant societies do not all have the same sorts of distinct ethnic histories; but they do have problems of conflicts between incoming groups and the dominant political cultures, including such issues as religious authority and the public role of women and children. Liberal culture avows openness and tolerance, especially by attempting to resolve cultural issues of identity through a principled neutrality among visions of the good life. But some cultural groups in an immigrant society may oppose this very liberal culture and its rhetoric of impartiality and scientific justification. Appeals to both forms of justification may not be publicly convincing in polyethnic societies and may stand in the way of fair compromises.

Besides the problem of arriving in a new culture with established practices of adjudication, immigrant groups face the problem of publicly communicating their new and different interests. This often leaves new immigrants politically poor and unorganized, even in the face of urgent needs. Such cultural inequalities can become entrenched in the public sphere when the pool of public reasons has not yet been expanded enough to transform the prevailing political culture. If the public sphere is restricted in this way, counter-publics form in which the public reason of a particular group can be exercised. Given sufficient time, these oppositional sub-publics can become entrenched and develop their own moral and epistemic standards and forms of public justification. Immigrant societies then begin to resemble more settled multi-nation states with many separate spheres of coexistence rather than a common and diverse public sphere.

Separate spheres may even be legally recognized, as when Muslims and Hindus in India developed separate public and legal domains. In periods of conflict, such as the present, each group tries to make its reasons public without reference to the reasons of the other group; neither is willing to engage in compromise or to find a basis for ongoing cooperation. Deep conflicts may be produced by such democratic failures in communication in the civic public sphere. Recent French policies forcing the integration of Muslims into the dominant French culture inevitably exacerbate cultural conflict by making seemingly public institutions culturally specific; minority cultures then have no choice but to develop their own alternative publics, and thus they no longer recognize France's deliberative institutions as legitimate. But this cannot be resolved by making the public sphere more "truly" neutral or by turning the issues over to the courts; both may inhibit not only deliberation but also accommodation. Rather than to avoid conflicts, the point of deliberation is to express values publicly and to search for ways to make the reasons of each group convincing to other citizens. In this way, each group can exercise its public reason in working out legitimate decisions and fair compromises according to its own conceptions of the good.

The solution to such culturally reinforced political poverty is once again like Sen's solutions to famines. Here, too, the best way to avoid culturally induced political poverty is through a public sphere, which can create the conditions for new social entitlements and expectations. First, the public sphere can provide a way to check the coercive power of the state in enforcing culturally specific policies. It has long been the function of the public sphere to overcome tyranny, and cultural tyranny or intolerance by a state is no different from other forms of exclusion.[56] Such a public sphere must encourage diverse forms of expression and a broad universe of discourse with alternative public reasons. Second, there must be constant and vibrant interaction among cultures and sub-publics in a larger sphere of common citizenship. Such dialectical interaction will enrich both publics; the public reasons of sub-groups will be enriched and become broader through interaction in a political public sphere of all citizens. In this chapter I have illustrated why overcoming political inequalities is part of the recursive process of a public sphere concerned with its own public character. So long as groups have some foothold in the public sphere and can initiate acts of deliberation, they can begin this recursive process; without it, the circular, or recursive, character of the public sphere may become a vicious circle for those who are already excluded.

The interaction among various publics in the political public sphere reduces the balkanization of pluralist societies produced by the combination of inequalities and conflicts. But, once in motion, dialectical interaction among publics cannot be controlled by any particular group or sub-public. For example, *sati* (the burning of widows) is now illegal but still common in multinational India and in other cultures with dowry exchanges. The dowry is supposed to compensate for resources lost to the husband's family when she arrives. With the death of her husband, she becomes an external burden. In view of the ineffectiveness of coercive law (since such burnings are now reported as kitchen accidents), the best way to eliminate this practice is precisely through interaction among publics, which may foster the creation of women's solidarity, social movements, and alternative institutions. Not only does collective action give rise to a critical public; more important, the public sphere makes new options and choices available to widows and, more generally, to women.

In a vibrant public sphere, new forms of solidarity can cut across cultural boundaries even in as dispersed a group as women in a pluralistic society. In shelters and cooperatives, such a movement can challenge the cultural basis of practices such as *sati* in ways that the centralized state cannot, committed as it is to a polyethnic compromise that leaves "private" or "family law" matters to religious authorities. The same problems also emerge in matters of divorce, which in India is not a subject for civil and criminal law.[57] Women in India can use a common, political public sphere to challenge the inequalities produced in the current multi-nation state compromise, for which they bear the burdens. Above all, women need these threshold equalities of capacities and resources to have exit options from the family and to become full participants in public life.[58]

Such examples show why cultural publics in pluralist democracies have to have permeable boundaries. The cost of interaction in the public sphere may well be the loss of some cultural forms of authority. The self-interpretations of such cultures and their traditions will be thrown open beyond their authorized interpreters to a wider set of participants, even to non-members with whom they engage in dialogue. If a public sphere is successful, communal boundaries will become more diffuse and membership more overlapping. In the public sphere, cultures survive by changing and incorporating a wider set of interpretations—that is, by becoming less well-integrated. Members of minority cultures fear that this openness will mean the loss of their identity (identity being one motivation for the rise of orthodoxy among religious subcultures). But these struggles do not mean that the interpretations of dominant groups are being imposed upon minorities; rather, interactions among sub-publics produce a greater variety of self-interpretations and of alternative self-descriptions, such as identifying oneself as a Muslim *and* a woman *and* a citizen. Political inequalities lead to impoverished public identities, making the political rhetoric of identity both more convincing and less democratic in demands for authenticity.

Such loosening of cultural integration may make culturally specific mechanisms of inequality less effective, including those within the sub-cultures. It is no accident that restrictions on women by traditional domestic law are challenged by women from within their own communities. The point of political regulation is to permit less powerful members of a pluralist society to participate in the public sphere without being defined either by others outside the group or by more powerful members within the group. A Muslim does not participate in the polyethnic public sphere only as a Muslim. In many instances, members of a culture may find after such interactions that their own practices cannot be justified in light of the expanded pool of public reasons at their disposal. The existence of even a small subpublic of women in India has had, at least to some extent, this effect upon the economic practices of marriage. Similarly, most Southerners in the United States now reject the practices of segregation that were widely supported during their lifetimes.

Many members of cultural groups may come to resent the effects of their interactions with other cultures in the public sphere; this resentment has spawned many conservative ideologies of cultural traditionalism and authenticity. European colonial practices actually encouraged such conservative ideologies, both by their Romantic ideals of authentic "native" cultures and by imposing their reasons from without; it is now the task of those participating in post-colonial public spheres to end these inequalities without undermining ethnic peace. There is no reason in principle that an autonomous public sphere will be homogenizing or oppressive, so long as there is a lively interchange between various sub-publics and the larger public sphere of free and equal citizens. The experience of post-colonial public spheres is that they thrive when they are pluralistic, as places in which citizens work out new patterns of mutual respect and openness to new influences.

The elimination of cultural inequalities is a necessary condition for the enrichment of the civic public sphere. With the emergence of new voices, old policies and laws (such as the prohibition of Muslim dress in public schools in France) will have to change and new ones will have to be created (as when women in India gain greater standing in family law). The dialectical interaction of sub-publics and the civic public is thus a necessary condition for democratically overcoming many persistent inequalities. In multi-national and polyethnic societies, the civic public must be continually checked for cultural specificity, or many groups will simply opt out and choose to address their grievances via non-cooperative strategies. When these strategies cease to address the public at large as a source of communicative power to solve shared problems, other groups become obstacles to be overcome, sometimes violently. In such cases the aggrieved group no longer addresses the public, because its members are not part of it.

Conclusion

In this chapter I have considered the various ways in which procedurally fair deliberative arrangements may produce and reproduce social inequalities. Communicative inequalities produce distorted political communication, that is, restrictions on public discourse about topics, themes, and interpretations caused by asymmetries of social power. So long as actors are able to participate in the public sphere and to address others in it by virtue of their common citizenship, they may rectify such restrictions on political communication. But such corrective and critical forms of communication are able to restart stalled deliberative mechanisms of dialogue so long as disadvantaged citizens can still make effective use of their procedural opportunities. Wide and persistent social inequalities make public deliberation more difficult. In such cases, citizens are not able to avoid being excluded from public deliberation or having their reasons consistently ignored. Such citizens have no reason to expect to be able to influence future deliberation and thus have no reason to continue to cooperate. But non-institutional means of collective action can give such actors access to the public sphere and, through effective participation, can reconstitute the public so that they are part of it. If power over decisions is widely dispersed in institutions (which also have a variety of channels for public input), excluding groups from deliberation is more difficult to accomplish; but this same fact also makes it easier for collective actors to influence and change institutions through reconstituting the public sphere.

The capacity conception of equality and political poverty developed here has brought to light an important feature of public deliberation that is missing from proceduralist accounts: effective freedom. Those who do not have the capacity to avoid political exclusion are not free to lead public lives. One of the important contributions of a non-procedural account is to show why participants in deliberation must be free *and* equal citizens. Proceduralism does, however, properly insist that no corrective mechanism should put any citizen or group of citizens in the position to determine deliberative outcomes non-publicly. At the same time, citizens must have the reasonable expectation that their public reasons may influence outcomes, so long as they are convincing to others. Deliberative democracy must fulfill demands for equality in the means for effective participation at least enough so that no citizen is so poor as to fail to influence outcomes or to avoid exclusion. I have given various examples in which this capacity account of deliberative inequalities illuminates problems of cultural conflicts involving the weakest members of non-dominant groups.

Besides cultural pluralism and social inequalities, other social "facts" raise further doubts about the practicality of the ideals of publicity. In modern societies, pluralism and inequality are often produced by powerful social forces and institutions that inflate the social power of institutions. For many social theorists, the complexity and the scale of modern society preclude effective participation of citizens in controlling the forces that govern their lives. Thus, social complexity places new demands on public deliberation that threaten to fracture and overburden the civic public sphere. At the very least, it creates a new dialectic: not between various sub-publics, but between informal and formal civic publics—between the informal and widely dispersed public sphere and the formal and more permanent public of political institutions invested with social power. These institutions, and not the citizens, seem sovereign.

In the next chapter I turn to a different set of social facts, having to do with the scale of modern societies. I argue that the "fact" of social complexity does not pose an insuperable practical limit on democratic public deliberation, any more than cultural pluralism or social inequalities do. But social complexity does demand that the public sphere itself carefully preserve a difficult requirement for deliberative democracies in complex societies: popular sovereignty. Complexity is best conceived not primarily in terms of civic participation in large institutions but rather as a question of the nature and the scope of political power in deliberative democracy and of the capacity of sovereign citizens to rule themselves, even while giving over much of their decision-making power to institutions.

4

Social Complexity, Deliberative Majorities, and the Limits of Popular Sovereignty

Because deliberation requires the public exercise of capacities for autonomy, legitimacy derives in the first instance from citizens' participation in decision making. In deliberation, citizens govern themselves and give themselves rules for common life. I argued in the last chapter that such a conception of legitimacy can be elaborated only in terms of a comprehensive conception of political equality. Above the threshold of political poverty, each citizen has equal public standing and may reasonably expect to influence deliberation. My goal in this chapter is to face one of the main sources of political skepticism about the ideals of deliberative democracy: the facts of social complexity. Too many social processes, such as the fluctuations of the global market, seem to operate behind our backs and out of our control. As currently structured, many political institutions seem to have very little opening for deliberation. The majority of expenditures in large nation states are already programmed, so that legislators actually debate a very small portion of the national budget. Expertise, the high degree of division of labor, new technologies, and many more factors also seem to put many current issues beyond the grasp of even the best-informed citizens. Popular sovereignty—the principle that the only legitimate government is by the people and for the people, or, more minimally, that decision-making power should be widely dispersed among citizens rather than concentrated in the hands of an elite few—seems to be the first casualty of complexity.

The "will of the people" seems conceivable only in direct democracy, as a unified "general will."[1] Such requirements for sovereignty are certainly too strong for contemporary pluralist democracies. But many critics of radical democracy extend their criticisms beyond the problems of political unity and stability. They suggest that the ideal of sovereignty itself has become irrelevant under contemporary conditions. In light of social facts such as those mentioned above, these critics argue that the voluntary organization of society is no longer possible in complex and pluralist societies. Complexity not only allows little to be a matter of actual public control; it also allows little room for deliberate choice. If most or all of these empirical claims about large and complex societies are true, they blunt the critical force of the ideals of deliberative democracy and lessen their applicability to large institutions; norms of free and open debate among equal participants seem practicable only in small organizations.

In this chapter I argue that such political pessimism about democracy does not follow from the facts of social complexity. It is certainly true that face-to-face assemblies and town meetings are no longer the best ways to maximize opportunities for active citizenship. Popular sovereignty does, however, need to be rethought under such circumstances, so that it squarely faces the issue of how to make majority rule more a matter of the public deliberation of citizens. But, I want to argue, the aspects of social complexity that supposedly challenge *any* form of popular sovereignty are not unavoidable features of modern social life. Instead, such arguments fail descriptively and normatively: while emphasizing one form of complexity over others, they ignore the *interdependencies* between social institutions and the publics that constitute them and constantly reinterpret their basis. The question for deliberative theorists is how to make these social interdependencies more democratic.

Social complexity does in fact unavoidably constrain current deliberative arrangements in many ways. Consider the sheer size and scale of most modern nation states. If decisions have to be made under time constraints, the number of actual participants in any political decision may turn out to be quite limited. As Robert Dahl and Edward Tufte put it, in a large society "the number of people who can participate directly in a decision by speaking so as to be heard by all the other direct participants is extremely small."[2] The largeness of modern institutions also makes it extremely difficult to coordinate deliberation in the usual back-and-forth manner of a debate. Such spatial and temporal limitations alone are real limitations on deliberative possibilities in large organizations. Deliberative democracy has too often been guided by criteria that make sense only on a small spatial and temporal scale. Unlike constraints of scale, most appeals to "functional" or systemic complexity, typical of most skeptical theories, do not pass their own rigorous criterion of unavoidability. Contrary to these critics, I argue that the spatial and temporal properties of large organizations and institutions in complex societies do not imply that popular sovereignty is either impossible or undesirable.

One response to such problems with radical democracy has been to separate public deliberation from decision-making power in complex institutions. Habermas, with his distinction of informal "opinion-formation" in the public sphere from the formal "will-formation" of political institutions, has elaborated this solution as the central feature of the constitutional state.[3] Similarly, Nancy Fraser distinguishes between "strong" and "weak" publics according to their decision-making power. The appeal of such attempts at demarcation is that they preserve at least one of the functions of popular sovereignty: critical public opinion at least can challenge the decisions of those whose power is sanctioned by their institutional positions. This view is taken even further by some recent critics of popular sovereignty from another direction: the "civil society" theorists, for whom the plurality of diffuse and informal associations serves to limit the power of an increasingly independent state and its bureaucracies.[4] The sovereignty of citizens must remain diffuse in order that state power does not attempt to reunify all social spheres. In effect, then, there can be no "strong" publics. But with too strict a separation of state and society there can be no democracy either: citizens are in the position of Kant's anti-democratic public sphere. Just like Kant's citizens, who must accept the decisions of already-constituted monarchical power, the contemporary citizens of weak publics can only criticize complex institutions; they cannot be the authors of their decisions. Without something analogous to popular sovereignty, complexity and differentiation undermine democracy itself, leading to a return to Kant's characterization of the public obligations of citizenship: "Criticize, but obey!"

In this chapter I closely examine the assumptions of this general line of argument against participatory democracy. Taken as an unanalyzed whole, the sheer size and complexity of modern society appear to undermine popular sovereignty and other democratic ideals, if not make them obsolete.

In the first section I show that the critics of radical democracy fail to distinguish properly between complexity and overcomplexity—that is, between complexity in its unavoidable and avoidable forms. On the one hand, social complexity is the product of the large spatial and temporal scale of social processes. On the other hand, overcomplexity involves the loss of human control over social processes. It has two (avoidable) forms: hypercomplexity and hyperrationality. Hyperrationality—excessive political will—is the actual target of most criticisms of more radical demands for popular control.

In the second section I analyze some claims about the "inevitability" of inequalities, such as the scarcity of resources and information, differences in competence and expertise, and the uncontrollability of non-intentional forms of integration and coordination. These antidemocratic claims about social complexity either are descriptively false or reduce to special cases of spatial and temporal limitations. Such limitations are, in turn, no basis for rejecting popular sovereignty.

Finally, I shall turn to Habermas's proposal of a "two-track" constitutional state for applying democratic norms in circumstances of social complexity. For all its merits, the two-track solution (a dispersed public and formal institutions) does not fully capture what is normatively distinctive about many constitutional states: the robust institutions of "dualist democracy." In dualist democracy, constitutional arrangements permit a variety of deliberative forums for "higher lawmaking," in which the conditions of "normal lawmaking" in existing institutions can be altered by the People.[5] I argue that Habermas underestimates the extent of popular sovereignty in the institutional design of dualist democracy, which contrasts sharply with his rather Kantian solution to the problem of complexity. For this purpose, I reinterpret the ideal of popular sovereignty as rule by "deliberative majorities" and suggest what such an interpretation might mean for maintaining the constant interchange between citizens and institutions necessary for democracy.

On Social Complexity: Hyperrationality and Hypercomplexity

Social theorists often simply assume that social complexity and democratic organization are inconsistent with one another. After all, the latter requires intentionality, while the former denies it. This common assumption is unfounded. Instead, democracy is more consistent with complexity than are non-democratic alternatives, which reduce rather than preserve complexity. If properly analyzed into distinct forms, complexity need not always be opposed to intentional and deliberative forms of coordination. In many instances, just the opposite is true: complex organization often depends upon such mechanisms in order to be sustained. Most political skeptics try to show that democratic organizational principles are inconsistent with and hence limited by the non-intentional mechanisms responsible for macrosociological order. If such descriptive theories of non-intentional integration are themselves inadequate, it is easy to see why complexity does not have the political and epistemological consequences that the skeptics believe it has. Their real target is not public reason *per se* but "excessive rationalism"—the belief that the deliberation of citizens of good will is able to solve every political problem.

The fact of modern social complexity that is most relevant to politics is the tendency toward ever-increasing social differentiation at many levels. This tendency is realized in various ways, including the segmentation of spheres of activity and the stratification of groups. But modern "functional differentiation," beginning with the differentiation of state and economy from society, culminates in increasingly distinct but interdependent subsystems, each with its own specific role and organizational structure.[6] According to these theories, each distinct system also develops its own "functional code" or language (such as money in economics or votes in politics) which determine the significance of actions within such a social system. The differentiation of such codes leads to a high degree of specialization and division of labor as well as to increasing impersonality and abstractness in the social system as a whole. The effects of markets and the code of money provide the clearest examples of this sort of depersonalization and abstraction. One supposed consequence of extreme differentiation is that there no "master code" (i.e., no generalized means of coordination among the subsystems). Increasing interdependence makes prediction more difficult, giving social intervention very little epistemic basis and, at best, "bounded rationality."[7]

What distinguishes functional differentiation from other forms of differentiation is the absence of a central coordinating mechanism in terms of which power and authority can be exercised. A functionally differentiated society is "polycentric"; that is, it has no single center or apex from which to exercise control over all the differentiated subsystems. The integration of complex institutions with differentiated spheres has been a critical question for the organization of the modern state since Hegel's *Philosophy of Right*, even as the state has become increasingly functionally differentiated. How can modern society be both differentiated and unified at the same time? Democracy, Hegel argued, is inadequate for the task.

This lack of a single "center" from which to regulate independent spheres of social action presents a basic challenge to democratic control. The apparent failures of planned economies have supplied much evidence for this view; their unintended consequences and their perverse effects have led many to conclude that market subsystems should remain independent and not be brought under conscious control by political institutions.[8] Furthermore, such control could only be had by restricting individual and social freedom. In order to gain the necessary certainty and full information, it is necessary for the political system to reduce complexity, primarily by restricting or eliminating the inputs of civil society. Civil society introduces further complexity by forcing the political system to adapt to new interpretations and to alternative patterns of decision making. Eliminating civil society altogether would, in fact, be the most direct way to reduce complexity and contingency. Nonetheless, systems theory and some forms of "civil society" theory make strange bedfellows to the extent that both argue against the application of democratic principles to all areas of social life; this insistence amounts to "democratic fundamentalism."[9]

Proponents of democracy seem trapped on the horns of a Hegelian dilemma: if the political institutions gain enough influence over all of society to bring about democratic integration and popular participation, then there is a corresponding loss of freedom and complexity; if freedom and complexity are preserved, then citizens must give up much of their influence and control. As formulated, however, the dilemma depends on the unstated premise that democracy and complexity are conceptually contradictory. Is there a more empirical way to conceive of their relationship?

The dilemma is a false one, on my view, because it fails to distinguish two distinct problems that complexity creates for democracy. The problem most critics of radical democracy identify is what Jon Elster calls *hyperrationality*, a pathological version of public reason that sees all problems as solvable by the *currently* available types of deliberation. It is an excessive rationalism to the extent that it ignores conditions that could make a satisfactory outcome of deliberation impossible, such as uncertainty and lack of information. Because deliberation is affected, democracy cannot remedy these conditions. Hyperrationality is thus an inability to recognize failures of rationality, as when deliberators ignore uncertainty, ambiguity and lack of full information and yet demand uniquely rational decisions.[10] But by irrationally believing in the powers of reason, including rational political deliberation, deliberators fail to acknowledge the limits of reason and thus to apply the self-critical capacities of reason to public reason itself. As Elster notes, the Kantian dictum is essentially correct: "The first task of reason is to recognize its own limitations and draw boundaries within which it can operate."[11] Typically, the critics of popular sovereignty discuss precisely cases in which the failure to draw such boundaries leads to excesses of political will. Social complexity is but one source of such limitations, and excessive rationalism is an issue for any form of democratic decision making, independent of any special facts of complexity and differentiation. Complexity may specifically limit efficiency and foresight to the extent that any means to some public end may have many unforeseen and interrelated consequences. However, the failure here is due to the agents' not being aware that the conditions for successful deliberative decision making are not present.

Excessive rationalism is a form of irrationality (rather than a form of public unreason, such as those discussed in chapter 2) that violates the self-critical basis of the public use of reason. *Hypercomplexity* is something altogether different: it is that degree of complexity which makes rational public decision making impossible. Many political skeptics do not distinguish between hypercomplexity and hyper-rationality, but instead simply assume that public reason is in every case operating outside its proper limits. Even when self-critical and aware of its limits, use of public reason cannot gain full knowledge of the hypercomplex effects on intentional forms of social coordination. Complex market interdependencies, for instance, are supposed to make conscious or intentional coordination unnecessary. But this example is exceptional and therefore misleading; it leads defenders of non-intentional, market-like complexity to consider the necessity of such mechanisms to be both inevitable and beneficial social facts. But "the invisible hand" is not always benign and not always invisible. This fact illuminates a very different account of public decision making under excessive complexity.

Consider a complex and highly interdependent technical system, such as a nuclear power plant connected to the power grid of a large metropolitan area. The complexity of these systems demands the opposite of an invisible hand: they need constant and intentional adjustment. Such systems are characterized by what Charles Perrow calls "tight coupling," which in turn lead to "normal accidents."[12] Tight coupling occurs when the interrelation of various sub-systems is so heightened that the need for control is increased. Adjusting the money supply may have immediate economic effects, which in turn require adjusting interest rates, and so on. The increased differentiation and independence of subsystems can often be maintained only at the price of raising uncertainty and risk. Under these conditions, such complex systems decrease freedom. This loss of freedom has nothing to do with the excessive will of political agents who seek to resolve uncertainty; it has to do with the increased risks associated with excessive complexity. We have already seen in chapter 3 that such subsystems also tend to promote inequalities and to lessen public freedom and eliminate the very possibility of deliberation.

Such tightly coupled systems must be closely connected to the social organization that monitors and maintains them. The greater the complexity of a technical system, the greater the number of non-linear connections between the system and its environment. The malfunctioning of a single unit, or such a unit's being unpredictably influenced by an external source, can have unexpected effects.[13] This unpredictability makes it necessary to *reduce* the complexity of the system's environment in order to maintain the system's complexity while avoiding a catastrophic breakdown. Thus, in tightly coupled systems there is constant monitoring of the environment, with minimal flexibility regarding the time and the resources needed for immediate intervention. Maintaining such a system demands increasingly specialized expert knowledge, which in turn multiplies experts' authority over decisions pertaining both to the system's maintenance and (more fatal to democracy) to the monitoring of the system's environment.

Technological systems are not a special case in this respect. To borrow an example from Joseph Rouse: once agricultural production becomes guided by technological interventions, decisions become more and more tightly coupled.[14] Every adaptation of the plant to the past intervention needs further corrective responses with fertilizer, insecticides, and so on. As a result, tight coupling has produced an "artificial complexity" in agricultural production, as compared to the looser form of complex interdependence typical of ecological systems. Artificiality refers to overcomplexity, in that every response is only a response to the previous intervention. With such complexity there is indeed "the slow decline into guardianship," to use Robert Dahl's apt phrase. However, this decline is not due to any intrinsic or unavoidable complexity, or even to specialized expert knowledge; it is due to the kind of interdependence that hypercomplexity produces. Why is this form of complexity desirable or inevitable? As with arguments based on the efficiency of subsystems, it is necessary to ask: complexity for what? Tight coupling is one mechanism through which functional differentiation undermines public deliberation, and it shows that certain forms of complexity are not always desirable.

A clearer analysis of the relationships among hyperrationality, hypercomplexity and democracy should make us question the assumptions of many criticisms of radical democracy. In the case of hypercomplexity, time constraints on decisions preclude any deliberative input if complexity is to be preserved. Overcomplex systems have anti-democratic consequences. But with regard to other forms of complexity the opposite is often the case: democracy preserves complexity, whereas anti-democratic measures are often attempts to reduce complexity for the sake of goals such as security and protection from risks. The empirical relation between democracy and complexity is not as unidirectional as critics of radical democracy have claimed. The in-principle argument against deliberative democracy makes the dubious claim that there is only one type of macrosociological complexity. It does not consider the ways in which democratic institutions actually promote and preserve complexity, at least to the extent that democracy is not excessively rational and political institutions are not overly complex. Both hyperrationality and hypercomplexity are anti-democratic (they inhibit effective deliberation and undermine democratic legitimacy), but certain institutions can maintain social complexity and the conditions of public deliberation at the same time.

In cases of hypercomplexity, the complexity of a subsystem (say, the technical subsystem of Perrow's example) may be preserved in only one way: by reducing the complexity of the environment. Thus, the system adapts the environment to itself, and not vice versa (as might be the case in the gradual destruction of the organic content of the soil through monoculture). This reduction of complexity limits the capacity of a deliberating public to hold decisions open until they have passed through public procedures sufficient to ensure some form of consent. *Hypercomplexity* aptly characterizes many problems facing contemporary democracies, including "ecological disequilibrium, nuclear disasters, demographic pressures, the problem of the food supply, the disposal of waste, the interconnection of financial systems, terrorism, and the worldwide circulation of drugs."[15] According to the theorists Danilo Zolo and Niklas Luhmann, these problems are too complex to be dealt with by the intentional and hence "linear" institutional mechanisms of democracy. Democracy and the popular sovereignty of citizens are therefore "obsolete" under such circumstances. In the face of such overwhelming risks, democracy "has become the most improbable and the most fragile, and the least realistic form of government conceivable today."[16] This claim leads to the inevitable Weberian conclusion that all non-elementary, complex political systems are "necessarily oligarchic," and thus to the conclusion that all claims for democratic consent, even those mediated through a constitutional state or civil society, are illusory. Claims about unavoidable complexity begin a steep and slippery slope, which eliminates possibilities of participation, then deliberation, then representation, and finally democracy.

This analysis of social complexity allows us to restate the basic dilemma which critics pose: democracy requires a certain degree of complexity in order for individual and public freedom to be possible, yet at a certain threshold of complexity this same freedom disappears. Does the second half of this dilemma mean that democracy is inadequate to deal with the fact of complexity and that something like oligarchy is inevitable? The conceptual mistake here is that oligarchy does not, in the end, preserve complexity; it is often the case that democracy maintains complexity by preserving the contingency of individual choice and the uncoupling of civil society from the economy or the state. Anti-democratic tendencies, such as the power inflation of the modern state bureaucracies that control social risks and the effects of scarcity, also aim at reducing complexity. As Zolo puts it: "The simplest and most effective mechanism for achieving such protection is a drastic reduction of social complexity."[17] Criticisms of democracy on these grounds call for increasing the scope of hierarchically structured political power. Conservative critics of democracy, such as Carl Schmitt, have long pointed out the inadequacy of democracy for the state functions of protecting us from evil.[18] Thus, there is no inherent functional antinomy between increasing democracy and maintaining complexity. The opposite is true: many of the same political mechanisms that reduce complexity also restrict democracy. It all depends on the type of complexity involved: the overcomplexity produced by non-linear feedback loops or the complexity that results from free and hence contingent decisions.

Hyperrationality is by no means inevitable when the people are sovereign. Some standard solutions, such as the familiar separation of powers, are institutional. This internal differentiation of the political system not only guards against the passions and interests of citizens; it also increases institutional complexity and preserves it from the overarching power of one branch. Instituting such internal complexity of the political system does two things at once: it restricts the capacity of each branch to intervene effectively in some social spheres, and at the same time it inhibits the escalation of political power. Such internal political complexity is therefore consistent with well-ordered democratic institutions. Similarly, hypercomplexity could be defined in terms of the inflation of power in one of these subsystems in order to meet an increased need for protection or for risk reduction. But this role ascribes to certain institutions (such as the executive branch) anti-democratic purposes. Hence, the conflict is not dependent on any level of social complexity but instead on the inherent tensions in political systems with purposes as distinct as effectiveness and consensus. Hypercomplexity often dovetails with hyperrationality through the escalation of hierarchical power necessary for carrying out political decisions.

Before I turn to more specific conflicts of democracy and complexity, one further general point needs to be made. Can there be democratic complexity? This term denotes the sorts of differentiated institutions typical of existing democratic institutions. The separation of powers is not merely a *functional* requirement necessary if government to fulfill certain independent purposes; it also exists to preserve private and public autonomy and thus to preserve the complexity of free and contingent decisions. In so doing, this form of complexity enables free and open public deliberation.

Such differentiation within deliberative institutions meets some challenges of complexity. It permits a variety of deliberative roles as well as an epistemic division of labor within deliberation and decision making. Exactly how one spells out the different deliberative roles depends on both the issue at hand and institutional constraints. Indeed, some issues, such as constitutional amendments, may require deliberative inputs from all citizens, whereas others may require only casting a vote for a particular representative in some decision-making body. Institutional mechanisms that preserve complexity by permitting diverse types of public input at various levels are necessary in any well-ordered society and for deliberation in the constitutional state. The mechanisms that help citizens avoid hyperrationality place limits on escalating political power. This is true to the extent that diverse public inputs keep the democratic process open and make it harder for institutions to see their policies as univocal expressions of the public will. Such institutional designs do not necessarily entail pre-commitment or self-binding; rather, they make ongoing intelligent planning, deliberation, and association possible.

Seen in this way, the separation of powers is a mechanism for preserving complexity and sovereignty rather than a merely functional or organizational device. It enables and limits popular sovereignty within the boundaries of democratic principles in that it establishes a recursive relation between public opinion and democratic decision making in institutions. By "recursive" or "self-referential" I mean that such mechanisms enable the public to reshape the institutional means it has for executing political decisions; at the same time, these institutions are necessary to organizing and carrying out the public will in large-scale societies, which require a dual dialectic between institutions and their deliberating publics. On the one hand, the decision-making power of the public is channelled into institutional mechanisms; on the other hand, the institutional mechanisms are influenced and limited by the public and its sovereignty. On the one hand, such limitations imply that the sovereign will of the people no longer has power to constitute the whole of society by its collective decisions; on the other hand, sovereignty limits political power in such a way that the will of citizens is its ultimate source.

Sovereignty here concerns the constitutional basis for legitimate political power in the deliberative process. The power of citizens is itself legitimate only if it is exercised through the limiting and enabling conditions of the constitutional state, and the constitutional state is legitimate only if it makes possible the constitution of power through the will of citizens. Whatever limits exogenous sources of complexity impose on democracy, the constitutional state preserves complexity by functionally limiting the scope of the use of hierarchical power and establishing mechanisms for the dispersal of democratic power. A constitutional framework is necessary not only to establish conditions and methods of deliberation but also to ensure that the exercise of political power by citizens does not violate the conditions of non-tyranny, political equality, and publicity.

Popular sovereignty shows the continued dependence of political institutions on intentional action and upon the belief of citizens in the legitimacy of politically generated power. Just as producers continue to practice monoculture only if they believe it to be more productive, so too the preservation of social complexity in politics depends on the intentional input of actors. "Tightly coupled" systems require monitoring; markets function best with consistent optimizing behavior and state intervention. Besides proper institutionalization, such as the separation of powers, deliberation requires that actors become knowledgeable participants capable of taking part in deliberation in a variety of ways, with a variety of roles. This broad participation is often quite efficient with regard to information pooling, thereby reducing the information costs of the process of public deliberation as a whole.[19]

But other forms of skepticism about democracy do not depend on the strong claims about the inverse linear relation between democracy and complexity or about polycentric, functionally differentiated societies. Rather, they claim that there are other forms of complexity that are "unavoidable" in modern societies. These forms of social complexity are equally anti-democratic, "democracy" being understood here as egalitarian decision making through face-to-face interaction among free and equal persons. By contrast, modern societies "unavoidably" depend upon centralized and hierarchical authority—on social processes that in no way can be reconciled with democratic norms of equality, freedom, and publicity. This "unavoidable" complexity leads to violation of these norms as well as to cognitive limits on the deliberative capacities of citizens. Given the complexities of institutional decision making and the cognitive demands of modern society, deliberation is supposedly found only in the informal public sphere. I turn next to such claims, arguing that they fail to distinguish between complexity and hypercomplexity—that is, between the limits of public reason and the dangers of excessive rationalism.

"Unavoidable" Complexity and Democratic Ideals

In the preceding section I disputed the general claim that increasing the scope of democracy *ipso facto* decreases social complexity. In this section I want to deal with a different sort of objection to participatory and deliberative arrangements: that "unavoidable" social complexity inherently limits the application of norms of political equality and the decision-making power of the democratic public. As in the skeptical argument discussed in the preceding section, this objection depends on establishing that the operation of mechanisms of non-intentional integration produces anti-egalitarian consequences and limits the effectiveness of intentional forms of political integration. The polemical purpose of these accounts is to show that socialism and other forms of "radical" democracy are inappropriate for modern societies.[20] In *Faktizität und Geltung*, Habermas affirms this harsh lesson of some critics of radical democracy; he agrees that the communicative organization of society as a whole is impossible, for the reason that democracy can no longer regulate the social contexts in which it is embedded.[21] Deviations from and even violations of democratic norms are inevitable once we abandon this false hope.

In order to reply to such compelling sociological objections, radical democrats must show two things. First, they must show that institutional complexity *per se*, such as the use of experts in deliberation, does not necessarily lead to the violations of democratic norms which critics claim they do. The epistemic division of labor as such is not inherently undemocratic and anti-egalitarian. Rather, it is a question of *how* the labor of decision making may be divided and still remain public. Second, radical democrats must show that popular sovereignty can be maintained even in institutions characterized by a high degree of social complexity. The problem is that most versions of these objections against popular sovereignty once again do not hit the target: they do not refer *social* complexity at all, but to a unified political will. Although some versions of participatory democracy do indeed founder on problems of excessive political rationalism rather than social complexity, macrosociology is hardly needed to see why this is true.

As a way of clarifying some issues, let me begin with a thought experiment proposed by Bernhard Peters in his *Integration moderner Gesellschaften*. I shall use it here only as a way of organizing the sociological objections to radical democracy typical of theorists as diverse as Weber, Luhmann, Lippmann, and Foucault. (Habermas, to whom I devote the next section, is a more complex case.) Peters's thought experiment proposes that we imagine a society characterized by "a fully conscious and discursive form of self-organization"; we are asked to consider what it would be like for a society to be structured entirely through the deliberation of free and equal citizens, without any external or internal limitations. Imagine that Marx's vision of the Paris Commune flourishes for more than a few months, or that deliberating citizens actually achieve some approximation of the ideal speech situation in their political institutions.[22] In every aspect and dimension, this society is fully consensual—Marx's ideal society of "freely associated individuals," each possessing the full range of cognitive and communicative capacities. What makes such a society an idealized version of deliberative association is that all *external* limitations—all spatial, temporal, communicative, and cognitive restrictions on citizens' capacities—have been lifted by abstraction, so that all problems of coordination can be resolved by conscious collective action. Such a society embodies egalitarianism in all its dimensions: "It is a structure which embodies the conscious, rational process of reaching understanding among equals; equality here signifies the fully reciprocal recognition of everyone, where everyone has the equal chance to participate in social life, in this case the equal opportunity to participate in the discourse of conscious will-formation."[23] Hyperrationality emerges before the norm of equality is even introduced, making it easy to confuse excessive equality with excessive rationalism.

However, the abstraction of a "purely communicative form of sociation" is not a mere thought experiment; it is also "a methodological fiction," useful for understanding necessary and unavoidable deviations from the norms of equality and publicity. This fiction, it is claimed, is also useful for criticizing the claims of democratic theories, such as those of Joshua Cohen and Robert Dahl.[24] Its "analytic" usefulness can be seen by gradually reintroducing "actual" social conditions of complexity and pluralism into the experiment until the facts of modern social complexity are reached. These facts make consensual association and dialogical deliberation impossible. We may expand this list of conditions to include all those which sociologists claim make democratic ideals impractical.

The first problem with this general type of criticism is that it is abstract: it is directed at an ideal of consensus and transparency that does not model anything like actual deliberation in democratic institutions and political discourse. It is based on the idealizing assumptions of *discourse*, and not on a reconstruction of democratic deliberation. Democratic self-governance can only in part be characterized as the institutionalization of discourses governed by mutual recognition. Thus, the *moral* idealization of full equality and recognition is not meant to be a model for actual public deliberation about conflicting values, interests, and principles. Indeed, the critics aim at a false target. They show what Kant knew already: that the "Kingdom of Ends" is not the basis for a workable political order. The fiction of pure communicative association suggests that these norms could be fulfilled only in a society without political power or institutions (which also suggests that there will be no need for democracy, either). In the end, the thought experiment only demonstrates the need to rethink overly strong notions of a unified rational will; it supplies no empirical argument against radical democracy or deliberative arrangements as such.

Once complexity is introduced into communicative forms of association, the first deviation that the thought experiment supposedly identifies is a direct violation of norms of equality. It is surprisingly strong: *unavoidable inequalities* emerge that would not be agreed to by everyone in deliberation. Radical democrats will have to admit that public deliberation certainly can produce and reproduce inequalities. However, the burden of proof is on the critic to show not merely that potential inequalities remain in such arrangements, but that these inequalities cannot be corrected by them (that is, that they are indeed "unavoidable"). A chorus of sociological critics of democracy propose a number of similar "deviations": "unavoidable" scarcity, inherent differences between and limits on the cognitive and communicative capacities of citizens, inevitable social coercion and non-democratic authority, and so on. The general structure of such arguments should now be clear. In each case, the critic proposes supposedly non-democratic solutions to such problems that, left unresolved, would threaten social integration: delegation, the division of labor, and non-intentional forms of integration such as markets. The critic then concludes that the democratic principle of equality must be abandoned if a complex society is to be integrated and organized at all.

Upon closer examination, these inevitable inequalities turn out to have little to do with social complexity. Such inequalities are generally

epistemic, having to do with "overburdening" intrinsic limited capacities or with ignoring "natural" differences in abilities. Many critics of
"mass democracy" have questioned the competence of the "masses,"
whose incompetence makes them need the guiding hand of benevo-
lent authority.[25] It is true that neither capacities nor acquired knowledge can be assumed to be evenly or widely distributed. Aside from
the fact that such limits give rise to inequalities in effectiveness in participation, knowledge and information are scarce resources in complex societies, so citizens surrender their autonomy to experts,
delegates, and other forms of the division of labor.

Mechanisms that are clearly intentional, such as delegation, do not
necessarily violate egalitarian principles, given proper selection procedures. Expertise seems to undermine the claim of all to participate
equally, and specialized knowledge seems to give unfair deliberative
advantages to some participants. Here the problem is misstated; effectiveness is a matter not merely of superior knowledge but of
greater access to the relevant forum. We then have to make a further
assumption about experts: that they use their knowledge to pursue
their own interests. It is certainly the case that such asymmetries per-
meate many of the social arrangements on which complex societies
depend, such as transportation systems, the distribution of food, ar-
chitecture, medicine, and many areas of specialized knowledge. Susan
Shapiro puts this epistemic dependency as follows: most ordinary citizens "are unable to render medical diagnoses, to test the safety and
purity of food and drugs before ingesting them, to conduct structural tests on skyscrapers before entering them, or to make safety
checks on elevators, automobiles or airplanes before embarking on
them; they must rely on the representations and assessments of experts."[26] Does this epistemic dependence on others show that complex societies cannot function with strict political equality?

This argument underestimates the effects of the epistemic division of labor on public activities. Experts themselves are in the same
position of trust in regard to their very own "expert" knowledge, not
just with regard to other experts.[27] Furthermore, social movements
have successfully challenged scientific experts both in the political
arena and, more important, on their own ground. These movements demonstrate quite well that epistemic inequalities are not an

"inevitable" result of the complex division of scientific labor or of the division of laypersons and experts in the public sphere. Act-Up and other AIDS-activist organizations have challenged experts' "representations and assessments"[28] and hence precisely the credibility of scientific experts in the public sphere. Although many areas of expertise remain unproblematic, the AIDS crisis took expert knowledge and assessments out of the uncontested domain. To resolve the crisis of trust and credibility, experts were forced to agree to take many aspects of AIDS treatment and research out of the exclusive domain of their expert authority and allowed them to become contested public issues.[29] This is not some exceptional circumstance; it is a political demand for access to the agenda of researchers who need both the cooperation of AIDS patients and the funding of public institutions. The division of epistemic labor depends on public trust. Mechanisms needed to maintain trust may also preserve *equality*, since experts cannot be effective unless they convince non-experts of their claims.

Perhaps even more important, public trust is a particular sort of resource in a democratic society. It is not a scarce economic resource that is depleted by use. Rather, it is a "moral resource" that *increases* through use.[30] The public testability and the moral character of trust as the social basis of expertise contradict the view that it violates norms of equality: expertise must be publicly convincing to be effective, and it can be lost through abuse and disuse. Furthermore, expertise increases the aggregate of available public knowledge, so long as it is treated as a *shared* resource. The more such knowledge is publicly used to justify democratic decisions, the more likely it is to become more widely distributed through deliberation and debate.

The phenomena of trust and the distribution of knowledge in deliberation raise other problems that lead to supposedly unavoidable violations of equality: problems of inevitable *scarcity*, such as the scarcity of information. Once again, an economic account of scarcity is needed to motivate the argument against democracy. All organizations and groups have a scarcity of cognitive resources to some extent, the main problem being simply the scarcity of time. There are organizational and distributive strategies for dealing with temporal constraints; these include setting limits on when decisions are made in order to meet the pressures of coordination and to minimize information costs in decision making. However, these limits do not result from complexity; they result from the limitations of time and information typical of ordinary intentional action. These same limitations constrain planning in democratic organizations.[31] Scarcity by itself does not create inequalities, since burdens can be shared equally. Analogous counterarguments can be made to dispute many of the critics' claims about cognitive inequalities.[32] Similarly, the time-saving routinizations typical of everyday decisions do not produce inevitable coercion. They only show that conscious deliberation is not possible for every decision and for every time some past decision is enacted or enforced. Instead of eliminating such efficiencies for the sake of consensual arrangements, in democratic arrangements there need only be opportunities for revision and review when routines become problematic and burdensome. If these practices are in place, the "inevitability" of coercion may only be temporary.

These public processes of participation, review, and revision can, however, themselves become routinized—a by-product that heightens the consequences of hyperrationality. Even if required, public hearings often have no impact on actual decisions, and only inputs that might lead to eventual court challenges receive deliberative uptake. Such proceedings would produce reform only if the alternative reasons are not defined automatically within the administrative system of significance. This system is developed precisely to ensure the smooth functioning of the organization, not to produce a diverse set of alternative proposals. Properly reformed, such hearings could become not only more deliberative but also a more efficient means for developing successful problem-solving strategies. Perhaps the greatest need for institutional reform lies in creating new forms of bureaucratic organization consistent with deliberation. Such forms of revision show that public scrutiny does not necessarily serve the functional purposes of institutions. Foucault makes such a claim in *Discipline and Punish*, in which he insists that the public scrutiny of the prison is just another level of surveillance and hence of disciplinary power.[33] The legitimacy of such a reduction of complexity can always be contested, especially since the institutions in which social order is created depend on the continuation of background cultural practices.

My line of argument has been to show that it is difficult establish "inevitable" complexities or violations of egalitarian norms by means of a macrosociological theory. The thought experiment is telling only for problems of hypercomplexity and hyperrationality, both of which require institutional mechanisms to be avoided. Thus, the argument of this section has been twofold. First, I have suggested that the relationship between democracy and complexity is not unidirectional. There is no empirical evidence or in-principle argument which shows that complexity inherently limits democracy. Second, I have argued that the relationship is actually bi-directional. Some institutions preserve complexity. Democratic institutions enhance and enable the positive features of complexity, such as the contingencies of freedom and plurality. Thus, my argument suggests that some institutions are capable of preserving both democracy and complexity.

What are these institutional alternatives? The general features of such a solution can best be described as lying between two poles: direct democracy and rule by experts, on the one hand, and hyperrationality and hypercomplexity, on the other. Habermas's recent account of the rule of law in modern constitutional states gives us a partial version of one such comprehensive solution. He sees the possibility of "two tracks" of democratic decision making, one in the informal public sphere and the other in formal institutions, which nonetheless are aimed at promoting public deliberation and communication.[34] Despite his focus on the institutional mediation of communicative interaction, Habermas's conception of democracy is still inadequate precisely because it assumes a unidirectional account of the relation between social complexity and popular sovereignty. The ideals of consensus and unrestricted public communication are not best defended by separating formal will formation within complex institutions from informal opinion formation outside of them. In place of this distinction, I propose a richer and more consistent principle of democracy, one that is more substantive yet still consistent with cultural pluralism. This principle also establishes a form of popular sovereignty that maintains the good features of social complexity (such as freedom and pluralism) and overcomes some of the obstacles that it presents to democracy (such as the escalation of social power and the loss of public control of large areas of social life).

Social Complexity, Institutional Mediation, and Popular Sovereignty: The "Two-Track" Model and Its Shortcomings

Habermas provides a good case study of a democratic theorist who has struggled to balance the demands of participatory democracy and social complexity. Whereas his earlier writings emphasize participation and the limits of formal democracy, in his later writings Habermas holds that the facts of social complexity undermine his own previous attempts to establish any stronger, more extensive form of democracy. Nonetheless, the centrality of democratic procedures and legal institutions in Habermas's critical social theory sharply distinguishes him from the previous generation of the Frankfurt School. As I noted in the introduction, the previous generation of the Frankfurt School defended a "utopian" notion of radical democracy very much like Marx's. Habermas defends a modified version of liberal democracy, incorporating what he thinks are the still-living parts of the radical democratic tradition. In this section I shall give the broad outlines of Habermas's "two-track" solution to the problem of complexity. I shall then argue that the institutional mechanisms described in this model do indeed provide the outline for a general solution to many of the problems of complexity. However, Habermas goes too far in reducing public deliberation to the merely informal bases of legitimacy, thereby emptying the radical democratic ideal of popular sovereignty of any substantive meaning. My criticisms of this claim provide criteria for developing a more successful version of the two-track solution.

In his recent writings on democracy, Habermas abandons his demand in *Legitimation Crisis* for some participatory and "substantive" form of democracy characterized by "the genuine participation of citizens in political will formation" to replace the merely "formal" one typical of welfare-state capitalism.[35] This stronger and substantive notion of a democratic will formed by citizens' participation was to continue the Critical Theorists' search for a wider notion of rationality with which to ground a richer and more demanding form of democratic politics. In *Between Facts and Norms*, Habermas rejects even this task for a Critical Theory of democracy. Democracy, he argues, cannot organize society as a whole, since it is embedded in contexts of social complexity that it can neither regulate nor control.[36] These contexts are constituted by a non-intentional social order of differentiated and systemically related parts. Without a component of the theory that describes the potentials of current practices for dealing with such order, deliberative democracy ignores the many "systemic constraints" on decision making: information and decision costs, asymmetries of competence and expertise, the uneven distribution of knowledge in the public sphere, the limits of public attention, and the cultural scarcity of deliberative resources.[37] Furthermore, the basic fact of polycentric power changes the nature of democratic institutions and political participation.

Once its implications are clear, this description of social complexity has a number of striking consequences for democratic theory. At the normative level, the strong analogies between the justification of moral norms and democratic decision making that were so prominent in *Legitimation Crisis* have to be abandoned. Exploring moral justification served the epistemological purpose of pointing the way beyond Weber, but it proved a misleading and undercomplex model for democratic deliberation. Besides leading to the subordination of law and politics to morality, the idealizations and abstractness of moral discourse set the standard of agreement too high for democratic theory.[38] This shift set the stage for Habermas's more modest approach and for his attempt to reintroduce complexity and contingency into the normative framework of constitutional democracy. At the very least, it means that both direct forms of self-rule and the application of democratic control to all areas of social life are impossible to achieve. Social life is now politically "unsurveyable"—so complex that it is beyond the grasp of actors who cannot control all the consequences of their actions. In their place, powerful institutions must organize highly differentiated and large-scale social processes and integrate them by means of non-intentional mechanisms. How can democracy avoid being overwhelmed by them?

According to the theoretical orientation shared by Parsons and Weber and developed further by Habermas, law is the solution: as an institution, it has special properties that make it a suitable means to solve these problems of integration and complexity.[39] Weber traces the rationality gains of modern, positive law, especially its development of formal and procedural forms of justification and bureaucratic organizations for enforcement and enactment of decisions. But Weber ties law to the bureaucratization of the modern state rather than to its increasing democratic potential. For all its weaknesses, Parsons's sociology of law provides a key descriptive term for Habermas's account of law as a medium for social integration. In complex and differentiated societies, the political subsystem, even if bureaucratically organized, cannot integrate all the many differentiated spheres. According to Parsons, "the societal community" identifies a whole set of spheres of action that serve integrative functions, from rituals that produce solidarity to second-order institutions (such as law and morality) that regulate conflicts.[40] For Habermas, the law is the central structure of the societal community, since it alone is able to transmit solidarity into increasingly abstract and institutionally mediated social relationships. It can do so not only because of its intermediary status but also because of its "self-referential" quality. As Habermas puts it: "Law is a legitimate order that has become reflexive with regard to the very process of institutionalization."[41] It is with this reflexivity that democracy becomes possible, since law is a medium not only for making specific decisions but also for determining the character of regulating institutions.

Political and legal institutions are now necessary to overcome the deficits in social integration that are empirical facts of modern societies: they compensate for "the cognitive indeterminacy, the motivational insecurity, and the limited coordinating power of moral norms and informal norms of action in general."[42] This need for institutional mediation means that political life will not consist merely of "free associations" based on communication, and that even the "sovereign will of the people" is no longer able to control or to constitute the whole of society. But communication by itself cannot perform this integrative role without institutional mediation. For democratic theory, it follows that whatever is left of ideals of participation and self-determination will have to be worked out within the context of liberal constitutionalism and its institutions, which in turn establish "a system of basic human rights." The rule of law is thus interpreted as both enabling deliberation and integrating complex societies.

If law is to perform this integrative function, political decision making and institutions must be oriented to the making of laws; politics is "jurisgenerative," as Frank Michelman puts it.[43] Political deliberation deals with issues that are so complex that it typically must employ all three of the following distinct aspects of practical reason[44]: political deliberation is "pragmatic" to the extent that it deals with achieving practical ends, "moral" insofar as it is concerned with achieving the fair resolution of interpersonal conflicts, and "ethical" when it is concerned with the interpretation of cultural values and identities.[45] Consider how the recent debate over health care in the United States has been conducted in all these dimensions in ways that are difficult to separate: questions of fairness, efficiency, and cultural values are all relevant. Moreover, the debate mixes together argumentation, compromise, and bargaining, as well. Political deliberation, therefore, does not take place within a specialized form of discourse, with its own logical structure and with an orientation to a single aspect of validity (such as truth or justice). Deliberative politics for Habermas is instead a complex "discursive network" that includes argumentation of various sorts, bargaining and compromise, and, above all, unrestricted communication and the free expression of opinions by all citizens in the informal public sphere.

Besides law as an institution, the second component of Habermas's solution is the role of rights in constituting and regulating the lawmaking process. Rights not only limit the power of institutions but also permit the generation of specifically democratic forms of power. Habermas gives an intersubjective interpretation of rights by appealing not only to the integrative function of law as an institution but also to the central role of law-making in establishing legitimacy. Even at the conceptual level, he argues, rights make no sense either as the properties of atomistic persons or as the shared values of communities; they make sense only as "elements of a legal order" based on mutual recognition and self-legislation. Rights emerge as conditions under which it is possible for citizens to collaborate in making positive law as free and equal citizens: ". . . 'subjective' rights emerge equiprimordially with 'objective' law."[46] Habermas claims to derive a whole system of rights from the discursive character of lawmaking— and these rights include negative liberties, rights of membership, and legal rights of due process, all of which guarantee private autonomy as well as rights to participation and social welfare. These conditions ensure that law "preserves its connection with the socially integrative force of communicative action."[47]

The final result of intertwining the ideal principle of discursive justification with the medium of law is the following principle: "Only those laws may claim legitimacy that meet with the agreement of all citizens in a discursive law making process that is itself legally constituted."[48] The agreement of *all* citizens, or the requirement of unanimity, does not yet distinguish the discourse principle from the principle of democratic legitimacy. This requirement, and the impartiality it demands, is precisely what characterizes law making as a discursive process. The discursive ideal is preserved, even if popular sovereignty is to be abandoned to make democratic legitimacy applicable to societies such as ours.

There is one further tension between social facts and democratic norms for Habermas to address: that between sovereignty and complexity. Even Habermas's modified principle of democracy as legal legitimacy seems oriented to face-to-face interaction rather than to large-scale institutions and societies. This is the problem of *external* tensions between facts and norms. Democratic theories must be normatively adequate and sociologically descriptive at the same time. Once again, there are two opposing positions that turn out to be two sides of the same dilemma: on the one hand, Habermas considers purely normative positions, such as Rawls's theory of justice, to be "sociologically naive"; on the other hand, purely descriptive sociology, such as Luhmann's systems theory, collapses into "legal positivism." Most versions of deliberative democracy are ensnared on the first horn of the dilemma. They develop ideal theories of democratic justification that specify necessary conditions and procedures for decision-making processes in all institutions. "Realistic" theories of democracy are caught on the second horn. Most of all, a good deliberative theory must avoid falling into both difficulties: deliberation cannot be based on impractical and unattainable ideals, nor should large-scale institutions be inconsistent with democratic self-rule and political equality. In contrast to both these approaches, Habermas thinks that a normative and sociological theory of democracy has to be developed at the same time. Here Habermas applies his method of "rational reconstruction," which attempts to combine normative and empirical analyses of social practices. Indeed, the "fact of complexity" makes it necessary to apply the conditions of discourse and standards of democratic legitimacy "in a more differentiated way."[49] The problem is that Habermas's two-track solution surrenders too much of democratic self-governance in order to achieve integration at the institutional level.

According to the two-track model, laws and political decisions in complex and pluralistic societies can be rational and hence legitimate in a deliberative democratic sense—that is, rationally authored by the citizens to whom they are addressed—if institutionalized decision-making procedures follow two tracks. They must be both (1) open to inputs from an informal and vibrant public sphere and (2) appropriately structured to support the rationality of the relevant types of discourse and to ensure effective implementation. That is, political decision making in institutions must be open to an unrestricted public sphere and yet structured in such a way as to be timely and effective (as well as coherent).

Here the problem of democratic participation in complex societies is a more basic one. In modern societies, citizens cannot literally come together to deliberate as a whole in any forum or particular body.[50] The process of discourse itself is inevitably dispersed across a variety of forums, including face-to-face interactions at home and work; larger meetings in the various informal voluntary associations and different levels of organization throughout civil society (clubs, professional associations, unions, issue-centered movements, and the like); the dissemination of information and arguments through the public media; and the complex network of government institutions, agencies, and decision-making bodies. Even before the problem of dissent is dealt with, a plausible concept of rational deliberation must somehow do justice to the complex and dispersed reality of actual public discourse under contemporary social conditions.

It seems to me that a deliberative democratic theory must hold three terms together if it is to solve the problem of complexity adequately: it must link deliberation and decision making with the citizenry. The sheer size and complexity of society could tempt one to relegate deliberation only to representatives so much that it would be difficult to call the account democratic. An opposite error would be to underestimate complexity and locate deliberation primarily in the public sphere. Here one does not take sufficient account of the institutional requirements for such deliberation to issue in effective decisions. At the same time, popular sovereignty and the public control of decisions can also be lost.[51] The facts of complexity seem to present deliberative democracy with a Weberian dilemma: either decision-making institutions gain effectiveness at the cost of democratic deliberation or they retain democracy at the cost of effective decision making. In either case, citizenship, deliberation, and decision making fail to be linked together.

Habermas solves this three-variable problem with his "two-track model," according to which Parliament, or Congress, provides an institutional focus for a broader, decentered "subjectless" communication dispersed across the public sphere and potentially involving all citizens. On this view, institutional decision making depends on a deliberation that is restricted neither to better-informed representatives nor to citizens who merely delegate power of will to representatives as their agents.[52] The public communication necessary for deliberation under these conditions is so dispersed that it is "subjectless" (or, as Habermas sometimes puts it, "anonymous"). Dualist democracy permits deliberation in both formal and informal settings. But the deliberating public is still sovereign only if it solves three main institutional problems of complexity: the problem of a political division of labor, the problem of the plurality of publics and their perspectives, and the problem of keeping formal institutions open to diverse substantive opinions and arguments on complex issues. In each case the model fails if one of the three necessary conditions of deliberative democracy drops out of Habermas's solution, primarily because Habermas thinks it must do so because of "unavoidable social complexity." It is in respect to the third problem of formal institutions that the weaknesses of Habermas's model motivate my alternative dualist proposal.

Political deliberation in complex societies involves something like a division of labor across levels of deliberation and decision. "*All* members must be able to take part in discourse, even if not necessarily in the same way."[53] Exactly how one spells out the various roles in a given deliberative process will depend not only on the issue of how a particular political system is structured but also on citizens' perspectives. Probably the most obvious and important distinction is that between "weak" and "strong" publics (to use Nancy Fraser's terminology), which in effect are the two components of Habermas's model—the informal public sphere and formal decision-making bodies. That is, a weak public is one whose "deliberative practice consists exclusively in opinion formation and does not also encompass decision making," whereas strong publics, such as parliaments, can reach binding decisions and are institutionally organized to do so.[54] This distinction is not hard and fast inasmuch as citizens also occasionally decide matters through referenda; in addition, the general election of officials is a kind of decision making, and it is often related to deliberation about issues.[55] In a similar way, one might further distinguish positions according to their *power to decide* and their *influence on deliberation*. Whereas political power (the ability to make binding decisions and execute government action) is found chiefly at the center, influence extends throughout society. Too strictly interpreted, this distinction could undermine self-rule. The presence of other centrally organized and powerful institutions gives actors (such as the heads of large corporations) more direct access to such centrally organized political power than any group of ordinary citizens. Critics and social movements can gain it, but only against the usual flow of influence among institutional actors. In this case, however, the solution accepts that institutions must become undemocratic in order to regulate complex societies effectively. This is a standard institutional problem of normal politics in constitutional states.[56]

The many mediations of institutional influence and the plurality of public spheres and roles suggest why Habermas turns to an interpretation of "subjectless" communication in informal public spheres. The public distribution of information and perspectives could be viewed as harboring a kind of communicative (or discursive) rationality, but not in a sense that would require full insight on the part of each citizen. The complexity of public spheres means that there will be a plethora of at best loosely connected and fragmented discourses in which many groups of individuals arrive at partial insights into issues through discussion. The idea of such subjectless communication suggests that a kind of public use of reason emerges from this diffuse network of discourses. If one assumes that for any given problem or issue there are a number of considerations (corresponding to the different validity spheres, as well as to different interest positions, values, etc.), then there "exists" a public "potential of reasons" that individuals draw on in different ways and to differing degrees—some stressing efficiency considerations, others moral ones, and so on. For this reason, Habermas calls such public opinion "anonymous," since it is not located in any individual or in any particular group of individuals. It is "decentered" into the network of communication itself, suggesting a different and weaker conception of publicity than the highly idealized one of discursive agreement. The problem is that one of the three terms of the solution to complexity drops out: public opinion in this dispersed sense cannot rule or govern; a reason is convincing in debate when it is somebody's public reason. Nor can an "anonymous public sphere" function as a societal community.

But there is an even deeper problem for deliberation. Political life under the condition of perspectival pluralism may not normally be so cooperative as the above image of information pooling suggests. On the contrary, one more often associates different social positions with a further type of pluralism: the plurality of conflicting opinions and arguments. Precisely this "fact of pluralism" is what makes majority rule necessary to conclude real deliberation. As I shall show, this raises more difficulties for democratic rule than Habermas seems to realize. But this means that *deliberative majorities* should rule, and the absence of such a conception in Habermas's model shows that he does not settle the question of who is the political subject (or agent) of complex deliberation. Even such a deliberative majority will not be a probable indicator of rational consensus if the conditions of deliberative equality are seriously violated. If pluralism leads to conflicting values and interests, the public sphere is also likely to collapse into competing publics ("subaltern counter-publics" to use Fraser's term); in the case of such a collapse, the public sphere cannot perform its epistemic function of filtering out non-public reasons. Multiple publics within a larger civic public sphere could have a positive role even in egalitarian and multicultural societies, in that they could help all citizens form their own identities and find proper expression for their needs.[57] Although the best argument does not always become the basis for a new majority, multiple publics can give voice to a diverse spectrum of public reasons. When these groups test the publicity of each other's needs and identities and thereby form a new majority, they may even begin to reshape and transform democratic institutions and the framework for deliberation.

This turn to discursive structures makes it possible for Habermas to state how he thinks the ideals of deliberation can be realized even in complex societies. Broadly characterized, it is precisely the presence of "discursive structures" that gives the rather chaotic mix of roles, positions, and arguments an epistemic character, so that one can be justified in supposing that the resulting political decisions are reasonable. This "structuralist approach" (as Habermas calls it) locates public reason not in a general will—which would have to be indicated by empirical majorities or discovered by representative bodies—but in the *discursive structures* that link the public with the legislature.[58] This characterization has somewhat different implications for the two main components in Habermas's model, the informal public sphere and formal decision making. In both cases, however, the basic idea is to foster processes of communication and to design institutional procedures that at least make it more likely that political decisions will be based on reasons that would correspond to those that would emerge from a discourse under ideal conditions.[59] These structures remain underspecified: their function is to promote interchange between publics and institutions, but they do little more than create channels of public influence.

In the next section I reject Habermas's "structuralist" model on the ground that it fails to solve the problem of social complexity for deliberative democracy. Here my finer-grain account of deliberation can bear fruit by revising the idea of majority rule; on this account the public remains sovereign (and not "anonymous") in two-track model of institutions, even in complex and pluralist societies. Above all, Habermas's version leaves out the constitutive interchange between publics and the institutions that organize them. This dialectic provides a more adequate reconstruction of Parsons's idea of a "societal community" as the source of legitimate laws, democratic self-organization, and institutional change. Above all, the societal community is still sovereign, and conceiving the problem as a relation of strong and weak publics skews a proper understanding of dualist democracy.

Unanimity, Majority Rule, and Deliberation: Dualist Democracy and Social Complexity

As these general solutions to various problems of complexity and size indicate, Habermas provides a plausible sociological framework for implementing his democratic ideals in a complex society. Moreover, there is no currently available model for institutional solutions to the problems of complexity other than the constitutional state, which enacts both enabling and limiting conditions on democratic deliberation. Although I am sympathetic to Habermas's account of the two-track nature of the constitutional state, it seems to me that too strong a separation of public opinion and formal decision making undermines popular sovereignty and effective public deliberation. This consequence follows from a combination of Habermas's idealized model of democratic agreements and his rather pessimistic diagnosis of the "fact" of complexity. These inadequacies are particularly apparent when Habermas turns to democratic theory proper, and especially when he turns to majority rule or institutional design.

With a different understanding of where popular sovereignty lies, it is possible to interpret majority rule as deliberative and to shift considerations of institutional design away from the traditional exclusive focus of deliberative approaches on the legislative process to the problem of making administrative and bureaucratic structures more deliberative and democratic. The fundamental issue here is whether representative mechanisms are the only form of mediation between the public and its organizing institutions. The mechanism here is not dialogical; it is primarily aggregative. I first develop a deliberative conception of rule by deliberative majorities as a way to make popular sovereignty an achievable ideal.

In legislative institutions, deliberation is carried on not only in reasoned debate but also through bargaining and compromises. One way in which deliberative theorists have attempted to raise the quality of reasons for such processes is to set the standard of consent high: that standard is unanimity, since *all* citizens must *agree*. Given the pluralism of standards and uncertainty of outcomes, it is hard to see why such procedures would necessarily lead to the agreement of all citizens in culturally pluralistic societies if by such agreement is meant unanimity for every particular law. Certainly, culturally specific elements of value interpretation will enter into such legislative processes; they do not admit of convergence toward consensus, especially as diverse and potentially conflicting cultural self-understandings enter into debates on particular issues. Such value conflicts cannot always be ignored or impartially resolved, especially if deep conflicts are manifested in the way the problematic situation is interpreted. And Habermas makes the task more difficult by insisting that citizens in democracies agree for "the *same* reasons" when they deliberate, rather than agreeing for different reasons, as in bargaining and compromises.[60] This convergence occurs despite the fact that social differentiation and complexity introduce diverse roles and perspectives into institutions themselves, not merely into the informal public. Merely to appeal to institutions is no solution; it merely restates the same dilemmas at a different level. Simply introducing compromise as a "second-best" democratic outcome, as Habermas does, is not enough to solve the problem of having an appropriate standard of legitimacy for legislative institutions.

The problem can be solved only by modifying the principles of democratic agreement while still seeking to improve the quality of reasons in public deliberation in a different way. This modification also permits us to understand the ideal of popular sovereignty differently. As indicated above, Habermas gives us a strong principle of legitimacy: "Only those laws may claim legitimacy that meet with the agreement of all citizens in a discursive lawmaking process that is itself legally constituted." In order to lower the requirement of unanimity without surrendering the norm of popular sovereignty, a participatory component needs to be introduced into the final clause of the principle. With this in mind, we can restate the principle as follows: a law is legitimate if it is the outcome of a participatory process that is fair and open to all citizens and thus includes all their publicly accessible reasons. The difference here is that citizens or legislators may not all agree, even though all may continue to cooperate despite their recognition of reasonable disagreement with one another. It is thus not necessary for *everyone* to agree with *every* particular law, goal, or decision. But more is demanded of citizens than mere conformity to the law. Deliberative consensus may be better defined in terms of continued participation in the ongoing public and legislative process, despite disagreement with any particular decision reached by deliberative means. In my first reformulation, the principle of democracy should read as follows: "A law is legitimate only if it is based on the public reasons resulting from an inclusive and fair process of deliberation in which all citizens may participate and in which they may continue to cooperate freely." Under this interpretation, the point of the democratic principle is to specify *how* citizens exercise their political autonomy together in deliberation. Political autonomy is exercised in the cooperative use of practical reason among citizens within a common public sphere and deliberative institutions.

Majority rule provides a perfectly acceptable basis for such cooperation so long as minorities have the reasonable expectation of being able to affect and to revise political decisions, including decisions about the character and the conditions of political participation. *Deliberative* majority rule also helps democracies deal with contingent demographic facts that may undermine cooperation. If such facts make minorities permanent, democratic institutions will not be well ordered in Rawls's sense; they will undermine the political equality necessary for mutual cooperation in the long run. In this way, revising democratic procedures to be more inclusive will make it possible to create various arrangements that, as Bernard Manin puts it, "compel the majority to take the minority into account, at least to a certain extent."[61] Citizens will then be more likely to overcome their myopia and ethnocentrism and to think of their democratic practices in an inclusive and future-oriented way, knowing that their decisions may have to be revised to maintain publicity and equality. They will also regard themselves as potentially occupying the minority position; even if they are in the majority for now, this alone does not lend their arguments epistemic force as necessarily the better ones. Majority rule can then be interpreted deliberatively.

Having criticized undercomplex and "direct" models of communicative association, Habermas must interpret the "ultimate" role of popular sovereignty quite minimally: political and legal procedures in institutions must remain at least open and accessible to the opinions of the general public sphere and to self-organized actors in civil society such as social movements. Whereas the informal spheres of opinion formation remain directly subject to the normative constraints of face-to-face communication, the formal institutions in which decisions are made do not. Social complexity thus requires a strong distinction between what Habermas calls "opinion" and "will formation." But if formal institutions are themselves democratic, such a distinction does not stand up to much scrutiny. The same processes that go on in the public sphere at large take place in these institutions to the extent that they may still be considered democratic. Sometimes representative bodies do deliberate, considering the public reasons for adopting particular policies. The legislative history of the "negative income" debate during the Nixon administration shows a surprising shift away from standard party preferences.[62] It is misleading to place much weight on this distinction since, in Habermas's own terms, opinion and will formation are *procedurally* identical. This is a distinction without a difference.

Since at least a minimal popular sovereignty now resides in the complex network of communication in the public sphere, it is still possible for Habermas to speak of continuing the radical democratic project of further democratizing the existing political system. In the final analysis, it may be that this sovereignty is too minimal and too indirect to preserve the radical contents of democracy. Kant thought that the will of the people could be expressed in the public sphere and then only indirectly affect independently and monarchically preserved political power. Hegel also preserves complexity by sacrificing democracy: sovereignty for Hegel is monarchical and not popular. Marx's criticism of the democratic deficits of Hegel's *Rechtsstaat* applies to Habermas's minimalist interpretation of the political content of popular sovereignty: "In a democracy the constitution, the law, the state, insofar as it is a political constitution, is itself only a self-determination of the people and a determinate content of the people."[63] The dualist character of deliberative institutions is precisely what gives the *Rechtsstaat* its democratic character.

Habermas's version of complexity is open to the same nominalist suspicion about agency that Marx raises against Hegel's highly complex and mediated constitutional state. With or without complexity, too strong a distinction between will-forming and opinion-forming institutions undermines any actual democratic sovereignty.

The distinction cannot be identical with that between institutional and non-institutional deliberation. As in the case of Hegel's civil servant, this separation of institutional and public power gives over too much effective political power to non-democratic political agents. "Will formation" is entirely given over to institutional actors who are only "influenced" by the public or "open to" reasons it puts forward. It also makes it difficult to see why Habermas continues to call his democratic theory deliberative, since the public is given only an opinion-forming (and thus an advisory and a merely critical) capacity.

Habermas admits that communicative power formed in the public sphere must continue to be sovereign, however mediated and constrained. Given the inchoate state of most citizens' opinions, it is true that a public will can take shape only in deliberative institutions of some sort. Even such a "public opinion," however, does not "by itself rule, but rather points administrative power in specific directions"; or, as Habermas sometimes puts it, it does not "steer" but "countersteers" institutional complexity.[64] Countersteering, or merely correcting for the interventions of independent institutional actors, is once again too minimal for democracy: these large and powerful institutions may simply overwhelm even well-organized public actors. The citizens rule in a democracy to the extent that they are the majority, and not administrators acting as proxies for institutions or "subsystems," who ultimately make decisions and have power. The rule of the majority is what institutionalized popular sovereignty means, and its weaknesses need to be corrected by rational counter-majoritarian institutions (such as judicial review), not by social complexity and the differentiation of administrative subsystems for decision making. Moreover, the majority must be a deliberative, informed, and rational one, in that its decisions are the outcome of fair and open public deliberation.

The cumulative weight of such problems means that Habermas's principle of democracy ought to be replaced. Popular sovereignty must be added as a third part of the discursive principle of democracy itself. I propose a three-part principle of democratic legitimacy as the most adequate to collective decision making in complex and pluralist societies: Laws are legitimate on the following conditions:

(1) if they result from a fair and open participatory process in which all publicly available reasons have been respected,

(2) if the outcome is such that citizens may continue to cooperate in deliberation rather than merely comply, and

(3) if this process makes the public deliberation of the majority the source of sovereign power.

Only in this way can decision making still be rooted in public participation. Only then do occasions for public input provide opportunities to resist the bureaucratic tendencies of taking more and more issues out of the public sphere and making them matters for administrative or economic efficiency rather than practical reason. In such cases, the norms for decision making are not deliberative: compliance is sufficient to ensure efficiency and in no way requires even implied consent. Public input makes a difference only if such institutions are themselves democratic and deliberative. Only if the procedures of the constitutional state pervade even administrative systems will popular sovereignty be based on more than an "anonymous" public. But democracy is not reconciled with social complexity by abandoning its core ideal of popular sovereignty, which is precisely the task of dualist, or two-track, institutional structure to defend. In the next section I show that this same structure can be generalized beyond current representative institutions and aggregative mechanisms for public input.

Making Institutions Deliberative: Some Proposals for a Public Division of Labor in Legislation and Administration

Deliberative theories of democracy have usually been interested in the associative life of civil society or in the details of representative and legislative institutions. Certainly, both are locations for the public use of reason, and for the formation of deliberative majorities. But the sovereignty of deliberative majorities in complex societies requires a complex series of interchanges between public and political institutions of all kinds. Under current arrangements and understandings of the constitutional state, this interchange is focused almost exclusively on the free and equal choice of aggregatively selected representatives who will form policies and binding laws. The problem is that the mechanisms of this interchange with the public are not adequate for ensuring deliberation, even in legislative institutions. By shifting the focus to a wide variety of public institutions, we can see that each of them needs to form its own political public sphere—a sphere at least as extensive as the one formed around legislative bodies and processes. Indeed, the interchange between public and bureaucratic and administrative institutions constitutes the biggest challenge for public deliberation. Democracy itself has made such institutions necessary in order for laws and policies to be exercised and enacted. Without their own political public spheres, such institutions are invested with too much unchecked power. At the very least, such political publics can make administrative institutions more reflexive and democratic, governed by public reasons.

Along with representation, the legislative process itself must be public, in the sense that it should demand the public use of reason. The American conception of representation and constitutional order is based on a particular theory of deliberative democracy. Its central proposition is that there are two kinds of public voice in a democracy: "one that is immediate or spontaneous, uninformed and unreflective; the other is more deliberative, taking longer to develop and resting on a fuller consideration of information and arguments—and only the latter is fit to rule."[65] This theory has influenced the institutional design of the legislative process, and it and the mechanisms that it suggested that are now often impediments to deliberation. Slowing down the legislative process by use of super-majorities and the filibuster has only increased the possibilities for their strategic use. Other features of the legislative process also inhibit deliberation. In the 1995 session of Congress, for example, laws were repealed without debate by cutting off their financing in general appropriations measures. Such anti-deliberative aspects of the legislative process could be changed without threatening the basic constitutional structure of appropriation by Congress, understood instead as the location for deliberation on the public issues of the day.

These and many other examples suggest that the process of producing legislation within such institutions needs to be made more public and deliberative. Most of the current rules are matters of convention, and many of the conventions need to be rethought for the reason that they do not serve the deliberative purposes for which they were intended. Other deliberation-promoting conventions, such as delegating certain authority to committees in order that they may acquire more informed and well-reasoned opinions, have fallen into disuse and should be revived. Public referenda on individual issues are not so important as opening the institutions to political debate and dialogue. The process has to make the institution itself an open and political public sphere, so that government does in fact rest on well-informed public opinion (as Lincoln put it). But the current design, which was to shield the people from their own excesses of political will, has evolved into a set of rules for strategic behavior among parties who seek to exclude one another's input in the decision-making process, rather than permitting a wider exercise of political power by a deliberatively formed majority.

The more pressing problem of social complexity has to do with the emergence of non-democratic, hierarchical institutions in administrative and bureaucratic sub-systems. Large-scale democracies cannot do without bureaucracies, since it precisely the demands of the public that give rise to the need for such administrative institutions.[66] Once again, it is important to see that democracy and bureaucracy are not inconsistent with each other; rather, vigorous public sovereignty requires problem-solving institutions. The problem is that such institutions have almost no public accountability; they have been structured so as to merely execute decisions efficiently. But executing decisions is not a mechanical process, the mere application of an algorithm or a formula. Administrative offices are based on the division of epistemic labor. The main shortcoming of current bureaucratic institutions is not that they have too much division of labor for democracies; it is that they have too little. Such institutions developed specialized competence and employ expert knowledge; however, they regard the citizens they interact with as objects of control and manipulation. In democratically structured administration, citizens should be regarded not as passive clients but as sources of information and judgments, especially concerning the contextual features of applying laws and agreements to specific local situations. Public administration is an achievable and efficient ideal, given gains in competence and information. Once again, the emphasis on the efficiency of administration, as merely carrying out commands, has undermined the deliberative potential of such institutions.

In order to achieve a truly public form of administration, each such institution needs to develop a political public sphere around it, much as legislative institutions already have. This public sphere could include public hearings and local meetings with those affected by problem-solving strategies. Such public hearings already exist in many instances, but what is lacking is any way to achieve public effectiveness in them. Having a hearing does not ensure uptake by the agents who exercise power in institutions. Various mechanisms could be developed to ensure that hearings do not end in non-decisions. Administrators could be held accountable through "public impact statements" that would state how the public reasons expressed by those affected were taken up in the decision-making process. Citizens' review boards that would act as trustees and oversight bodies could also be created. The problem here is to develop relations of trust between administrators and public, not to create a counter-administrative set of institutions. This trust can be built up by assigning certain deliberative roles to the public, which will then build up a cooperative form of problem solving. Administrative institutions then must be more reflexive in their application of rules and policies. In contrast with the older models of following rigid and formal rules, such reflexive administrative is more open to a variety of public input, which it does not pre-package into certain institutional categories. Such decisions, too, must be governed by the same sort of revisibility and publicity constraints discussed in cases of persistent minorities, which also foster cooperation here even when particular segments of the public ultimately disagree with the decisions made. The situations are analogous: processes of public input must be created so that deliberators within the framework of administrative institutions are compelled to take diverse perspectives into account as they constantly revise their basic framework for decision making.

The basic problem of complexity is that institutions no longer seem to be under public control. Various sociologically motivated skeptics claim that the facts of modern society entail that this must be so. My claim is that the interchange between publics and institutions has been restricted almost exclusively to representation mechanisms for choosing representatives. Even there, the legislative process itself does not promote deliberation, nor is it as open to public input as it could be. The main consequence of complexity is that new institutions, particularly administrative institutions, have emerged to coordinate large-scale social processes. These institutions have been modeled on formal rule following and efficiency rather than on deliberative division of labor. There is no reason that such a division of labor based on the principles of dualist democracy could not increase the interchange between the public and institutions, thus harnessing the power of these institutions to the constraints of popular sovereignty. Popular sovereignty thus provides an alternative to the reactive and powerless mechanism of "countersteering," proposed by Habermas as the replacement to public control. On my view of dualist democracy, the execution of plans cannot be separated from public deliberation. Rather, administrative institutions, too, can become more or less deliberative, as they create problematic situations which become themes in the public sphere. Because of the dependence of complex systems on agents' interactions, the public always has a foothold from which to introduce new forms of intentionality. In these cases, deliberation opens up a space for greater freedom as a way to introduce public control over unintended consequences.

Conclusion

Habermas's strong distinction of opinion and will formation does not answer the question of popular sovereignty in complex and pluralistic societies. In light of the persistence of cultural conflicts and a certain degree of functional differentiation, popular sovereignty is neither unified collective will nor something formed independently of interaction of citizens in institutions. Thus, complexity and pluralism do not exclude the normative core of radical democracy; they still permit popular sovereignty in the less idealized (but still demanding) sense of deliberative majority rule; it can still be maintained in light of the "fact" of complexity. The future task of deliberative reform is to expand the scope of public deliberation beyond merely representative and legislative institutions. Popular sovereignty requires mechanisms that promote the agency of citizens and the uptake of their public reasons, even if decisions are the product of majority rule and the division of labor in institutions.

This interpretation of popular sovereignty avoids the predicament of overcomplexity with which I began this chapter. By weakening the demand for unanimous agreement and replacing it with ongoing cooperation, rule by a strong public can be characterized by cultural diversity, epistemic division of labor, and institutional structure. The solutions to the potential fragmenting consequences of pluralism and the social distribution of knowledge are quite similar: experts, too, have to enlist the ongoing cooperation of the public to keep their enterprises functioning. Neither experts or administrators claiming epistemic authority nor representatives claiming the sanction of the general will can govern complex societies in which public cooperation and trust require constant renegotiation and revision. The need to enlist cooperation across both functional and cultural boundaries limits the excessive rationalism endorsed in some radical democratic theories. At the same time, democratic cooperation is more demanding than the mere compliance that is required in hypercomplex forms of social organization and integration. In that extremely complex systems require a high degree of compliance, they are vulnerable to being reorganized by public actors, who reopen the framework of deliberation about a certain problem and about ongoing technical solutions.

Overcoming problems of complexity does not require the redesign of the constitutional state. Although sometimes submerged, the dualist structure of many democratic practices—of a public of citizens structuring and being structured by institutions—needs to be extended to many different contexts. There is an institutionalized equivalent to such public agency in existing democratic arrangements: majority rule, which best approximates the basic principle of deliberative democracy. Even if there is no form of collective agency that could regulate every aspect of complex societies, it is possible to avoid both hypercomplexity and hyperrationality while establishing a political system based on constant interchange between a strong public and open institutions. The employment of public reason cannot reside in the informal public sphere alone—nor is it exercised only in voting for legislators according to judgments about the common good. Within a more dynamic and dualist structure for ongoing political cooperation, it is also possible to see popular sovereignty as the achievement of sufficient legitimate power in deliberative processes so as to achieve collective goals. On such a formulation, majority rule is not an approximate realization of an ideal consensus. Rather than approach this rationalist ideal, deliberative majorities emerge as the political will is formed and re-formed within institutional boundaries. This popular will cannot be known independently of such processes of deliberation; there is no independent test other than more and better deliberation.

Popular sovereignty also provides a way to discuss the forms of social integration that political institutions can still provide despite complexity and pluralism. In this respect, Habermas is correct when he argues against those who see the polycentrism of modern societies as resulting in autonomous subsystems without any society-wide forms of integration; democratic institutions provide for the possibility of a "societal community," in Parsons's phrase. Without such integration, there is no social basis for popular sovereignty, and thus no basis for democratic power. In this case, majority rule is what Dewey calls "mere majority rule[67]": the rule by some groups or coalitions of groups that happens to be the strongest. But with the need for organizational resources to solve complex problems, such integration remains a functional necessity for large-scale societies. Dualist democracy creates the condition for the emergence of a sovereign societal community in large and complex societies: a free and open sphere of public deliberation and a set of formal organizations and institutions in which decisions can be made effectively and can be backed by resources. The framework of these deliberative and majoritarian institutions must so structured that the problems of overcomplexity and hyperrationality can be solved without eliminating the societal community as the origin of democratic political power.

In the dualist framework of the political public sphere, majority rule can become the expression of an epistemic, informed public opinion even when it is determined by aggregative mechanisms such as voting. 'Deliberation' describes the public way in which majorities are formed. As Dewey puts it, it is *how* a majority is formed that is the significant normative feature of any such decision-making mechanism: "The means by which a majority comes to be a majority is the most important thing: in antecedent debates, modifications of views to meet the objections of minorities, and so on."[68] Even so, reasonable disagreements may still persist. That, however, is just the point:

that all *un*reasonable disagreements, as well as unreasonable *agreements*, be eliminated.[69] Only a variety of publics with a wide range of dissenting opinions could test for public irrationality. Minority opinion has an important epistemic role in public deliberation, even if it is not correct in light of the ultimate opinion of the deliberative majority. Dualist democracy therefore must ensure that minority opinion not only is respected but also is taken up in the relevant forum and in the appropriate institution.

With regard to the deep conflicts that result from the fact of pluralism, I argued that public deliberation entails the elimination of unreasonable appeals to fear, prejudice, and ignorance. Making reasons public and answerable to minorities may "launder" them, filtering the inputs of deliberative majorities about conflicts through public testing. In the case of unreasonable agreements by powerful majorities, however, this may not be enough to give minorities equal deliberative footing. Furthermore, the presence of permanent minorities is an indication that democratic institutions may not be "well-ordered" in Rawls's sense. When institutions and normal politics fail to this extent, the sovereignty of citizens over their institutions is of paramount importance. In these cases, only a change in the framework for public deliberation can compel the majority to take the minority into account. Such revisions must correct for inequalities that produce the permanent minority status, at least so much that members of the current majority may come to regard themselves as potentially occupying the minority position; being in a deliberative majority does not make any argument about what public reason requires the better one.[70]

What makes these conditions possible? Certainly, laws and rights as set out in a dualist constitution establish general conditions for the free exercise of public reason by all.[71] But ensuring these general conditions of deliberation does not overcome specific blockages of public-opinion formation or restrictions in public communication, such as the lack of mutual comprehensibility, the restriction of information pooling, or the undetected exclusion of points of view from public discourse. Even if law can provide constant, recursive tests to check if deliberation is free and open, it is still up to participants in deliberation to address specific problems and limitations: this is indeed the role of social critics in the public sphere. Since such limitations and restrictions are truly unavoidable in complex and pluralistic societies, the conditions of communication and the methods of persuasion can never be completely transparent, even under fully realized legal conditions of public and private autonomy. It is also one of the central civic concerns of citizens to seek to improve the conditions and methods of debate and discussion.

Changing the conditions and methods of public debate can be difficult. The civil rights movement, for example, shows the ambiguities of the public sphere as it is now constituted. The constitutional state and its institutions are not as open or "porous" as the two-track model seems to suggest, and it required a great deal of collective organization for the civil rights movement to gain enough public attention to initiate a period of higher lawmaking about the structure of formal institutions. Further, achieving inclusion and reform has been much more difficult than achieving mere legislative success, since both citizens and the state have used many avenues to resist enforcing civil rights legislation. Not only that: both powerful institutions and the citizens themselves may resist improving the conditions of public debate and deliberation.

How it is possible to improve the conditions of the public sphere, especially if the majority of citizens is limiting and restricting its own deliberation and is blind to the objections of the minority? Deliberation may be restricted by ideologies and passions in ways that citizens may not even be aware of; at the same time, publicity demands that citizens be able to transform these very conditions. Ideologies and other such restrictions seem to make impossible the very public acts of criticism that might overcome them. Critics are then always in the cognitive minority with regard to their public reasons. The need for such criticism and the lack of public agency once again raise practical doubts, especially concerning the cognitive demands of deliberative democracy for self-interpretation and reflection by all citizens. This chapter has shown the importance of the constant interchange of formal and informal public spheres in deliberation, especially in correcting the limitations that non-democratic sources of power place on institutional decision making. The further question is not how to overcome the difficulties for democracy related to the size of modern societies or the complexity of current social problems; it is how it is possible for public deliberation to be reflexive enough to remain free, open, and capable of self-transformation.

5
Social Critics, Collective Actors, and Public Deliberation: Innovation and Change in Deliberative Democracy

I argued in chapter 4 that the "fact" of social complexity does not present insuperable barriers to realizing the ideals of deliberative democracy. These problems can be resolved institutionally through a dualist democracy that establishes rule by deliberative majorities. Furthermore, I challenged the sociological account of complexity upon which much contemporary skepticism about radical democracy is based. There is no "inevitable" conflict between democracy and complexity; democracy preserves rather than reduces complexity. Properly understood, complexity need not produce violations of democratic equality. Rather, it requires dualist institutions that make possible a division of deliberative labor among citizens and vibrant interchanges between the public and all political institutions. The focus of political theory on representative institutions has underestimated the potential for public deliberation in other settings, particular in bureaucratic and administrative institutions. The growth of these institutions is a by-product of complexity, but there are many ways in which they, too, can become locations for public deliberation.

The flaw shared by most pessimistic and skeptical accounts of social complexity is that they ignore the interplay between publics and institutions, postulating needs for efficiency, expertise, and integration that preclude public input into functionally determined decision-making processes. But the interchange must go both ways. On the one hand, institutions and their resources cannot remain under democratic control without some mechanism for giving public input the ultimately determining role. On the other hand, the public cannot form itself into deliberative majorities without the methods and constraints of democratic institutions. Thus, the state requires constant public input in order to solve problems and to be legitimate; but some institutional structure is needed to collect the diverse inputs from civil society. Institutions provide the formal constraints of fair procedures for input and the amplified resources and capacities that are needed to overcome problems of scale, while the informal public sphere ensures that deliberation is open to all salient interpretations in civil society. Still, a people cannot be sovereign unless they are able to deliberate together successfully and unless they have something to say about the conditions under which they deliberate. Dualist democracy ensures that these conditions are met, especially when its design for majority rule and public sovereignty is applied to all political institutions.

In this chapter I consider some of the conditions necessary for deliberative democracy that cannot be guaranteed by institutional rules, designs, or procedures. Deliberative democracy needs not only to be stable but also to provide periodic renewal of its institutions when public reason begins to fail to produce agreements. Some designs may inhibit renewal by making democratic change too difficult or too easy. But deliberative democracies need to find ways to promote the emergence and formation of new publics, which in turn may change existing institutions and their rules or even produce new ones. Some of these publics may become deliberative majorities. This potential for innovation is necessarily decentralized and set in motion by the problems and needs of citizens in their everyday lives. Out of the public expression of these problems and needs, some citizens begin to formulate new understandings of themselves and of institutions, all the while seeking to modify the current framework for deliberation.

The goal of this chapter is to offer a fine-grained analysis of the process of producing new and innovative understandings in deliberative dialogue. A dynamic public sphere must be able to do more than change particular beliefs and attitudes in deliberation; it also must be able to alter the framework of deliberation. Such processes depend on the emergence of new publics, which then alter the relationship of citizens to democratic institutions. Just as the analysis of deliberative inequalities required a more substantive account of political poverty, so, too, the spontaneous process of forming new publics and new understandings cannot be fully captured without specifying how moments of popular sovereignty and institution building are democratic, even as the constraints of normal politics are sometimes put out of play. The challenge here is to understand how the societal community—the public core of civil society, which is reflexive about the process of institutionalization—can remain open to new forms of association emerging in everyday life, and thus to the new cognitive possibilities they make available. In this chapter I shall show how public deliberation enables and constrains constant institutional change and what it can do when public reason seems to fail.

Even in "normal" politics, the interplay between institutions and the public sphere can pull deliberation in opposite directions: whereas institutions and their procedures constrain the public agendas so as to make timely decisions possible while organizing a majority opinion, the public sphere functions to keep debate open and to introduce revisions of decisions that have already been made. This tension between the public and its organizing institutions is constitutive of a vibrant democracy; it is necessary both for its stability and for its capacity for innovation. Certainly, the state can promote the conditions necessary for a well-functioning public sphere. But even with well-ordered democratic institutions, a public can still fail to deliberate well; its citizens may not be able to produce publicly acceptable solutions to the problematic situations that initiate their deliberation. If such cognitive failures cannot be traced back to institutional flaws, the public can only examine itself for failures of public reason.

Throughout this book I have discussed the many empirical social conditions that work against successful deliberation. In view of the array of problems facing deliberative democracy, such difficulties in resolving problematic situation may even be quite likely. What does a public do when its deliberation fails? How can citizens restore to deliberation its public character and make it more likely to succeed in achieving cooperative outcomes? I want to show that the connection between the public sphere and institutions that is unique to democracy makes possible a special sort of collective learning among citizens. When deliberation fails, citizens may need to change their public reasons; but they also may need to change the situation itself, the framework in which they deliberate.

A public's concern with itself as a public—as an unlimited audience to which political speech is directed—has played a central role in the historical emergence of the public sphere in civil society. The public sphere is not merely a collection of spaces or forums, such as salons, clubs, theaters, union halls, or other meeting places, but also a set of self-understandings by which a group of persons see themselves as a public. The participants in public discussion should not think of themselves as *the* public or an exclusive elite of aesthetic experts; they "always understood and found themselves immersed within a more inclusive public of all private persons."[1] This self-understanding and self-reference affected the structure of discussion within the historical public sphere: in terms of interest, importance, and accessibility, the issues discussed were of "common," or general, concern. The topic was, more often than not, the public itself, its reception of works of art, its behavior, or its lack of certain virtues. These "public" issues included tolerance, civic morality, and public morality; the letters and articles were primarily critical, as were the reviews of cultural events, and aimed at overcoming "ill-informed judgment," "dogma," and "fashion." Thus, the public "that read and debated these matters read and debated about itself"—not only about its own opinions but also about itself as a practically reasoning public.[2] The self-critical and self-reflective character of public reasoning can be a source of innovation and change in democracies.

This self-reflexivity has a broader function than merely maintaining the public sphere, limited as it is, in any given historical period. To be self-critical, it must be part of a larger and dynamic public process that is inherently oriented toward forming and testing the public's attitudes and beliefs. Becoming accustomed to this sort of self-scrutiny and self-examination is a crucial part of the public culture of deliberative democracies. When community-wide biases restrict the scope of such self-scrutiny, usually by leaving relevant problems off the public agenda, deliberative institutions can lose their problem-solving capacity and public communication breaks down in unnoticed ways. Institutional filters and constraints require that the public sphere itself be functioning well, and they are often insufficient in these problematic situations. In such cases, a new public must emerge to create new institutions and new opportunities for deliberation. As the dualist conception of democracy suggests, political institutions, oriented as they are toward solving problems and processing available public input, are not by themselves capable of ensuring flexibility and innovation, particularly in the form of needed cultural innovations and learning. Deliberation within institutions usually rearranges, rather than changes, the set of feasible and available alternatives. When deliberation and "normal" problem solving are blocked, the public can no longer deliberate in this constrained, means-ends way. Rather, the public can only act self-referentially; it changes the conditions of political deliberation by changing itself. Or, as Dewey puts it in *The Public and Its Problems*, the public changes institutions indirectly by forming a new public with which institutions must interact.[3] In the process, institutions are changed in a variety of ways: in their concerns, in their ongoing interpretation of rules and procedures, in their predominant problem-solving strategies, and so on. These periods of democratic renewal depend on new publics, which then organize and are organized by the new deliberative institutions.

But such innovation can be blocked or inhibited by current political institutions, which are oriented toward and structured by a different political public. There is a temporal lag between the emerging publics, which seek to reorganize institutions, and the existing publics, which have shaped the current set of institutions. For example, the relatively weak state institutions that emerged after the American Revolution reflected a dispersed and decentralized public. Certainly, minimally democratic institutions ensure some stability and continuity; nonetheless, when the existing state loses touch with the dynamic public in complex societies, it no longer fulfills or expresses that public's needs. Dewey saw this tension between stability and innovation as the driving force behind the formation of each new public and each new political form. It is a difficult process: "To form itself the public has to break existing political forms; this is hard to do because these forms are themselves the regular means of instituting change."[4] The new public must not only form itself as a public; it must also change the forms of existing institutions. As Dewey notes, change in democracy is still difficult, since "an adequately flexible and responsive political and legal machinery is so far beyond the wit of man."[5] Yet deliberative institutions must resist the tendencies toward overcomplexity and routinization that are part of their stabilizing function. Institutions that do not remain responsive to new publics lose their legitimacy.

In this chapter I discuss the main processes by which democratic institutions can remain flexible and open to change, short of constant revolutionary activity. This interchange between new publics and stable institutions takes two main forms: the speech of social critics in the public sphere and the emergence of social movements. (Dewey called the latter "the formation of a new public."[6]) These sources of innovation become necessary precisely when institutions become routinized relative to the public sphere, so that the current public might no longer be the public that had created them. But it is precisely in this situation that the formation of new publics and new institutional forms may be all the more difficult, since it is blocked by the very inadequate institutions and forms of power that make innovation and change necessary. However, given the existence of a public sphere marked by free association and expression, I argue that these obstacles to deliberation may be overcome.

In my discussion of political equality, I argued that certain background conditions undermine the conditions for successful public dialogue. Here I turn to the ways in which such restrictions can be lifted and the interchange between publics and institutions reestablished. First I shall discuss the effect of social critics on public deliberation. When successful, critical discourse can open up restricted public communication. Next I shall consider the critical discourse needed for the formation of new publics by emerging social movements. They influence political discourse in various ways: by introducing new themes and topics, by focusing public attention on pressing problems and unrecognized needs, and by offering new interpretations that "frame" the issues in new ways and ultimately reshape institutions. There is, however, a dialectic at work in democracies: as soon as institutions have stabilized again, they are reformed by a successive public that has been left out even in the new institutional arrangement, and so on. In the final section I shall consider how radical criticism is still possible in the public sphere. When the problematic situation of deliberation itself limits possibilities of new public input, critics and movements must "disclose" new social worlds and new forms of interaction. Innovation begins when a public forms around such critical discourse and successfully frames public debate in such a way that it may reshape democratic institutions.

Social Critics and Public Discourse

Critics act just like any other participants in the public sphere: they discuss the issues of the day and seek to sway public opinion. But they want to do more. They want to have certain effects on their hearers in the public sphere. Critical discourse attempts to overcome blockages of and restrictions on communication, to let citizens see things in new ways, to help in the formation of new publics, and thus to overcome the restricted forms of institutionalization and routinization typical of the state in its current form. Critics achieve results through speech, by persuading and convincing others. Such effects are not easy to achieve, particularly in situations in which existing deliberation is not adequate to solve the problems at hand. Especially prominent problems for critics include the ways in which institutions of public deliberation have already restricted the scope of opinion. Not only existing rules and procedures, but also many of the biases and blind spots of current forms of deliberation favor the most effective and advantaged members of the public. If the public is to see such biases and limitations and undertake to correct them, critics and other actors must convince them that their public reasons are in fact non-public and thus not answerable to others.

In democratic contexts, the speech of social critics is best seen as contributing to the joint action of public deliberation. We have already seen that social inequalities in the public sphere may freeze the dialogical mechanisms by which citizens deliberate and in so doing may restrict the uptake of relevant reasons. In such situations, the task of the critic is to unblock dialogue by changing the conditions of communication. By using the self-reflexive character of critical public speech, the critic can aim to raise not only "consciousness" but also the level of public debate, particularly by changing its underlying and often implicit interpretive assumptions and understandings. Successful institutional change in democratic societies depends on emergent publics, which spread such new understandings throughout society and in so doing alter the relation of the public at large to existing institutions.

Successful critics in the public sphere must do something very specific with their words. Speech-act theories inspired by J. L. Austin provide a well-developed apparatus for analyzing speech as a kind of action embedded in ongoing contexts of action and interaction. We do things with our words, according to Austin: we marry, advise, threaten, give orders, make assertions, and so on. But speech, as an action, also has ends or aims that we may achieve: we frighten, persuade, or change the beliefs or attitudes of the hearers. As Austin puts it: "Saying something will often, or even normally, produce certain kinds of effects on the feelings, thoughts or actions of the audience, or of the speaker, or of other persons."[7] These effects may, but need not, be produced by intention or by design; they may be a form of "uptake" that results simply from comprehending the utterance. Uptake may be public or non-public. If such an aim of the utterance is publicly avowable, Austin classifies the utterance as an "illocutionary act"; if it is not so avowable, then it is for Austin a "perlocutionary act."

Certainly critics in the public sphere must have avowable intentions. The success of their criticism, in fact, depends on the audience's becoming aware of the intention of the speaker to criticize existing practice and finding such criticisms so persuasive as to join in demands for change. Current ways of regulating the exchanges between institutions and their public do not promote this sort of success. Aggregative mechanisms for decision making, in particular, produce incentives to use whatever tactical means to gain more votes. The task of changing public discourse and interpretation is much more difficult. But how does a critic succeed? As a first approximation, we might consider that a critic's success might be similar to the success of any speech act. Austin considers the capacity to do something with words to be a matter of "conforming with a convention."[8] Here Austin has in mind acts based on certain conventional formula, such as "I apologize" and "I promise." But often critics want to undermine the basis for existing conventions that they find intrinsically biased and restrictive. There is no recipe for ending the use of conventions, and a critic does succeed simply by announcing his or her intention. Even if the critic's expression must have an avowable intention, its success does not depend on the intention's merely being recognized.[9] But if this is the criterion of success of illocutionary acts, what can be done when the openness of communication breaks down? How is it possible for critics to change the conventions that organize speech and hence organize interaction in the public sphere?

The answer is that there are some illocutionary acts whose success is not based on conventions; they are "institutionally unbound," to use John Searle's phrase.[10] At the same time, there are perlocutionary acts that do not require that speakers' intentions be covert, or nonavowable, in order for them to succeed. As might be expected in light of the complex goal of criticism, such speech mixes illocutionary and perlocutionary features of success. If the conditions of public discourse about a topic make it difficult for all speakers to achieve similar uptake (as when deliberative dialogue is disturbed by social inequalities and power asymmetries), it is often the case that speakers must resort to an indirect or strategic form of communication to get any sort of uptake.

Such forms of communication aim at restoring the conditions of direct communication in order to make mutual understanding in public dialogue possible once again. When cooperative communication begins to break down, competent speakers may begin a phase of meta-communication, or communication about communication, to restore cooperation between speaker and hearer about mutual understanding. If for any reason this is no longer possible or effective in restoring cooperation, as when actors are deceived by their own ideologies and other self-deceptions, then speakers still have recourse to other means of achieving understanding. These means include irony, jokes, metaphors, and other jarring ways of expressing something, as well as narratives expressing the experiences behind someone's political or normative claims. Such forms of communication are typical of attempts to unblock the capacity for perspective taking in an audience—one of the dialogical mechanisms of public deliberation. These modes of expression can also be a phase in dialogue in which strategic elements are employed to restore the conditions necessary for non-strategic success.[11]

When public communication is blocked by entrenched cultural practices or institutional routines, critics have to engage in precisely this sort of speech to achieve their desired effect: to reopen dialogue and thus to restore the self-referential character of public speech. But such speech requires more than just the strategic aim of contesting certain existing but inadequate public understandings. It must also create the conditions under which agents can begin to contest the current understandings that are embodied in institutions. To do so, the critic aims at a new audience: an emerging public in which new forms of interaction and new kinds of interpretation are already publicly available. These new forms of interaction point the way toward restarting stalled processes of cooperation and deliberation. The critic articulates new possibilities of expression and understanding, and in so doing may elaborate an alternative understanding that can inform a new relationship between citizens and institutions. Here again procedural opportunities for deliberation are insufficient. The same blockages to informal public communication repeat themselves on the reflective level of institutionalized deliberation—even in deliberative settings, such as the legislative process or court proceedings, in which reflection on the basic rules and conditions of political association is supposed to occur.

The intervention of social critics and other public actors is possible because their acts of deliberation are embedded in larger sequences of politically structured talk and discussion, the organization of which is guided by formal and informal rules and procedures. To the extent that they are democratic, these procedures create a forum in which reciprocal critical dialogue can emerge. Through communication in the larger public sphere critics try to achieve a particular effect: "to initiate processes of self-reflection," as Habermas puts it in *Theory and Practice*.[12] The civil rights movement brought various issues to public awareness that had been submerged in the ideology of "separate but equal." This communication in the larger public sphere found its way into institutional forums which were previously closed by various mechanisms of exclusion and initiated deliberation in those institutions, including the passing the Civil Rights and Voting Rights Act in Congress. Such legislation in turn also initiated reflection in the Supreme Court, which had long defended the constitutionality of racial segregation. Here Thurgood Marshall's effective use of social-scientific description of the experiences of children in segregated schools helped achieve such institutional reflection. In effect, such critical discourse reconstituted state institutions, which now could be informed by a new, multiracial public. It altered voting procedures and made them more inclusive, created special bodies for the enforcement of civil rights legislation, and so on. As this example shows, there are also myriad ways in which citizens and institutional actors may disrupt such successful intervention in the interchange between the new public and decision-making processes.

Such public reflection is not merely on some common theme, but also indirectly about the public itself: critics try to get the public to think about itself as a public once again, to change citizens' self-understandings in such a way that a new public must emerge. Once the public sphere is large and pluralistic, it is not only critics who initiate such processes of reflection; more important, this is now done by groups of public actors in social movements and associations which are oriented to the political public sphere. These collective actors, such as the civil rights movement, the ecology movement, or even neighborhood associations, understand themselves as part of a larger public sphere made up of groups of citizens. Given the sorts of resources necessary to capture public attention and to motivate large institutions to employ their resources on the behalf of less advantaged citizens, it is no longer possible to conceive of the public sphere primarily as consisting of "private persons embedded in the larger public of private persons," as Habermas described the salons of the Enlightenment. Rather than as an exclusively private person, a citizen understands himself or herself as part of a public sphere that consists of other citizens, each with group identities and allegiances, who are potential cooperators.

If we look at any list of effective social critics in the twentieth century, such as Michael Walzer's *Company of Critics*, we see that each has been part of a larger social movement, such as the workers' movement, the civil rights movement, or the anti-apartheid movement.[13] In large-scale societies, groups more than individuals originate the new forms of communication and initiate reflection. They typically do so by introducing new themes to public discussion, by acquiring the means to capture public and institutional attention in deliberation, and by framing issues in such a way as to make them comprehensible and significant for the larger public sphere. If these actors succeed, a new civic public has a new understanding not only of a particular issue but also of the terms of their common life.

New Themes and Different Frames: Collective Action and the Public Discourse on Social Problems

As I noted in discussing political inequality, the pooling of resources, information, and voices may make it possible for impoverished citizens to influence the deliberation of the larger public. But it would be a mistake to see new social movements only as organization for pooling resources to achieve particular goals; they are also a public in formation. In influencing the deliberative process, social movements introduce new themes into public discourse and express new needs that are not met by public institutions. These are not merely strategic tasks; such movements must formulate reasons that persuade nonmembers that their needs or problems deserve *public* attention. Thus, participants in such movements understand themselves as part of a larger public to whom their claims are addressed. As I noted in chapter 1, being answerable to an unrestricted audience introduces norms of publicity into political discourse, such as constraints on overt manipulation.[14] However, many prejudices, ideologies, and biases may be too widely shared to be eliminated, even if all citizens intend their reasons to be public, unless new publics emerge and change the context of deliberation.

Groups that become successful public actors must be able to employ and appeal to norms of publicity, such as reasonability and generality, in their efforts to convince the larger deliberating public. Unlike their currently more successful rivals, their public activities are thus constrained, even for strategic purposes, precisely because of the requirement that public dialogue and discourse be "jointly maintained by the participants."[15] This joint maintenance of the public character of discourse is incumbent even on movements and publics-in-formation that are seeking to expand and change the existing democratic institutions. The demands of joint maintenance constrain strategic communication, even while the strategic use of public reasons aims at mobilizing new public opinion. Nonetheless, maintaining cooperation does not make innovation impossible. Rather, social movements can do both: they can, for example, create the occasions, settings, and events about which the public deliberates. More often than not, the event that forms such a public occasion is not directly in the movement's control; consider the effects of the Three Mile Island accident on the movement against nuclear power. But it is through contesting the interpretation of such events in public discourse that changes in public opinion occur.

An emerging new public encounters special difficulties in establishing its opinions. The stability of institutions alone supplies inertia against change, and embedded power relations give sanctioning power to current interpretations. If this public consists of previously excluded and unequal groups or entirely new needs and interpretations, even raising a new theme or changing current interpretations in public discourse may be difficult. Such obstacles go beyond the cycles of political poverty. As William Gamson notes, cultural codes entrench taken-for-granted meanings, making them given "facts" rather than social constructions; they "appear as transparent descriptions of reality, not as interpretations, and are apparently devoid of political content."[16] Such transparent descriptions and accepted meanings guide definitions of problematic situations, and in so doing they limit the possibilities that are available to deliberators. Collective actors in social movements have to challenge this taken-for-granted character and show these meanings to be only some of many possibilities, as the women's movement has done with gender identity. Moreover, by being taken for granted, such features of problematic situations do not receive public attention; they seem natural, unavoidable, or out of everyone's control. Often public concern can be gained only by creating a sense of the public's own responsibility, as Joseph Gusfield points out in the case of the social construction of drunk driving as a "public" problem with social causes and assignable political responsibility.[17]

Once the emergent public has succeeded in placing an issue in the "contested" public realm and in focusing public attention upon it, it must then also construct a new set of interpretations or a new public framework. As a challenger to accepted definitions and practices, the new public must also provide a new "frame" for public deliberation, an alternative interpretive schema that includes a definition of the problem and available solutions. For example, Gamson identifies a shift in the way in which nuclear power has been publicly framed. Before the Three Mile Island accident, "progress" was the basic framework, "nuclear power" itself being "an uncontested symbol of technological progress."[18] There was very little challenge to this understanding until it came to be replaced by the frame of "public accountability," in which the nuclear industry is characterized as untrustworthy, self-interested, and actively involved in eliminating all other energy alternatives. Of course, framing can go in any political direction. The frame for affirmative action shifted during the last few years from one of justice and inclusion, or remedial action, to one of preferential treatment. The contestation of public definitions is thus the key to the debate. As the frame shifts, the state's support for previously uncontested policies slips as a new public emerges. Supporters of affirmative action must now recapture the public frame. Similarly, the American Medical Association has opposed virtually every attempt at health-care reform by framing changes as "socialized medicine." This frame did not hold public attention when the interchange between the public and Congress pushed Medicare through, but it has found new life as a way of inhibiting newer problem-solving strategies and the formation of a new public in more recent debates.

In analyzing the ways a collective actor can constitute itself as a new public capable of shifting institutional goals, it is important to see that such frameworks are not merely sets of beliefs or values. In order to distinguish them from beliefs or attitudes, I shall adopt Frederic Schick's term "understandings."[19] Often, no new values or different beliefs are necessary for a change in framework; rather, the current values or beliefs must be understood differently. To use Schick's example: if the same person who saw his life as half over now sees it as half yet to come, "no change in belief need to be involved, not even indirectly, as to what caused him to change."[20] Schick reports one of George Orwell's experiences in the Spanish Civil War as an illustration of the difference between beliefs and understandings. On sniper duty, Orwell sees a Fascist soldier run across the top of the trenches, half-dressed and holding up his trousers with one of his hands. This detail keeps Orwell from shooting and changes his understanding of the situation: "I had come here to shoot at 'Fascists,' but the man holding up his trousers isn't a 'Fascist'; he is visibly a fellow creature similar to yourself."[21] Conversely, our understandings also blind us, as when we do not recognize that two facts are identical (or, in Schick's terms, "co-reportive"). Oedipus wants to marry the Queen of Thebes, but soon realizes that this understanding is defective and incomplete; he did not know that this meant that he then also desired to marry his mother, since this is also a fact true of the queen. An understanding, then, is this whole set of facts which are "co-reportive" with what the agent wants or believes; in light of a limited understanding, the agent does not fully grasp the full set of facts about the social world that his or her actions are involved in and influence. For both Orwell and Oedipus, that these facts go together is revealed in an experience that opens the agent's eyes and enables him see his situation in a different light. It is this level of public understandings that collective actors seek to change, as when the civil rights movement used the framework of equal rights to achieve a new understanding of the facts of the practices of segregation and the scope of the Constitution.

Both Orwell and Oedipus experienced events which opened their eyes to the need to change their operative understandings of the world. Shifts in public understandings can be marked by particular events, or "crucial discourse moments," around which these new public understandings coalesce.[22] These events enable public discourse to change and new publics to be formed. Owing to the presence of a social movement seeking to form a new public, such events focus attention on some potentially "public" problem both inside and outside institutions. Different groups of challengers to and defenders of the current understanding then contest the meanings of such events in various public forums. The Three Mile Island accident was just such an event for the anti-nuclear movement; previous, equally serious accidents were not. The *Bakke* decision was such a critical moment in the discourse on affirmative action; Israel's invasion of Lebanon was such an event in public discourse about U.S. policy in the Middle East. Each of these became a focal point around which a dense network of public discourse formed, and the struggles over their interpretations in many respects determined the successes and failures of challengers and their new frames.

The mass media may play a role during these periods, but neither the media nor collective actors are able to manufacture such discursive shifts on command. Because these critical moments receive enormous media attention, they can greatly expand the potential audience and thus the constituency of the new public in formation. Although the mass media are effective in reaching many different actors and settings, actors discover that the media operate with their own systems of meaning and representation (such as "sound bites") and with non-public purposes (such as mass entertainment for the sale of advertising). These facts make the media another institutional force that can resist changes in frames that do not serve the media's purposes or meanings. The non-public character of such structures of significance makes the media more open to direct manipulation and less open to challengers; their understandings, too, must be contested, and they shift only with very broad shifts in public culture.

In periods of great activity in the public sphere, cultural codes, understandings, and even the very character and texture of the social world may become contested as the public's dissatisfaction and unfulfilled needs are mobilized to change understandings and form a new relationship between citizens and powerful institutions. Sociologists have noted that there are "cycles of protest" as the new understandings introduced by social movements spread through various institutions, groups, and regions.[23] Indeed, such a spread is an indication of the public character of the movement's new understanding, as was the case when the generalizable message of the civil rights movement spread to other social movements.

Public challengers to widely shared cultural norms and codes must create new understandings rather than simply appeal to already-accepted ones, and the more radical the challenge the greater this disadvantage. Appealing to all good citizens to face some very abstract problem, such as poverty, hunger, peace, or war, may not be a very effective way to form a basis for a new public. Such challenges create what Gamson calls an "aggregate frame" whose potential participants are merely a pool of individuals taking personal responsibility rather than a public or collective actor.[24] If abstract problems do not mobilize a new public, then effective frames are usually more specific, with a clearer grievance and a clearer goal. In the case of publics that pursue broad cultural change, the responsibility for a solution may be "diffused throughout civil society" and hence "structurally elusive."[25] Besides disadvantages and inequalities that put challengers in the minority, the complication of elusive grievances and goals is typical of the process of public innovation, in which new publics challenge the understandings operating in many political settings.

In the section that follows I shall focus on the emergence of critical discourse, particularly surrounding events that produce a problematic situation for a deliberating public. In it, I refer generally to "social critics," and my use of the term includes collective actors such as social movements. Cultural innovations by critics, I argue, change understandings by creating new patterns of relevance. Such changes in assumptions about what is relevant in a problematic situation can clarify why it is effective to introduce new frames into public deliberation, since they disclose new possibilities of interpretation and action. In order to describe this cognitive process, I shall adopt the controversial Heideggerian terms "disclosure" and "world disclosure." But I shall distance myself from overly strong requirements for innovation associated with the concept, as in the interpretations of Martin Heidegger and Richard Rorty. Disclosure has little to do with things "being revealed" to us; it has more to do with the opening up of new possibilities of human freedom and transformative agency. Disclosure designates radical change in the ordinary interpretation of the world—just what is needed for innovation in public deliberation. Once I have clarified the public role of the critic, I shall give a broader account of democratic innovation in the interchange between publics and their organizing institutions.

Radical Criticism and World Disclosure

If institutions organize the publics that then shape them, democracy opens a possibility for innovation through new understandings: the changes in understandings that occur in critical discourse moments reshape the social world and reconstitute its institutions. Heidegger, the postmodernists, and most other philosophers interpret such cultural innovation primarily in aesthetic rather than political ways: artists, they say, create new vocabularies and new languages, more like the oracles of the gods. Van Gogh's famous painting of a peasant's shoes may have let us see the shoes more fully, but poets do more: they "disclose" the world. The poet, Heidegger claims, "lets truth itself originate."[26] In this section I want to show the way in which critics and collective actors such as social movements illustrate a more ordinary sense of innovation—that is, innovations as changes in public understandings—against the more emphatic notions of disclosure and innovation shared by Heidegger, Rorty, and many others. Critics and movements in the public realm "disclose" even radically new possibilities in an ordinary way: in the free and effective exercise of capacities of understanding and cognition, as when ordinary communication with others can sometimes make us change even deeply entrenched understandings and assumptions.

With their many diverse meanings and uses, the terms "world-making" and "world-disclosure," or their equivalents, have come to carry a lot of philosophical weight. Though originally used primarily in aesthetics, they have migrated by analogy into philosophy of language, epistemology, and even cultural anthropology. "Making" or "disclosing" a world is claimed to be the domain of poets, artists, natives, children, and others who are outside the public realm; it is also more often than not done without explicit knowledge, by languages and cultures as a whole. Generally, quite different phenomena, from ordinary classification schemes to novel artistic and poetic language and epochal-historical experiences of radical innovation in whole cultures, are included under the term. Disclosures traverse across both "making" and "finding," both the construction and discovery of worlds, and sometimes even both at once. Above all, the concept of disclosure is a certain way of talking about changes in cultural codes and understandings.

The main question that the concept of disclosure is meant to answer is this: How is it that we can experience new facts or embrace new values, if the world is experienced as already interpreted within a shared cultural framework? Various answers to this question show an unresolved tension between two quite different, although related, senses of disclosure. On the one hand, a language or a culture

discloses a "world" in that it already shapes how we see and question
reality through its habitual categories and presupposed practices.
"Things" or "facts" are not so much given as they are ordered within
a familiar categorical space; for example, the dangers of nuclear
power only recently were interpreted in the cultural category "accidents." Heidegger considers the "public" world as uncontested and
given; disclosure is therefore always directed against "publicness."
"Publicness primarily controls every way in which the world is interpreted, and it is always right."[27] The world that is disclosed in this
sense is the world that is taken for granted and unreflectively experienced. Call this disclosure$_1$. On the other hand, innovators and poets
are said to disclose the "world" in the opposite sense. Poetic language
discloses the world to us in new ways, as when new and successful
metaphors connect disparate experiences or objects never before
brought together. Innovations in general disclose the world by break-
ing down old patterns and illuminating new possibilities of seeing,
thinking, or speaking, as when the new greeting "Citizen!" articulated the Jacobin ideal of equality and disclosed a social world without
deference. The world that is disclosed in this sense is a whole new set
of possibilities for thinking and acting. Call this disclosure$_2$. It is precisely because the world is disclosed in the first sense that we need disclosure in the second sense: innovation rearranges such cultural
frameworks in order to make new experiences and different meanings possible. But how is this possible, if disclosure$_2$ is always dependent on disclosure$_1$, if innovation makes sense only within
some settled framework? Does disclosure$_2$ imply some framework-
independent reality and thus the denial of disclosure$_1$?

Let me illustrate the tension between these two senses of disclosure
by a few examples involving institutions and their collective frameworks. In 1966 a little-known partial meltdown of Detroit Edison's
nuclear reactor was reported in the press as a "mishap" disclosing an
engineering flaw soon to be corrected in progress toward the future
of "power too cheap to meter."[28] In 1979 the less severe Three Mile
Island incident was not buried in the back pages of the paper, but instead was categorized as a "nuclear accident" revealing the grave risks
of this form of power and the lack of public accountability of the industry. Was a new fact discovered between 1966 and 1979, or was it

merely that a new interpretation became culturally accepted? Why does Chernobyl now without question belong to the category of nuclear accidents and not engineering mishaps? Consider also the institution of science and its operating assumptions. We can date precisely when the first supernova was observed in the West: by Tycho Brahe in 1572. But these celestial lights had been "seen" before as atmospheric phenomena. If Tycho, then, did not "disclose" them as "out there," what did he do? Similarly, Boyle constructed an apparatus that produced a vacuum, and Galileo's telescope made visible the phases of Venus, sunspots, and the moons of Jupiter; both disclosed new non-Aristotelian facts. Eventually, their discoveries did have wide effects on scientific beliefs and practice. But what did they disclose? They not only touched off debates about how their facts were to be interpreted theoretically (Boyle's apparatus leaked, and the phases of Venus could be coherently explained away), but also about the standards and methods of inductive and deductive proof in the sciences.[29] What brought about this shift in public practice?

I do believe that something like disclosure occurred in the cases that I just mentioned. I think that it is tied primarily, although not exclusively, to the innovative use of cultural meanings and to the openness of our cognitive faculties to experiencing the world in new and different ways. It is quite misleading, however, to think of disclosure independent of ordinary capacities. Such stronger versions of the concept lead to an anti-democratic and elitist view of the limits of democratic politics. Most of all, these views of disclosure and innovation make it impossible for us to understand the rationality of social and political change. They lead, for example, to Rorty's split between "public" critics, who appeal to shared values, and "private" innovators, who make up new vocabularies. To use another analogy to the philosophy of science: in this section I defend a "logic of discovery" for public deliberation.

Against these views, I propose two redescriptions of the process of disclosing new possibilities. First, it is not the artist as much as it is the critic who provides the best paradigm for the analysis of what it means to disclose new possibilities of action and thought. Artists, too, can be critics, and their art is disclosive to the extent that it is critical. Second, what this means can best be analyzed not in terms of a contrast between innovative and everyday discourses but in terms of the contrast between a *disclosive* relation to the world and a *rigid* one—a contrast found by analogy in pathologies of reasoning, perception, and speech, which are often marked by a special rigidity and lack of multidimensionality. My view is that analysis of such pathological phenomena, and not exceptional cases of epochal innovation or artistic expression, offers the best and richest description of the phenomenon of disclosure—not by way of exceptional cases on the order of artistic genius, but by way of a perspicuous contrast to cases in which openness and the capacity for change are clearly absent. This also happens in the public world, especially one that is exclusive and closed. According to Heidegger, disclosing a world (*Erschliessung*) in public language use is turned into a closing off (*Verschliessung*) as we begin to see a standard set of beings, statements, or ways of doing things as the only right and meaningful ones—the only possibilities.

But there is another sense of closing off of the public world that is not so tied to rigid and inegalitarian cultures. For this reason, public criticism is always necessary, even in the most democratic of cultures. First, any change begins as an open-ended process that gradually restricts possibilities as it begins to take shape. As an emergent public forms its relationships to institutions, it becomes as inevitably selective as the public it is replacing, even if only in different ways. The power of large institutions can always be exercised in restrictive ways, and in this sense the utopian hopes of permanent renewal are illusory. Second, the public that wins at the end of a struggle over institutions may be merely different rather than better. Nonetheless, the process of change, if it is truly public, is constrained in certain ways that I have already outlined. A public will be able reshape large institutions only if it succeeds in mobilizing a deliberative majority. New publics formed by collective actors that do not meet the requirements of deliberative majority rule are neither democratic nor stable. Here we might think of groups that use democracy to abolish it, or that opportunistically use public openness to create new restrictive regimes, such as fascists and some fundamentalist religious groups. Third, the requirement of ongoing cooperation places crucial constraints of stability on even the most innovative processes of democratic change.

Once so described, epochs of democratic innovation can also be captured without the overblown claims of Rorty and others that "strong poets" must invent "new vocabularies" or languages to show the limits of inherited ones.[30] Rather than invent new languages and new vocabularies, innovative critics and artists create the context in which new beliefs are possible and relevant; they formulate their ordinary language communication in such a way that it has the broadest contextual effects on the implicit assumptions we use to understand them. In political terms, they transform "normal" lawmaking by opening up new understandings of democratic possibilities. Critics are thus disclosive in the sense described by one of Kafka's narrators: they don't talk like the rest of us, but they show us things that we cannot yet fully describe in quite ordinary ways.[31] Kafka's parables show indirectly how a shift in communicative context permits us to see things in a new and different way—to see the relevance of what is not yet important to us.

Disclosure as Truth, Disclosure as Relevance

Some philosophers, most notably Heidegger, equate truth with disclosure. Heidegger's view is non-epistemic, since disclosure simply *is* truth in its "original" or "primordial" sense, independent of justification; it is anti-public because it occurs only in exceptional circumstances. In both of these features, disclosure seems to have little to do with public deliberation in which people are called upon to answer and respond to others. If innovation is simply the same as truth, we then have no criterion for deciding among different competing disclosures of something new. To use one of Heidegger's own examples, it cannot be said on this account both that the Galilean law of falling bodies is true and that the Aristotelian doctrine that light bodies strive upward is false; "the Greek understanding rests upon a different interpretation and hence conditions a correspondingly different kind of seeing and questioning natural events."[32] The one is not "more correct" than the other: one interpretation of nature does not uncover more than the other, just different aspects rather than correct ones. Contrary to Heidegger, picking out some new aspect of a situation may make an epistemic difference: what is true under one description may be false under another. In this case, to see things in one way is to exclude seeing them in the other way as *true*. Learning in general requires that we have what Heidegger seems to deny is possible: the cognitive capacity to consider various aspects and points of view and then to compare and coordinate them. Disclosure is necessary only if one perspective has become so entrenched that only one aspect is available, so that interpretations are always of the same sort. To have any critical significance, then, a disclosure need not offer a new truth but must offer new possibilities of interpretation. Still, innovations may offer new standards of evaluation and justification. In this way they may take on cognitive significance in deliberation, especially if the community of deliberators is unaware of some truth or of some form of justification that may reject the currently available ones. Consider how often the Supreme Court has offered such new understandings of basic constitutional principles, despite the narrow basis of justification to which it can appeal.

In order to avoid the anti-critical consequences of "strong innovation" or disclosure, I want to propose a third view: that disclosure and thus innovation are not equivalent to or independent of truth but conditions for it. In my view, disclosure makes something relevant against the background of current public beliefs and practices. Hilary Putnam expresses this notion of relevance when he notes that a being that did not have any values would not know any facts.[33] More than that, the capacity to see something as relevant is a necessary condition for an open relation to the world, a condition that is present in ordinary and healthy cognitive functioning and that is crucial to all learning and innovation. The problem is not that every truth is also an untruth or that the public world is always unquestioned; rather, it is that our values, modes of questioning, and ways of seeing things can become rigid and fixed, so that new aspects, new experiences, novel variations, and minority viewpoints are not even considered to be possibly relevant to deliberation.

Analogies to certain aspects of perceptual experience best introduce what disclosure as relevance and openness might mean. Gestalt psychology has long analyzed the holistic nature of the disclosure of the perceptual field. The vacillations between two figures (such as between the duck and the rabbit) as our gaze seeks some equilibrium reveals that we are not in full conscious control of our own activity. But this involuntary way of experiencing a world has a negative side, which is manifest in well-known cases of extreme pathologies. As in

Leon Goldstein's analysis of the case of Schneider,[34] in pathologies the perceptual world is given not in a living gestalt but in explicit acts of judgment and interpretation; when asked to move his arm, for example, Schneider moves his whole body until his movements are confined to his arm, which he then "finds." The result is a rigid and fragmented relation to the world, a world that is defined in narrow categories of literal judgments that lose all richness and ambiguity. Rather than being in a dialogue with the objects around him, Schneider must really impose significance on the world (as some philosophers think we do), with the result that the perceptual field becomes rigid and "loses its plasticity." Not only does the world make no "sense" to Schneider, he has also lost all freedom in relation to it— in particular, the freedom to modulate his way of seeing it or to orient himself in it. The world is something that he can only undergo. Under certain circumstances, our cognitive capacities can lose the freedom and ambiguity that make them disclosive of something or receptive to others claims and objections.

These sorts of contrasts, I argue, are not limited to cases of extreme illness. There are analogous phenomena in ordinary life that constitute equally strong limitations on freedom and learning. From Francis Bacon's "idols of the cave" on, many philosophers have pointed out the pervasive human tendency to see the world in terms of accepted beliefs. This is the restrictive side of the ordinary prereflective cultural interpretations of the world. We often do not even see the evidence that refutes our theories, as many examples in the history of science demonstrate. In *Human Inference*, Nisbett and Ross appeal to a rich variety of experiments that all show a strong confirmation bias in processing evidence.[35] People see the relevance of confirming evidence more readily rather than they see that of falsifying evidence. Especially when they are "degenerating," past theories and beliefs can become like rigid gestalten to which evidence must conform, much as the world conforms to Schneider's imposed judgments. In such cases, normal science's productive problem solving deteriorates into theoretical blindness and *ad hoc* gerrymandering. Scientists then do not see new or contradictory evidence, or, if they do attend to it, they interpret it falsely to fit their current paradigm. The dialogical and open-ended interaction of theory and experience becomes frozen in a rigid framework. Such scientists one-sidedly assimilate the world to their theories, rather than accommodate their theories to the world. Their theories are therefore instances of rigid cultural expression, in that all the evidence that is perceived as relevant will always prove them right. Whereas rigid beliefs and expressions are caught in a circle of self-confirmation, disclosure opens up the possibility of perceiving falsifying evidence as relevant to one's theoretical beliefs and assumptions.

The role of dialogue in deliberation and testing gives special significance to cases of linguistic rigidity. Unlike the world of objects, the public world is maintained by linguistic interaction as human relationships are constructed and mediated in speech. This world of relationships, too, can become fixed and rigid, especially in cases of pathological interaction. Here schizophrenic families might offer a proper analogy to the extreme cases of aphasia. So, too, would a rigid culture with a strict code of interaction and conventions, constraining agents to constitute their interactions with narrower and narrower interpretations of the code. Bourdieu's analyses of *"Homo academicus"* and of the class character of matters of taste provide many examples of this phenomenon.[36] Citizens of democracies must be capable of making such codes fluid, at least insofar as they affect their capacity to see cooperative solutions to problematic situations.

Relevance as a Contextual Effect: Criticism and Disclosure

If the linguistically constituted public world can become rigid, it can also become fluid in deliberative dialogues when speakers try to correct failures in interaction. As Habermas points out, the social world can be reanimated by new self-interpretations and other self-referential forms of communication.[37] If deliberative democracy is in part built up in dialogue and maintained in common acts of self-interpretation, then there is an ongoing process in which social critics may intervene, especially as such common dialogue and interpretations become fixed and entrenched. This is not an extraordinary event, but part of the process of reaching understanding, coordinating actions, forming common beliefs, and sharing a whole form of life. Social actors achieve such coordination, according to Habermas,

by raising various sorts of intersubjective validity claims in communication, including truth claims. Such claims may be accepted or rejected in a fluid process that may continue indefinitely. Once speakers
reflect upon and discuss the dialogical process itself, they are engaging in discourse, in which they can test the assumptions behind the
shared world of public understandings. But Habermas has neglected
important limitations on such forms of public self-reflection, and a
pragmatic concept of disclosure plays an important role in delimiting
the scope of such reflection. Such interaction must itself be disclosive
to the extent that it permits multiple possibilities of self-interpretation—possibilities that allow speakers to invest the social world with
significance through their common acts of interpretation, dialogue,
and judgment. All these activities require contrasting, alternative possibilities as their subject matter.

If this is the proper analysis of the dialogical construction of deliberative contexts, disclosure is not any sort of mysterious event in
this context. It is best understood as a certain *effect* of expressive
speech, and indeed a certain effect on a specific type of audience.
The effect is best described through the concept of relevance: in any
sequence of talk, an utterance is relevant to the extent that it affects
the understanding of the hearer. To the extent that an utterance is
relevant, it has contextual effects; that is, it orders the subsequent sequence of talk and interaction. It follows, then, that the greater the
relevance the greater the contextual effects that an utterance has on
the background assumptions of the hearer. New information has just
such an effect, whereas already-processed information does little to
change the context of an utterance in a sequence of talk. In most
cases, relevance is a matter of degree; some utterances are more relevant and thus have greater effects than others. Heidegger seems to
be most interested in massive contextual effects in his conception of
new ontologies. I want to show that such contextual effects are possible even in ordinary communication, and in this way to give a micro-
foundation to the explanation of large-scale changes in the relation
of institutions and their publics.

Perhaps it is time to give a clear definition of ordinary relevance
and to explain why it can be best understood as a certain type of effect that lies on a continuum between changing individual beliefs

and transforming deep cultural assumptions and understandings. In their book *Relevance,* Dan Sperber and Dierdre Wilson analyze the role of relevance in communication and formulate a "principle of relevance" in analogy to Grice's cooperative principle for interpreting communicative intentions.[38] Grice's principle states that talk exchanges require some mutually accepted purposes, so that at least some possible contributions must be excluded for failing to accord with these mutual purposes and intentions.[39] This principle has to be supplemented for various reasons, not the least of which is that interpreting an utterance involves more than identifying the assumptions explicitly expressed as the information content of the conversational contribution. It involves "working out the consequences of adding this assumption to a set of assumptions that have themselves already been processed. . . . It involves seeing the contextual effects of this assumption in a context determined, at least in part, by earlier acts of comprehension."[40] Such effects include any modification of the cognitive environment of the hearer, such as establishing new synthetic implications, manifesting implicit contradictions, or weakening or strengthening of the beliefs that make up this background set of assumptions.

However, a speaker cannot just aim at maximum effect: the utterance must be relevant in the context, and if the cognitive effects are too large the hearers will not change their assumptions. If I say "You are all now dreaming" and if I am not lecturing on Descartes or Buddhism, my statement will have little cognitive effect, since the assumptions of such an utterance have too little connection with the background beliefs hearers usually employ to understand any utterance at all. Relevance is then a matter of degree along a number of dimensions. As Sperber and Wilson put it, "Other things being equal, an assumption with greater contextual effects is more relevant; and, other things being equal, an assumption requiring a smaller processing effort is more relevant."[41] Disclosures must be optimally relevant along both innovative and conservative dimensions. Much as learning requires both accommodation and assimilation according to Piaget, having little relation to the audience's current assumptions lowers the net cognitive effects of the information contained in a message. As the ethnomethodologists' many natural-setting experiments about nonsense and rule-breaking behavior show, we cannot help but be relevant; the communicator always makes a presumption of relevance.[42] But a message or some new information is or is not relevant precisely through its contextual effects on common knowledge and assumptions. The total cognitive environment of such shared assumptions can be called a "world" which speakers construct and reconstruct in their ongoing acts of speech and comprehension.[43]

The cases that are most interesting for my purposes are instances of introducing new assumptions into the background set of common knowledge, so that the audience of the message acquires a modified interpretive framework. Should these assumptions be sufficiently in conflict with existing ones, the common world must be repaired or altered. This activity requires a certain openness of the audience to placing new assumptions communicated by others in a number of possible, accessible contexts. By engaging in communication that demands precisely such variation and extension of the context of understanding by their audience, social critics disclose aspects of the initial context and offer ways in which we can recontextualize our beliefs so that the assumption is relevant. Suppose I wish to point out the dangers of nuclear power in 1966 after the Detroit Edison incident. The accident had a certain relevance in the initial context of the age: it was a "temporary" engineering problem that experts could solve. But in an extended political (rather than technological) context of democratic decision making and control over risks, the danger of nuclear power becomes accessible and relevant. Similarly, Martin Luther King Jr. and others extended the assumptions about religious and constitutional equality relevant to the statement "all men are created equal" to show the narrow assumptions of segregationist ideology, and thus they succeeded in making racist beliefs unacceptable to large segments of the American public.[44]

Each of the above examples represents more than simply the introduction of a new topic into public discourse. Some facts about accidents at nuclear facilities and about black poverty and social exclusion appear even in the technocratic and racist "worlds." The failures not simply due to logical errors or to lack of empirical validation but of a lack of public accounability; critics create the context for such new accountability. The critic tries to make these facts relevant in such a way that they are discrepant with the common "world." Usually, such "disjunctures" cause us to discredit the "facts" as perceptual or cognitive errors.[45] But these facts, according to the critic, cannot be reconciled with that world, and it is that world and its assumptions and practices, not the relevance of the facts, that must be changed.

In the context of a dialogically constructed social world, a critic's expression is disclosive if it can express and thereby change the relation of the hearer to the social world—to the existing set of beliefs, practices, and norms that actors animate and reproduce in their common activities. Social criticism is thus a paradigmatic instance of disclosure: if it is successful, then it has such a contextual effect, which in turn is correct when the possibility so disclosed is validated in a discourse that publicly reorders our assumptions. The audience is then reoriented to the social world, and it can take up a different attitude toward the world of cultural meanings and possibly a new position in its holistic interpretive field. Negatively, critics show that the existing field of meanings and beliefs has become, at least in part, pathologically rigid, in that it fails to permit the expression of certain possibilities (for example, solutions to problems or new interpretations) in the current situation of cultural self-expression and dialogue. A disclosure could reveal that the current set of social facts does not include all the possible ones; the critic devalues some of the possibilities relative to some new but still relevant context. Segregation was no longer an acceptable interpretation of the constitutional guarantees of rights, but only because those rights were made relevant in new ways in an extended political context by the civil rights movement.

This process need not call for innovation in any strong sense, since possibilities of meaning are already present in the social world and need only be given a certain pragmatic twist. Much like the aphasic who has to substitute elaborate narrative for the effect of a simple word, critics often achieve such effects indirectly by jokes, irony, storytelling, and other indirect forms of communication. What unites all these forms of speech is not that they raise a certain claim—say, to truth or correctness—but that the hearer comes to see things in a new way, take up a different perspective, or change attitudes. They are not merely accepted but tried and taken on, and in considering them the hearer is opened up to a new pattern of relevances—to a new perspective on what may count as potentially good reasons. Against Rorty, the activities of both artists and critics can be understood in this way. Critics do not simply "change the subject." Rather, they change the context of public assumptions about justification. Such disclosive effects made possible what Ian Hacking called new "truth-candidates"—that is, a new set of statements about the world that could be true or false.[46]

Because criticism is disclosive only if it expands currently available cultural forms of expression, it carries with it the danger that it may become non-public (that is, idiosyncratic and incommunicable). To avoid this problem, critical-disclosive acts must be verified in a second act of reflection by the audience to which they are addressed. It is not enough to open up possibilities, although that may be a first reflective step; these new possibilities must be reflectively tested and appropriated, as is the case in the aesthetic sphere as well. Thus, to be critical, the expression must have a reproducible effect on the audience, as well as open up possibilities and relevances.

That truth and disclosure are not identical in acts of criticism should now be clear for two different reasons. The first has to do with why disclosure is not, strictly speaking, an epistemological notion: disclosure is audience-relative, whereas truth in the strong, normative sense is not. Some expressions are disclosive in some communities but not in others. This fact does not overlap with the truth or falsity of the sentences so expressed. The sentence "The planets move" is disclosive to ancient Greek science and cosmology, but it has no such pragmatic effect on the modern scientific community. The sentence "West Germany annexed East Germany" is not literally true, but it asks the hearer to take a certain perspective on the unification process and to relate unified Germany to its Nazi past; this is achieved through the jarring use of the verb "annex." Thus, many examples of literally false sentences, including many of the conceits of political poets and satirists, are disclosive.

This last implication is the second reason to distinguish truth and disclosure. Often the possibilities so disclosed do not have specifiable truth content, even if they are different from the fixed cultural schemata that they overcome. A correct diagnosis can be made for the wrong reasons in both medicine and social criticism. For instance,

Heidegger may be right about the dangers of modern technology's dominating our perception of the world, and this fixation may well be disclosed in his image of the power station on the thoroughly tamed Rhine. But as disclosive as this image is for the fixating powers of the technological way of looking at the world, upon reflection there is every reason to reject his positive notions of the "earth" and his revival of polytheism. Disclosure is thus clearly an effect that, upon reflection, can be rejected by the audience; without the invitation to reflection, disclosure is simply a powerful form of rhetoric employed by social critics in situations of restricted communication. In these situations, disclosure describes an effect that certain ideas and expressions can have on the audience inhabiting a restrictive culture. Nonetheless, the "truth content" of this disclosure is contained not in its effect but rather in its verification in the further reflection on what is disclosed that it initiates. Disclosure is not truth itself, but it enables truth to emerge in public reflection. Consider aphasia as an analogy. Aphasia does not affect the truth of the sentences uttered, but rather the disclosive capacity of the aphasic's speech. A severe aphasic cannot utter some or all true sentences (depending on the severity of the injury), because he or she lacks the very preconditions for making either true or false utterances. Disclosive criticisms aim at creating just these preconditions. In problematic situations that require the initiation of non-routinized public deliberation, disclosive criticisms can open up new possibilities and establish the conditions under which dialogical mechanisms of deliberation might begin to function in public discourse.

In political terms, periods of public verification that follow upon disclosive events or criticisms may also have conservative effects, allowing older publics and their powerful institutions to restrict the effects of new patterns of relevance. The democratic requirement of public verification is part of the test of whether the new understanding can elicit and promote continued cooperation. At the same time, however, these periods open up channels for resistance by which citizens and state actors can mobilize to contest the public in formation. We can see just such effects upon the civil rights movement in the United States, which achieved its formal goal of voting rights and equality before the law only to see gains against segregation at other levels lost through informal resistance and the retrenchment of power. Such resistance also occurred after the initial constitutional advances in another period in which "normal politics" was suspended: the post-Civil War period of Reconstruction. Challengers often see this dialectic between the democratic demand for public verification and the capacity to mobilize counter-powers to resist or blunt the public impetus for change. The capacity of older publics to mount such resistance is the price of the stability of democratic institutions in periods in which innovation is not required and the price of the interchange between publics and institutions. The power that institutions now exercise on such a large scale is the product of some past public interchange with previous institutions and their forms of power.

This distinction between truth and relevance also makes clear that the many different forms of possible disclosure are not exhausted by the intentional acts of critics. If disclosure is defined primarily in terms of its effects on the audience, then it is clear that many forms of expression and even some things are disclosive to an audience: visual images, new technologies, art, historical events, and much more. These broader, often non-intentional forms of disclosure capture the sense of the historical-epochal form of disclosure that I discussed above. Nonetheless, even here the epochal significance of such events must be communicated to an audience; their disclosive effects do not just happen, but are related to the way in which such communication makes relevant information that shakes our core beliefs. For example, the event of going to the moon and seeing pictures of the Earth had a profound disclosive effect on a generation of Americans. But this example shows a further feature of disclosure: it can lose its pragmatic effect. Like a dead metaphor, the commercial reproduction and wide use of the image of the Earth made it part of the available cultural framework. Like the sentence "Planets move," images can lose their disclosive effects, perhaps even more rapidly, as they become assimilated into the dominant cultural forms of expression. Yesterday's disclosures become today's clichés, the material for new fixed cultural schemata. In this sense, it is no accident that latent and oppositional meanings and images tend to be disclosive, and that once assimilated they lose their disclosive power.

By focusing on the relation to an audience, the paradigm of the social critic makes the somewhat mysterious notion of disclosing a world
relevant to public deliberation. First, disclosure is, on this view, an act
of expression that opens up new possibilities of dialogue and restores
the openness and plasticity necessary for learning and change.
Second, disclosures are not disclosures of truth; they are prior to truth,
and they concern what makes truth possible. Disclosures are not self-
justifying or self-verifying, but require public reflection to test them for
idiosyncrasy. These same tests open up a new dialectic, however, between public verification of the new forms of democracy and the resistance by the older publics and its stable institutions, between older
and newer forms of publicly generated power. Third, disclosures often
take the form of indirect expression, since the effects they aim to
achieve often cannot be achieved in direct forms under conditions of
social and cultural restriction. Fourth, the disclosure as concerned
with relevance identifies the proper role of social critics: criticisms
point to new possibilities, but always relative to the limits of existing
possibilities of meaning and expression. All these elements make some
cognitive and communicative act of disclosure necessary when there
are community-wide biases. In these situations, neither the procedural
rules for initiating debate nor the self-reflective capacities of the majority are sufficient to get public deliberation going, no matter how
well ordered the institutions or how competent the citizens.

Dualist Democracy and Institutional Innovation

The public activity of the critic is to point out new patterns of relevance. In disclosing new possibilities, critics are not simply announcing a new truth or a new form of justice; they are addressing an
audience and expanding what it considers relevant to deliberation.
The ultimate test comes in the reflection on these new possibilities in
public deliberation: the practical question of how we should live. The
disclosive capacity of a culture is therefore not only a precondition for
truth but also, and perhaps more important, a precondition for
freedom. As in the case of learning, disclosure indicates a necessary
condition for the autonomy of an agent within a cultural context,
that is, an open and "dialogical" relation to the conditions of joint

public activity. Such an open relation permits reflective agents to change these conditions, even if one piece at a time. All critics open up the fields of meaning and action of a culture by introducing new themes or facts; but radical critics, by doing so, do not merely interpret "worlds"—they change them. The world here is the cultural background and context that informs institutions and their taken-for-granted understandings. Only a public can create a world, in organizing itself and the larger public around these new understandings. Such innovative publics make democratic deliberation a dynamic and historical process.

These emergent publics can be accommodated only in new institutional frameworks, often radical and innovative enough to constitute new "constitutional regimes." Such changes alter the possibilities of "normal politics," as much as the scientific revolutions discussed above historically change the conditions of normal science. In the case of such political changes, the source of many extraordinary periods of democratic lawmaking is the reassertion of popular sovereignty against the resistance of rigid forms of institutionalization and entrenched relations of power. Bruce Ackerman has argued that there have been at least three such "revolutions" in American history, and that they have crystallized around paradigmatic historical experiences, such as the founding of the republic, the Civil War, Reconstruction, the Great Depression, and the New Deal. In these cases, popular sovereignty asserts itself, even within ongoing democratic regimes, in such a way that the people employ extraordinary means. Around such "critical discourse moments," a public successfully forms outside of the Framers' formal institutional design of dualistic democracy, even with its multiple institutional tracks for deliberation within and between branches of government.[47] Capturing such dynamism once again shows the superiority of a dialogical account and the limitations of the proceduralist and precommitment models (even in the context of constitutional deliberation).

According to the analysis I have offered in this chapter, these "revolutions" or democratic renewals succeed in large part because public actors discover the right political rhetoric and critical discourse with which to initiate community-wide deliberation about crucial events. Such popular rhetoric is necessary in order to overcome the impasses of public deliberation that occur at critical junctures when the public finds community-wide biases and restrictions in communication keeping its input out of normal institutional channels and routinized problem-solving strategies. In these cases, a contest for public opinion begins, as can be seen by the enormous periods of struggle and conflict before each such transformation. Once the source of public opinion become contested, possibilities for public deliberation in which the basic framework of association would be considered emerge outside institutional channels.

It is not unusual in such periods for "constitutional politics" to be characterized by moral appeals, which are often called "higher" than existing law and which draw attention to an existing injustice. The injustice itself becomes problematic, initiating public deliberation and demands that the framework of the fundamental democratic norms be rethought. In critical discourse moments, historical experiences may "disclose" new forms of democracy and new democratic principles. Part of the public testing of these principles comes after the new regime becomes more stable and is directed to ensuring the continuity of the old regime with the previous ones. This continuity is, however, not the strict continuity of tradition but the weaker continuity of a learning process. Learning requires coherent development, but it also is discontinuous to the extent that whole new types of reasons and principles may be introduced into the public basis of justification. The term 'disclosure' is meant to signify the innovative side of social learning, which is typical of the public use of reason.

In the phases prior to these historical periods of learning, government and other public institutions are no longer able to reflect, articulate, and organize public opinion. In these periods of change, deliberation is no longer focused around institutional locations. Rather, the public opinion formed in such periods of society-wide deliberation reorganizes and recreates the public basis of institutions. Critical discourse moments need not be about a global crisis of the institutional regime; they can also form around particular issues in ongoing political life. In these smaller-scale cases, only specific institutions are transformed (such as regulatory agencies in the case of nuclear power, or the specific cultural codes that governed them, such as the ideology of inevitable technological progress). In these

moments, radical democracy and popular sovereignty are briefly re-
asserted, even in the existing institutional framework. The public
exercises its fullest rule in these periods: democracy is truly "radical"
only during periodic constitutional and institutional crises, to the
extent that the operative interpretive and institutional frameworks
change through public deliberation and learning. The space for
radical democracy depends on the publics' being able to appeal a
self-critical principle of popular sovereignty precisely at those moments when institutions are no longer open to the full spectrum of
public opinion. Normal lawmaking is usually not opposed to popular
sovereignty. Although stability is a democratic value as well as a functional necessity, it must be balanced with the interplay between
publics and institutions—between moments of popular sovereignty
and the constitutional order that makes them possible.

Conclusion

In this chapter I have argued that the public sphere is the primary
source of innovation and learning in deliberative democracy. In order
to function properly in deliberative settings, a public must be able to
articulate alternative interpretations to problems that find resonance
with citizens. Thus, one of the roles of a vital public sphere is for citizens to be able to detect and problematize the ways in which deliberation fails as a result of cultural understandings and institutional
limitations. After formulating their way of looking at the problem in
their voluntary associations, citizens can then address the larger public sphere, the broadest possible forum for the exchange of arguments and perspectives. At the very least, at those crucial moments in
which the "disclosure" of new understandings is needed, it must be
possible for new publics to emerge, to place new themes on the public agenda, and to challenge available understandings. Only then can
deliberative impasses and limitations on public reason be overcome.

In large and complex societies, the mass media replace the reading
public of the eighteenth century. They have come to play a central
role in the dissemination of arguments and information to a wider
and wider audience. That pluralism as an ideal challenges the idea
that the public is singular does not mean that the audience to which

public reasons are directed ought not be unrestricted. This public is the collective body of all citizens, not just in society-wide deliberation but also in deliberation across institutional boundaries. In this pluralistic and dynamic sense, we can still speak of the formation of world public opinion and of various ways in which even this largest of publics may be politically organized. Such a public sphere already exists in nascent form, although it is already well developed in some multicultural states.

Some new democratic renewal may succeed in producing such public deliberation about crucial events and historical experiences that now must be conceived as international problems. In these cases, a contest for international public opinion begins, as can be seen by the enormous periods of struggle and conflict before each such transformation within constitutional states. In a vibrant public sphere with an international civil society, these channels may often be cosmopolitan. As I noted above, such periods of what Ackerman calls "constitutional politics" are often characterized by novel moral appeals, which are often called "higher" than existing law and which draw attention to existing injustice.[48] Making violations of human rights public is precisely to make such a moral appeal that questions the legitimacy and sovereignty of current legal institutions. If my analysis of the interchange of publics and their institutions is correct, Kant's ideal postulates something like a period of "cosmopolitan politics" among the enlightened publics of each republic, analogous to Ackerman's constitutional politics. But, as opposed to Kant's view, such a politics questions the sovereignty of nations, even if it affirms the sovereignty of citizens (now citizens of the world).

The main reason that a world public sphere does not exist is that global institutions are international but not yet cosmopolitan; because they are based on negotiating interests among nation states and their representatives, they are only very indirectly open to democratic input. In such meta-institutions, citizens are not sovereign—states are. But not all trans-national institutions need to follow this model. The European Parliament already bypasses states in assigning policy decisions to its representatives. Moreover, under proposed ideas of European unity, this parliament can deliberate and set policy. Rather than an inaccessible bureaucracy, the European Parliament may become a focus for the organization of collective action in European civil society. When the parliament debates farm policy, the associations of civil society concerned with related issues (farmers' organizations, environmentalist groups, and so on) can organize around the debate, attempting to influence not only the representatives in the parliament but also the citizenry that elects them. In this case, then, it is possible to see how a cosmopolitan public can begin to be organized by and in turn reorganize a deliberative institution. International civil society is not enough; it is too punctual and too divided spatially and temporally to affect decisions. Only the cosmopolitan public sphere can become a location for the public use of reason across international civil society. When organized around international deliberative institutions, a public sphere of democratically organized international associations could shift the location of sovereignty in the international sphere from nations back to citizens. These citizens would then be world citizens by virtue of their rights to political participation in a world civic public sphere.

But what is this public at large? In complex societies, it may be difficult to see this public as anything more than an abstraction, a placeholder, an episodic event (as Hannah Arendt thought), or even a "phantom" (as Walter Lippmann put it).[49] Indeed, for Habermas it is only a "structure of communication," an anonymous and subjectless network of communication and discourse. I have argued that it must be seen as taking shape in a deliberative majority formed around any particular issue if it is to be connected to the ideal of popular sovereignty. But the public at large also plays a functional role in the constant interchange between large institutions, such as the state and its sovereign citizens—an interplay that has produced changes in political forms, such as universal suffrage. If the civic public is a phantom, it is because we have inherited substantialistic ways of thinking about the public that are not appropriate to large nation states. Rather, as Dewey notes, our conceptions of democracy are too often limited to "local town meeting ideas and practices." For Dewey, the public in a modern society seems "amorphous and unarticulated . . . as uncertain about its own whereabouts as philosophers since Hume have been about the residence and make-up of the self."[50] In the place of a large and unmanageable assembly, Dewey thinks about the democratic public as a series of local communities within a larger societal community.

The problem of reconceiving the public on a large scale involves the seeming contradiction between the interactive debate of a town meeting and institutionally mediated deliberation. In complex societies, public deliberation is mediated not only by the powerful institutions of the state but also by the electronic mass media, which have the capacity to reach a large and indefinite audience. As difficult as it is to separate the idea of democratic participation from the town meeting model, it is also difficult to imagine the public sphere without modeling it on the circulation of printed material. According to the current diagnoses of the decline of the public sphere (such as Habermas's) that favor a model of the critical debate among members of the reading public, the media-structured public sphere is "degenerated," and the commercialized media institutions turn citizens into passive consumers.[51] Though such critical analyses often overestimate the power of techniques of persuasion, they do point out just how problematic the mass media are as public institutions. There seems to be little interaction between the public and the media analogous to the constitutional mechanisms structuring public input into the state, with citizens having less control over the systems of meaning and the purposes the media embody.

The problem is not that the media do not make information available. Rather, it lies in how they do so—in the underlying purposes and criteria media personnel employ in structuring public attention. These norms force collective actors to choose dramatic and symbolic strategies to make their complaints known, thus adapting their public contributions to these non-public requirements for attention. But focusing attention in this way may shape their own political communication and make it not only less effective but also less transformative. Given constitutional constraints on the direct regulation of public speech, the only practical solution may be to decrease the influence of any particular medium or group, such as the major television networks in the United States. But it is important to see that collective actors use the mass media to address the larger public. As currently constituted, the mass media structure their messages to address another indefinite audience: the average consumer. Commercial media are certainly no longer governed by norms of civility and sociability that might act as public filters; they do not demand of consumers the joint activity necessary to maintain the existence of common deliberation. Nonetheless, the transformative power of commercial media should not be exaggerated. Only already-successful public actors receive media attention, thus producing yet another institutionally caused cycle of political poverty that can be corrected only by the emergence of a new public.

So what is the answer to Lippmann's question: Where is the "phantom" public in complex and pluralist societies? It is certainly the case that the democratic public is organized for decision making by political institutions. So organized, the inchoate public may become a deliberatively formed majority. But the public in this sense is constantly changing as emerging new publics eventually become deliberative majorities. In well-ordered and pluralistic democracies, the emergence of publics is not rare at all; it is a constant feature of ongoing public discourse. Unless it is responsive to public opinion, political power cannot be generated and regenerated in public interaction, nor can institutions successfully promote deliberation. The emergence of new publics therefore ceases only when cultural understandings become rigid and when normal politics within institutions becomes non-deliberative and non-democratic.

This view of democratic innovation fits the model of deliberation I have been defending throughout this book. According to this view, the democratic public sphere is not a structure but a process: it is the process by which emerging collective actors appeal not to a "phantom" public but to other citizens in ways that are consistent with the requirements of equality, non-tyranny, and publicity. Sometimes this process creates a new constitutive public which interacts with democratic institutions in ways that change how the public is formed into deliberative majorities. Once again this public is no phantom; however, it may not yet be formed, and it may or may not even eventually emerge. The close connection between the emergence of new publics and processes of change should not be surprising. In order to remain democratic and open to popular renewal, complex societies require institutional learning in open, dynamic, pluralist forms of public deliberation. Even if innovations begin outside of institutions, they prepare the way for learning and renewal in them when institutional deliberation fails.

Conclusion: Deliberative Democracy and Its Critics

Deliberative democracy places great demands on both ordinary citizens and political institutions. For this reason, many of its critics have argued that deliberative democracy is an unworkable ideal under any circumstances, indeed one that accentuates all the typically mentioned weaknesses of democracy. Such criticisms often hit the mark of those theories of deliberative democracy that fail to consider relevant social facts of pluralism, inequality, and complexity. Communitarian and associative theories fail in this respect, although for quite different reasons. Communitarians attempt to enrich democracy by restoring a shared conception of the common good according to which citizens make politics one of their highest values. Such a deliberative perfectionism demands that political judgments meet the test of public virtue rather than the test of continued cooperation among groups with different values and beliefs. Although not perfectionist, associative and civil-society theories also demand much from citizens, most especially their voluntary participation in a variety of associations and organizations. Such associations are insufficient in the face of the complexity and scale of modern societies. Whereas communitarians demand too much of citizens, associative theorists demand too much of civil society. I have proposed a conception of public deliberation and its dualist institutions that is an alternative to both of these one-sided conceptions of democracy.

Neither communitarian nor associationist models offer workable solutions to the main difficulties facing deliberative democracy that I have discussed in this book: cultural pluralism, which undermines the possibility of a general will, a unitary common good, and a singular public reason; social inequalities, which may produce a vicious circle of exclusion from effective participation in deliberation; social complexity, which makes it necessary for deliberation to take place in large and increasingly powerful institutions; and community-wide biases, which may restrict public communication and which also narrow the scope of feasible solutions to social conflicts and problems. I have argued that overcoming these obstacles requires going beyond the civic-republican and Kantian origins of deliberative democratic theories. These conceptions of public reason cannot solve the challenges to democracy that are typical of a pluralist and complex society having a high degree of social conflict and inequality, large and powerful social institutions, and a highly contested public sphere.

The success of a deliberative form of democracy depends on creating social conditions and institutional arrangements that foster the public use of reason. Deliberation is public to the extent that these arrangements permit free and open dialogue among citizens, who make informed and reasoned judgments about ways to resolve problematic situations. In chapter 1, I outlined the dialogical mechanisms that make convincing public reasons and cooperative agreements more likely. In basing this process on the pragmatic goal of continued cooperation of politically equal citizens, I have offered an ideal of deliberative democracy that is less normatively demanding than either the Kantian or the communitarian alternatives. My argument nonetheless tries to save the core of such egalitarian and participatory (if not radical) theories of democracy and their critical orientation toward current institutions. As opposed to Kantian and communitarian theories, I see public deliberation primarily as a joint social activity. Public deliberation is a dynamic activity performed by a plural subject, precisely the sort of activity that is maintained in the give-and-take of reasons that enhances the quality of justification for political decisions. At the same time, I have argued that such a dialogical process must take place in a revisable institutional and interpretive framework; the ongoing dialogue between the deliberating public and the institutions that organize their deliberation keeps this framework open and democratic. Without this dialogue, democracy loses its capacity to generate legitimate political power. First, when public opinion is not institutionally organized, it remains inchoate and ineffective. Second, when there is no public input and no public control, these same organizing institutions become dependent on non-democratic forms of power. This sort of interchange between institutions and their publics is as important to deliberative democracy as the quality of public discussion and debate among citizens. Not only does it permit innovation and democratic change; it makes the institutions that organize deliberation more responsive and more effective.

Besides claiming that deliberation requires political perfectionism and amorphous popular power, the critics of deliberative democracy see public opinion as too indeterminate to be a norm for political rule. According the Hegel's well-known remark in *The Philosophy of Right*, public opinion must be "as much respected as despised."[1] For Hegel, public opinion is nothing more than "unorganized opinion and volition" reflecting the current conflicts in civil society. Habermas sees the commercialization of the public sphere as producing the same result. Contrary to such indeterminate and rhetorically influenced opinion, Hegel contends that only the sciences offer a rational alternative: in them, rational beliefs are "not a matter of turns of phrase, allusiveness, half utterances and silences, but consist in the unambiguous, determinate and open expression of their meaning and significance."[2] Lippmann too saw expert authority as a way to counteract unstable public opinion.[3] Similarly, Joseph Bessette has recently argued that deliberative majorities need an "external basis," which is to be found in a body of traditional republican principles and in the periodic emergence of extraordinary statesmen who resist the temptations of unreflective public opinions and passions.[4] Bruce Ackerman likewise calls for periods of "higher lawmaking" to be judged by higher moral standards, sometimes found in the Supreme Court's or the president's ability to ignore limited public opinion.[5] Such sympathetic and unsympathetic critics of deliberative democracy alike insist there must be an external standard to limit and define public opinion, and thus that deliberation cannot define its own guiding norms and procedure-independent standards.

In chapter 5 I argued that public opinion emerges outside organizing institutions when the needs of the public are no longer met in the existing framework. But this does not make public opinion that has been formed in this way somehow more rational according to some non-political and ultimately undemocratic standard. Morality and science are tempting standards by which to judge the vagaries of public opinion, especially in comparison with "higher" moral laws or "scientific" truths. But such ideals prove difficult if not impossible to institutionalize, given the facts of pluralism and complexity. Too often such appeals to external standards may violate the demands of the norm of publicity. Moreover, it is hard to see how these independent norms of rationality actually operate in already-existing and more or less successful democratic practices. In contrast to such overly strong reconstructions of rationality which ignore existing practices, Rorty argues for a "priority of democracy over philosophy."[6] By this phrase, Rorty means that stronger epistemic and moral standards that are established independent of the historical conditions and thus not addressed to a specific society—like those sought by philosophers from Plato to Hegel—cannot meet the practical demands of democratic politics. My more pragmatic and non-skeptical view of public reason also leads us to rethink what is required by reasonable agreement. In contrast to stronger and ultimately non-pragmatic norms of rationality, my account accepts deliberatively formed compromise as a crucial feature of democratic life in which norms of reason themselves are publicly contested. Citizens, I have argued, have no other choice but compromise when public deliberation fails, and not to recognize the limits of public reason would be a sign of excessive rationalism.

Besides answering the skeptic, the motive for devising a more pragmatic and less idealizing account of deliberation is the recognition of heterogeneous standards of justification operating in democratic practices. Democratic deliberation ought not depend on any single epistemic or moral norm, such as liberal neutrality or moral impartiality, to define its rational character or to delimit the range of reasonable forms of cooperation. The basic task of critical public reason should be thought of in more practical terms: the point of political deliberation is to solve social problems and to overcome political conflicts. The criterion for successful deliberation is, therefore, that it restore the conditions of ongoing cooperation in problematic situations. I have identified the mechanisms of dialogue and the conditions of equality needed for public deliberation to be successful. When successful, deliberation produces outcomes that all might reasonably accept and also expect to be able to revise in the future. The success of public deliberation should be measured reconstructively—that is, in light of the historical development of democratic institutions and practices—rather than by external standards of justification. I have employed such an approach in my philosophical reconstruction of deliberation, analyzing existing practices for their potential for rationality rather than constructing new ones on the basis of a practice-independent standard. The test of this reconstruction should be pragmatic: its proposed norms have to be able to overcome the obstacles that democratic deliberation now faces. Many philosophical approaches to public reason still have very little to say about reasonable disagreement; they suggest that contentious issues simply be excluded. The reconstructive approach that I have taken here argues that deliberation guided by public reason can answer such questions in ways that promote cooperation.

While I do not offer institutional blueprints, my reconstructive approach is not silent about possibilities of reform. Rather than a utopia projected into the future, it provides a way to think about improving actual deliberative practices as they currently exist. In the periods of learning and change initiated by social critics and collective movements, innovations and reforms of this kind have already occurred. Democracy creates the social conditions for such learning by facilitating a flexible relationship between institutions and their constitutive publics. Whatever the consequences of social complexity, this flexibility is possible with democratic institutions of any scale. Against Marx, "real" democracy, on this account, does not require the complete transformation of society; rather, it is a project of piecemeal reform that builds upon the constitutional and institutional achievements of past frameworks.

In this reformist democratic practice, the role of critical social theory is to provide a critique of public reason, an analysis of the potentials and limits of the public and autonomous employment of practical reason. On this view of participatory democracy, public reason is exercised not by the state but primarily in the public sphere of free and equal citizens. In the American civil rights movement, for example, citizens collectively changed the legal interpretation of political equality and its enforcement. To the extent that critical theory is defined by an ideal of consensus, its proponents search for greater democracy—that is, for increased scope for public deliberation and popular sovereignty.

The example of the civil rights movement reveals a further aspect of the public practice of reform. According to the model I have developed, public actors and movements emerge in the public sphere and change institutions, particularly those "new" social movements that contest the very nature and definition of "normal" politics. But the civil rights movement also shows the ambiguities of the public sphere and democratic deliberation as they are now constituted. The current constitutional state and its institutions are not as open or as "porous" as dualist democracy demands. Furthermore, the public process of inclusion and reform has been much more difficult for the movement to bring about than has mere legislative success. Both citizens and the state have also used many avenues inside and outside institutions to resist enforcing civil rights legislation. My approach's mixture of reconstructive and pragmatic elements can help to analyze the historical ambiguities of such processes and outcomes. When it is both descriptive and normative in this way, a theory of public deliberation permits a better critical understanding of actual deliberation. As neither normal social science nor a recipe for political action, this critical approach can identify potentials and barriers to citizens who seek to expand their opportunities for effective public deliberation.

Historically, many different democratic reforms have improved the conditions of deliberation. In view of the varied and complex circumstances of public deliberation, it is not surprising that monistic accounts of democracy, such as those based on the single principle of maximizing direct citizen participation, are unable to guide criticism and reform. In institutions that operate through large-scale spatial and temporal processes, for example, it is more important to make the division of labor more democratic than to abolish it for the sake of maximizing more direct participation. Nor is it always the case that openness to the observing public of spectators always promotes the quality of deliberation in representative bodies. In fact, "sunshine laws" meant to promote publicity have arguably increased representatives' strategic posturing to the gallery, thus decreasing the quality of reasoned argument and informed debate in legislative bodies as well as the representatives' willingness to compromise.[7] These examples show that some seemingly appropriate reform efforts may have perverse consequences for public deliberation. I have already noted how participatory arrangements may sometimes only worsen social inequalities and cultural conflicts, especially when they reinforce existing inequalities of social influence, community-wide biases, and shared unreflective assumptions. Above all, reforms that do not address the phenomenon of political poverty will not help those who are least effective in deliberation.

That said, it is certainly true that current arrangements in most complex democracies do not promote the sort of public deliberation that is needed in complex and pluralistic societies. Important issues related to social inequalities and their impact on democratic decision making have hardly been addressed, and threats to eliminate the welfare state, rather than make it more accountable to the public and its clients, only exacerbate the problem. I have proposed a number of ways to correct for deliberative inequalities. Similarly, I have proposed solving the problems of pluralism through changing voting practices and through creating distinct local jurisdictions in some cases of enormous inequalities. It is clear that winner-take-all, one-person-one-vote elections will produce permanent minorities in the absence of institutional reforms and changes in voting procedures. Furthermore, moral compromises of the sort that I have proposed as solutions to deep moral conflicts have yet to become common in the public sphere; under current conditions they will be viewed with suspicion by opposing parties, who will see them only as another instance of their losing ground rather than finding common ground with others. The escalation of power in institutions due to complexity also remains unaddressed. Only through the concerted efforts of many citizens, such as AIDS activists, have there been any notable successes in harnessing powerful institutions (such as scientific review of human experimentation) under public control and accountability. As the case of AIDS activism shows, this success depends on finding the proper points in the long chains of complex interactions that are open to deliberative intervention by the public and its legitimate interests.

Some deliberative theorists have made more specific proposals for reforms than I have offered here. James Fishkin has proposed and recently even begun to implement the idea of a "deliberative opinion poll."[8] In such a "poll," a representative sample of citizens get together, inform themselves on a particular issue, and discuss it with one another in front of a national television audience. Such a procedure overcomes some of the basic weaknesses of current practices for measuring and discussing public opinion: rather than being "the cool and deliberate sense of the community" that Madison sought, current polling practices measure opinions that are as unreflective, quickly formed, and easily changed as Hegel thought public opinion to be. Fishkin argues that his deliberative poll can have an advisory and educational function, but it could potentially restore the concern of the public for itself that was once so typical of the reading public. Fishkin's proposal also emphasizes how the process of deliberation might change public opinions rather than reflect the current set of beliefs and spontaneous sentiments. Such polling might even encourage candidates to engage in campaigns of a more deliberative character; campaigning on this model is directed not to *current* preferences but to a *future* reflective equilibrium among voters. This sort of procedure might also encourage representatives to act in a more deliberative way, voting for legislation which they believe their constituents would have agreed to had they also gone through the same deliberative process, or had they the same opportunities for informed and reasoned judgment. In any case, one of the merits of Fishkin's proposal is that it creates a new deliberative forum for articulating the public opinion of non-expert citizens, one that is broader and more public than the like-mindedness of most memberships in voluntary associations.

Refinements in institutional design may also promote more deliberation. I have discussed the most general requirement that there be multiple pathways and possibilities for public influence on formal processes and institutional actors. A single mechanism of deliberative input into institutions may make relations of power more rigid than ever and enable those who are more effective to use it even more opportunistically. On the one hand, the general structure of American dualist democracy and the separation of powers generally promote just such an idea of multiple and overlapping decision-making processes. On the other hand, the use of direct referenda (such as in California) has had mixed results in promoting deliberation and has the ambiguities of direct democracy. As has been shown in recent anti-tax, anti-gay, and anti-immigrant referenda in the western United States, such referenda are more often appeals to popular prejudice and political alienation than to community-wide deliberation. Because of the ease of proposing them, referenda are just as episodic and unreflective as current opinion polls.

Mechanisms for increasing public input are not enough to avoid breakdowns in well-functioning deliberative institutions. Any institution in which citizens deliberate relies not only on formal rules but also on informal norms of interaction. For example, Bessette identifies a series of informal norms that helped to promote deliberation in Congress, including the fostering of specialization and expertise in parties, deference to committees and their deliberative work, and constraints on publicity seeking in debates.[9] His analysis points to the breakdown of these informal means of promoting ongoing cooperation, rather than deficient formal rules or institutions, as having led to a precipitous decline in the deliberative quality of congressional debate. The constraints provided by informal norms were crucial to establishing the sorts of relations of trust that were necessary for voting down ill-conceived but potentially popular measures and for thinking in future-oriented ways. A deliberative body should at least increase the temporal horizons of deliberation and promote long-term, rational planning. Without it, a lack of constraints on opportunism in deliberation only penalizes those who seek to compromise and cooperate. Besides procedural opportunities, the incentives built into deliberative processes in representative institutions should be structured to promote, rather than disadvantage, those who are willing to give the public reasons of others their proper uptake and respect.

Despite its current limitations and fragmentation, the public sphere remains the source for any reforms and innovations in deliberative arrangements. Such reforms become radical only in periods when the problematic situations with which public deliberation begins concern the very nature of political institutions. In a well-functioning public sphere, the issues of the day are discussed from a variety of perspectives. Usually, such discussion and dialogue, however critical, is more mundane and concerns particular beliefs and practical goals. But in periods of great innovation and change, basic understandings and assumptions that underlie institutions are called into question. In well-ordered societies characterized by the rule of law, such periods of change will be marked by reflection on constitutional essentials, since the current understandings are no longer an adequate basis for planning and cooperation. Such changes begin as "legitimation crises" that can be resolved only through public deliberation on the basis of political life. Without this possibility of radical change built into constitutional democracy itself, it is difficult for democracies to maintain the dialectical interplay between emergent publics and institutions that is the key to their vitality. Such periodic renewals of popular sovereignty keep institutions from acquiring independent forms of power that merely organize public opinion from above. They may also challenge the assumptions that guide even the most participatory and local arrangements, the hidden anti-democratic biases and exclusions of the operative public culture that could emerge unchecked in direct democracy.

I began this book with Max Horkheimer's claim that a society is democratic only if it is guided by the ideal of rational agreement, that is, to the extent that it makes "all conditions controllable by human beings depend on real consensus." Many critics have claimed that the problems of complexity and pluralism cannot be solved democratically and that their consequences cannot be controlled by consensual means. The cumulative argument of this book is that such claims are false. Such conditions do not necessarily "overburden" institutions and the capacities of deliberating citizens, nor do they make the ideals of deliberative democracy obsolete. Rather, they show how important it is that the principles of democracy be applied across the board to all institutions. Certainly, many of the utopian hopes of radical democratic transformation have to be revised once the many dilemmas of pluralism and complexity are faced more squarely. These unresolved problems show the dependence of some participatory democratic theories on false anti-institutionalism as well as on excessive political will and hyper-rationality about political decision making. Without a doubt, the fall of bureaucratic socialist regimes in 1989 has been a sobering experience for proponents of thorough democratic reform. But there are other traditions and practices of radical democracy to draw upon in implementing the ideals of public deliberation. These historical failures and successes show that these ideals should now be located within modern institutions and their publics, rather than outside of them and opposed to them. Once we look to already-existing practices and their potential for deliberation, we can see that increasing the scope of democratic participation and equality in decision making is still an indispensable goal for pluralistic and complex societies.

When facing the current challenges of complexity, inequality, and pluralism, citizens do not encounter insuperable obstacles to deliberative democracy. Just the opposite is true: what is most significant in our historical period is the potential to expand the ways in which citizens cooperate in the public sphere. Cultural pluralism, social complexity, and growing inequalities represent the greatest challenges to democracy today, and they have brought about many popular anti-institutional and anti-democratic movements. These challenges can be met only by inventing new forums and reformed institutions in which citizens deliberate together and make public use of their reason in new ways. When understood pragmatically as the results of these historical experiences, democratic consensus, equality, and participation are not only the most appropriate norms for Critical Theory today; they are also achievable political goals to be realized in feasible practices of actual public deliberation.

Notes

Introduction

1. John Dewey, "The public and its problems," in *The Later Works*, volume 2 (University of Southern Illinois Press, 1988), p. 365..

2. See O'Nora O'Neill, *The Constructions of Reason* (Cambridge University Press, 1989)—especially the first two essays—for an account of Kant's version of publicity as unrestricted communication and of his self-reflective justification of reason publicly justifying itself.

3. Judith Shklar puts it this way: without considering the best available historical and social scientific accounts of such facts, a political theory "cannot expect to have anything significant to contribute to our political self-understanding," and "stands in acute danger of theorizing about nothing at all except their own uneasiness in a society they have made little effort to understand." See Shklar, *American Citizenship* (Harvard University Press, 1991), p. 9. Similarly, John Dewey pointed out "the immense gap between facts and doctrines" in social philosophy—see "The public and its problems," p. 238. On the conception of political possibility see Jon Elster, *Logic and Society* (Wiley, 1978), pp. 48–49.

4. For more on the connection between deliberation and democracy discussed in this section see William Rehg and James Bohman, "Discourse and democracy: The formal and informal bases of legitimacy," *Journal of Political Philosophy* 4 (1996): 79–99.

5. Perhaps the two main statements that guide the theory of deliberative democracy developed here are that of Jürgen Habermas (*Faktizität und Geltung: Beiträge zur Diskurstheorie des Rechts und des demokratishen Rechtsstaats* (Suhrkamp, 1992), especially chapters 7 and 8) and that of John Rawls (*Political Liberalism* (Columbia University Press, 1993), especially chapter 4). See also Joshua Cohen, "Deliberation and democratic legitimacy," in *The Good Polity*, ed. A. Hamlin and P. Pettit (Blackwell, 1989). For more specific institutional proposals see James Fishkin, *Democracy and Deliberation: New Directions for Democratic Reform* (Yale University Press, 1991); for a more historical approach and a case study see Joseph Bessette, *The Mild Voice of Reason: Deliberative*

Democracy and American National Government (University of Chicago Press, 1994) and many other works that I will cite throughout this book.

6. Rousseau's account of the "general will" in his *Contrat Social* is sometimes interpreted this way; for Habermas's critique see *FG*, pp. 130–134. For a historical overview of republicanism and its influence see Frank Michelman's foreword to a special issue on the 1985 Supreme Court term: "Traces of self-government," *Harvard Law Review* 100 (1986): 4–77.

7. For an accessible introduction that is quite critical of Rousseauian positions and to ones broadly similar to the one that I defend here see William Riker, *Liberalism Against Populism: A Confrontation Between the Theory of Democracy and the Theory of Social Choice* (Waveland, 1982).

8. On this contractualist and counterfactual idea of democratic consensus see T. M. Scanlon, "Contractualism and utilitarianism," in *Utilitarianism and Beyond*, ed. A. Sen and B. Williams (Cambridge University Press, 1982).

9. See Cohen, "Deliberation and democratic legitimacy," pp. 24–25.

10. For the deliberative theory of representation in the U.S. Constitution see Bessette, *The Mild Voice of Reason*, chapter 2.

11. See Joshua Cohen, "An epistemic conception of democracy," *Ethics* 97 (1986): 26–38; also see David Estlund, "Making truth safe for democracy," in *The Idea of Democracy*, ed. D. Copp et al. (Cambridge University Press, 1993).

12. See Cohen, "An epistemic conception," p. 32.

13. This is also a definition of autonomy as the public exercise of all such self-governing capacities. See Joshua Cohen and Joel Rogers, *On Democracy* (Penguin, 1983), p. 151ff. Because public deliberation is an activity, I use a capacity-based account of various basic normative terms, including equality and autonomy, throughout this book.

14. For a sketch of these procedural idealizations see Robert Alexy, "A theory of practical discourse," in *The Communicative Ethics Controversy*, ed. S. Benhabib and F. Dallmayr (MIT Press, 1990).

15. Rawls, *Political Liberalism*, p. 137.

16. Danilo Zolo, *Democracy and Complexity* (Pennsylvania State University Press, 1992), p. 77ff and p. 120ff; see also Norberto Bobbio, *The Future of Democracy* (Polity, 1987), p. 25ff. Both argue that modern democratic institutions gradually sever the connection between representation and democracy as they adapt to the conditions of large, functionally differentiated, industrialized societies. See also Niklas Luhmann, *Legitimation durch Verfahren* (Suhrkamp, 1969).

17. As Rawls puts it in *Political Liberalism* (pp. 65–66): "We should have to see whether acceptable changes in the principles of justice would achieve stability." In his exchange with Rawls, Habermas appears to reject the entire political turn in Rawls's conception of justice. The emphasis on practicality, Habermas thinks, undermines the epistemic sense of agreement essential to the theory: "Overlapping consensus would

then be merely an index of the utility, and no longer a confirmation of the correctness of the theory; it would no longer be of interest from the point of view of acceptability, and hence of validity, but only from that of acceptance, that is, of securing social stability." See Habermas, "Reconciliation through the public use of reason," *Journal of Philosophy* 72 (1995), pp. 121–122. However, Habermas also insists that his theory is concerned with institutionalization and argues that ideal procedural accounts of democratic justification are "sociologically naive." Thus, the issue here is not whether an adequate political theory must have a practical and empirical component but whether it should distinguish more sharply between de facto acceptance and rational acceptability. Rawls is unable to make this distinction central because of the particularly functionalist sociological perspective built into his practical theory, not because he sees usefulness as a criterion of theoretical adequacy and normative justification.

18. This is Marx's characterization of the Paris Commune. See Marx, "The civil war in France," in *Selected Writings*, ed. D. McLellan (Oxford University Press, 1977), p. 539ff. This form of democracy was achieved by the elimination of the "systematic and hierarchical division of labor" (p. 539) and by "the reabsorption of the state power into society" (p. 555).

19. Marx, "On the Jewish question," in *Selected Writings*, p. 522ff. Similarly, Marx argues in the "Introduction to a critique of Hegel's *Philosophy of Right*" that the bourgeoisie "frees the whole of society only under the presupposition that the whole of society is in the same situation as this class, that it possesses, or can easily acquire, for example, money and education" (1975, p. 71).

20. Rawls, "The idea of an overlapping consensus," *Oxford Journal of Legal Studies* 7 (1987): 2–3.

21. See James Bohman, *New Philosophy of Social Science: Problems of Indeterminacy* (MIT Press, 1991), p. 194ff.

22. Max Horkheimer, "Traditional and critical theory," in his *Critical Theory* (Seabury, 1982), p. 244.

23. Since there are "democratic" emotions, democratic persuasion need not appeal only to reason and constraint: "If fear and destructiveness are the major emotional sources of fascism, eros belongs mainly to democracy." (See T. Adorno et al., *The Authoritarian Personality* (Norton, 1953), p. 480). See also Herbert Marcuse, *Eros and Civilization* (Beacon, 1966), for a fully developed depth-psychological account of liberation.

24. For Horkheimer, the reduction of democracy to majority rule shows the "illusory triumph of democratic progress that consumes the intellectual substance upon which it has lived" (*Eclipse of Reason* (Seabury, 1987), p. 21). When reduced to majority rule (which is the mere quantitative aggregation of subjective preferences), democracy is so standardless that it easily dissolves into dictatorship when it fits subjective interests of the masses and blind functional forces. Habermas's version of this argument in *Legitimation Crisis* is more dialectical and Weberian; he argues that only a notion of practical reason richer than formal or instrumental reason can make sense of the cognitive character of democracy. He is opposing two "positivist" interpretations of law and democracy: mere decisionism and simple proceduralism.

25. Habermas, *Legitimation Crisis*, p. 36.

26. Habermas, "Legitimation problems of the modern state," *Communication and the Evolution of Society* (Beacon, 1979), p. 186.

27. Habermas, *Faktitizät und Geltung*, p. 370 (hereafter cited as *FG*).

28. *FG*, p. 63ff. I am arguing that the Kantian side of Habermas's philosophical project, so prominent in his moral theory, is far in the background here. Indeed, Habermas considers Kant a liberal who endorsed "the improbable idea that society as a whole can be governed as a free association of originally free and equal citizens" (ibid.). Rather than try to figure out how to put this moral idea into practice in new arrangements, Habermas now asks Hegel's question: where is the place for free agreement and deliberation among citizens in the complex society that has developed historically, with its large institutions and its massive accumulation of social power?

29. *FG*, pp. 395–398. In this section of chapter 7 of *FG* Habermas adopts a thought experiment proposed by Bernhard Peters in *Integration moderner Gesellschaften* (Suhrkamp, 1993), p. 230ff. The thought experiment asks us to imagine a society that was entirely organized democratically; Peters calls it "pure communicative association," similar in many respects to Marx's image of the Paris Commune. Below I distinguish two different problems which Habermas and Peters confuse: hyperrationality and hypercomplexity. For an argument that participatory democracy is not necessarily less adequate in situations of social complexity see John Dryzek, *Discursive Democracy* (Cambridge University Press, 1991), chapter 3.

30. *FG*, p. 397.

31. *FG*, chapter 7; see especially section III for the discussion of internal-communicative and external-social forms of complexity.

32. Rawls argues that the sanctions of state power are necessary for social unity and stability so long as there is sufficient pluralism. See "The idea of an overlapping consensus," p. 22; see also "The fact of oppression," in *Political Liberalism*, p. 37. Similarly, Habermas argues that "coercive law" is necessary for the social integration of complex societies through political institutions; see *FG*, chapter 2.

33. Rawls, *Political Liberalism*, p. 38. In this section of *Political Liberalism* Rawls has pared down the relevant facts and conditions of modern society to four, including the three social facts mentioned above and the presence of certain intuitive ideas of fairness in the general public culture. In "The idea of an overlapping consensus" Rawls lists seven facts, five of which concern cultural pluralism.

34. Rawls, "The idea of an overlapping consensus," p. 1. Richard Rorty argues that Rawls turns away from stronger normative justification for liberalism and adopts a more pragmatic one: "Rawls, following Dewey, shows us how liberal democracy can get along without philosophical presuppositions." See "The priority of democracy to philosophy," in *Philosophical Papers*, volume I (Cambridge University Press, 1991), p. 179. I do not see this pragmatic turn as "thoroughly historicist and anti-universalist" in Rorty's skeptical sense. Quite to the contrary: there is no inherent anti-universalism in such pragmatism and pluralism. Rather more like Critical Theory and Dewey before him, Rawls teaches us that referring to empirical facts and considering the addressees of a theory are both important parts of the justification of a political theory.

35. For proposals on ways to increase the scope of public participation in decision making see Fishkin, *Democracy and Deliberation* and Dryzek, *Discursive Democracy*; for the

relation participation to representation see Cass Sunstein, "Interest groups in American public law," *Stanford Law Review* 38 (1985): 29–87; for an account of participatory democracy that draws on examples of town meetings and workplace democracy see Jane Mansbridge, *Beyond Adversary Democracy* (University of Chicago Press, 1980).

36. For the best and most complete versions of such lists see Robert Dahl, *Democracy and Its Critics* (Yale University Press, 1989), p. 307ff; see also Cohen, "Deliberation and democratic legitimacy," p. 17ff. Fishkin develops a more parsimonious list in *Democracy and Deliberation*, chapter 1. For a long discussion of such necessary but not sufficient conditions for fair deliberation see Habermas, *FG*, chapter 7.

37. See Jean-François Lyotard's arguments against Habermas in *The Postmodern Condition* (University of Minnesota Press, 1984).

38. For Sen's fullest statement of the central role of capabilities in an adequate conception of equality, see chapters 1–5 of *Inequality Reconsidered* (Harvard University Press, 1992).

39. Bruce Ackerman, *We the People*, volume 1 (Harvard University Press, 1991), p. 131ff.

Chapter 1

1. T. M. Scanlon, "Contractualism and utilitarianism," in *Utilitarianism and Beyond*, ed. A. Sen and B. Williams (Cambridge University Press, 1982), p. 110. Habermas's formulation is from his *Legitimation Crisis* (Beacon, 1979), part III. For reasons that I elaborate below, I weaken the strict requirement of unanimity implicit in Scanlon's and Habermas's principles of legitimacy. I take seriously here Habermas's repeated claims that an adequate democratic theory would have to account for how norms of publicity structure *actual* deliberation; I also take seriously his claims that only "participants themselves" can ultimately determine what is fair and just. Both of these claims, however, can be developed only through a more adequate account of the conditions of success for actual public deliberation. For a good summary of the objections that any theory of deliberative democracy must answer see Jon Elster, "The market and the forum," in *Foundations of Social Choice Theory*, ed. J. Elster and A. Hylland (Cambridge University Press, 1984).

2. Such hypothetical agreement as a form of justification is developed by Scanlon in "Contractualism and utilitarianism." For an elaboration of this form of justification in relation to making one's actions "answerable" to others see Samuel Freeman, "Contractualism, moral motivation, and practical reason," *Journal of Philosophy* 88 (1991): 281–303.

3. See William Gamson, *Talking Politics* (Cambridge University Press, 1993), especially p. 19ff. Gamson recorded peer-group conversations about political issues in which the participants were aware that their statements were directed to a "gallery." The also knew that "remarks people would make in a strictly private discourse violate norms of public discourse" (p. 19). This awareness of the differences between the audiences of public and private discourse was particularly evident in topics where race played a role, such as affirmative action. Gamson reports that the awareness of the gallery produced higher degrees of solidarity among blacks, while it made whites

clarify their remarks when they thought their opinions might be perceived by others as prejudiced.

4. On p. 285 of his *Political Liberalism* (Columbia University Press, 1993) Rawls defends his constructivist approach to ideal theory in this way: "In the absence of such an ideal form for the background institutions, there is no rational basis for continually adjusting the social process so as to preserve background justice, nor for eliminating existing injustice." An ideal theory is, on my view, useful for the critique of existing institutions, rather than for the construction of a theory of democratic deliberation.

5. For a discussion of Madison's desire to limit the scope of deliberative arrangements see James Fishkin, *Democracy and Deliberation* (Yale University Press, 1991), pp. 14–17. On problems of stability first discussed by Arrow see William Riker, *Liberalism Against Populism* (Waveland, 1982). See also Joshua Cohen's reply to these criticisms: "An epistemic conception of democracy," *Ethics* 97 (1986): 26–38.

6. For an excellent overview of the history of these arguments see Carole Pateman, *Participation and Democratic Theory* (Cambridge University Press, 1970). Pateman defends the ideal of a "participatory society," or democratic participation as a decision-making mechanism in all social spheres.

7. Many democratic theorists defend the transformative power of deliberation. See Jane Mansbridge, *Beyond Adversary Democracy* (Basic Books, 1980); Seyla Benhabib, *Critique, Norm and Utopia* (Columbia University Press, 1987), chapter 8; Benjamin Barber, *Strong Democracy* (University of California Press, 1984); Mark Warren, "Democratic theory and self-transformation," *American Political Science Review* 86 (1992): 8–23; Cass Sunstein, "Beyond the republican revival," *Yale Law Journal* 97 (1988): 1539–1590. For arguments for the need for civic consciousness to hold together diverse associations see Joshua Cohen and Joel Rogers, "Secondary associations and democratic governance," *Politics and Society* 20 (1992): 420–421. For insightful criticism of such usually unsupported empirical claims see Jack Knight and James Johnson, "Aggregation and deliberation: On the possibility of democratic legitimacy," *Political Theory* 22 (1994): 277–294. Against Knight and Johnson, I argue that such transformation is less concerned with individuals' beliefs and desires than with changing the background beliefs and desires of public culture.

8. For the contrary view see chapter 8 of Jean Cohen and Andrew Arato, *Civil Society and Political Theory* (MIT Press, 1992).

9. On the limits of pure proceduralism see John Rawls, *A Theory of Justice* (Harvard University Press, 1971), p. 85ff. For cases in which such "pure" procedures are fair and binding see Jon Elster, *Solomonic Judgments* (Cambridge University Press, 1989). But Elster discusses only cases in which deliberation does not improve the outcome or decision; often this is true simply because of the time it takes to arrive at an informed judgment, as in child-custody cases.

10. For these lists see Joshua Cohen, "Deliberation and democratic legitimacy," in *The Good Polity*, ed. A. Hamlin and P. Pettit (Blackwell, 1989), p. 22ff; Robert Dahl, *A Preface to Economic Democracy* (Oxford University Press, 1985), p. 59ff; Dahl, *Democracy and Its Critics* (Yale University Press, 1989), p. 112ff. Disagreements between the two lists center on the issue of the equal consideration of interests, but these do not concern me here. See Cohen's review of Dahl's *Democracy and Its Critics*: *Journal of Politics* 53 (1991): 221–225. Cohen's and Dahl's lists are remarkably consistent with each other.

11. Dahl, *Preface to Economic Democracy*, pp. 59–60.

12. Besides Mansbridge, Fishkin, Barber, and Dryzek's defenses of deliberative democracy, see Bernard Manin, "On legitimacy and political deliberation," *Political Theory* 15 (1987): 338–368. In particular, Manin gives good arguments why deliberative theories do not depend on unanimity, even as a political ideal. See also Cass Sunstein's criticism of preference based theories of democracy, "Democracy and shifting preferences," in *The Idea of Democracy*, ed. D. Copp et al. (Cambridge University Press, 1993). For an account of deliberative democracy at work in the U.S. Congress see Joseph Bessette, *The Mild Voice of Reason: Deliberative Democracy and American Government* (University of Chicago Press, 1994).

13. Kant, *Critique of Pure Reason*, A487 and B766.

14. See chapter 1 of Fishkin's *Democracy and Deliberation* for a similar set of conditions. My conditions here are more minimal than his, since I reject his "insulation condition" as he has formulated it; this condition has more to do with the violations of equality that I will treat in chapter 3. For a more elaborate attempt to specify this type of condition see Robert Dahl, *Democracy and Its Critics* (Yale University Press, 1989), p. 307ff.

15. Fishkin, *Democracy and Deliberation*, p. 32. Fishkin calls this the "insulation condition." However, some civic republicans, including Fishkin, think that this insulation is also meant to exclude all appeals to self-interest and other self-regarding motives; however, the dialogical model of public deliberation does not require such exclusion. Indeed, the very stuff of deliberation are the needs and interests of citizens, some of which can be made into publicly convincing reasons. Not all interests need to be generalizable to be the appropriate topic of public deliberation. In the next chapter, I will criticize exclusions of liberal notions of neutrality for similar grounds, in that they exclude the very issue of conflict in pluralist societies.

16. Nancy Fraser distinguishes between "weak" and "strong" publics with regard to their decision-making power; weak publics are informal and oriented to opinion formation, while strong publics are in formal institutions with decision-making powers. My distinction has to do with the strength of the norm of publicity; even an informal public can have strong publicity. However, informal publics do not require that reasons necessarily be acceptable to all, but only publicly intelligible. See Nancy Fraser, "Rethinking the public sphere," in *Habermas and the Public Sphere*. ed. C. Calhoun (MIT Press, 1992), p. 134ff.

17. On p. 213 of *Political Liberalism* Rawls puts it this way: "Public reason is public in three ways: as the reason of citizens as such, it is the reason of the public; its subject is the good of the public and matters of fundamental justice; and its nature and content is public, given by the ideals and principles expressed by society's conception of political justice, and conducted open to view on that basis." Rawls expresses a broader, more capacity oriented view on the previous page that accords better with the sense of deliberation here: public deliberation is "a way of formulating the plans (of a political association), of putting its ends in order and making its decisions accordingly. The way a political society does this is its reason. . . ." (ibid., p. 212)

18. "What is enlightenment?" in *Kant's Political Writings* (Cambridge University Press, 1970), p. 38ff.

19. For a full development of this interpretation of Kantian publicity and its foundational role in the critique of reason see O'Nora O'Neill, *The Constructions of Reason* (Cambridge University Press, 1989), pp. 42–48.

20. O'Neill, *Constructions of Reason*, p. 34.

21. Kant's maxims are found in section 49 of the *Critique of Judgment*. For a clear discussion of the political implications of Kant's notion of universal judgment see Hannah Arendt, *Lectures on Kant's Political Philosophy* (University of Chicago Press, 1982). See also the useful discussion of the themes of public communication and the central role of publicity throughout Kant's works in Hans Saner, *Kant's Political Thought* (University of Chicago Press, 1983).

22. Kant, *Critique of Judgment*, section 49. On p. 136ff. of *Situating the Self* (Routledge, 1992) Seyla Benhabib argues that the capacity for enlarged thought is central to the intersubjective interpretation of Kant; but the maxim of seeing things "from the standpoint of everyone else" is not necessarily intersubjective. Moreover, it is not an account of judgment (but the basis for certain judgments in common sense) and hence only indirectly related to deliberation.

23. For Kant, publicity is determined by the exercise of reflective judgment and not by discourse; O'Neill's appeal to the role of communicability does not resolve this problem. Communication with others only serves to "enlarge" the capacity for judgment.

24. Habermas, *Theory of Communicative Action*, volume I, p. 10. See also p. 125 of volume II for the use of the term "problematic situations."

25. Habermas, *Theory of Communicative Action*, volume II, p. 125.

26. Jürgen Habermas, *Faktizität und Geltung* (Suhrkamp, 1992) (hereafter *FG*), p. 435ff.

27. Jürgen Habermas, *The Structural Transformation of the Public Sphere* (MIT Press, 1989), chapter 2.

28. These version of formalism include Rawls's "veil of ignorance" and Bruce Ackerman's notion of a "constrained conversation" governed by a strict neutrality principle. For Ackerman's discussion see his *Social Justice and the Liberal State* (Yale University Press, 1980), pp. 11–12 and 44–45. For good criticisms of formalism, especially of Rawls's version, see Charles Beitz, *Political Equality* (Princeton University Press, 1989), p. 104ff. Scanlon's contribution to this debate is that contractarian justification (or appeals to the "informed and unforced agreement of all") works even when formal constraints such as these are stripped away.

29. T. M. Scanlon, "Preference and urgency," *Journal of Philosophy* 72 (1975): 659–660.

30. In *Political Liberalism*, Rawls considers the Supreme Court to be the "exemplar of public reason" in our society (p. 231ff). For all his criticisms of Ronald Dworkin's emphasis on the judge, Habermas does not offer a detailed account of legislative deliberation in *FG*. The focus on law as an institution misleads both Rawls and Habermas when they theorize about public reason. For a close study of actual deliberation in the U.S. Congress see Bessette, *The Mild Voice of Reason*.

31. *FG*, p. 411.

32. In a reply to critical discussions of his recent work on law and democracy see Habermas's reply to contributions to the symposium on his work in *Cardozo Law Review* 17.

33. See chapter 1 of Martha Minnow's *Making All the Difference* (Cornell University Press, 1990).

34. See Jon Elster, *Ulysses and the Sirens* (Cambridge University Press, 1984), p. 36ff. Besides Elster's analysis of such examples see Thomas Schelling, "Ethics, law and the exercise of self-command," in *Liberty, Equality and Law: Selected Tanner Lectures* (Cambridge University Press, 1987), pp. 163–200.

35. Elster, *Ulysses and the Sirens*, p. 37.

36. Samuel Freeman,"Reason and agreement in social contract views," *Philosophy and Public Affairs* 19 (1990): 122–157; see especially 143ff.

37. Elster, "The market and the forum," p. 113. However, the norm of rationality is often the subject of public debate and hence cannot be its presupposition.

38. Freeman, "Reason and agreement in social contract views," p. 143.

39. Ibid., p. 145.

40. On the idea of a conception-dependent desire as one dependent on a comprehensive moral doctrine see Rawls, *Political Liberalism*, p. 81ff. Rawls characterizes "the desire to have a shared political life on terms acceptable to others as free and equal" as conception-dependent (p. 98).

41. This is one of the main results of the study of the emergence of cooperative behavior. All that actors can do to bring about cooperative behavior in others is to make it clear that they will act consistently in following norms or rules. It is my commitment to a certain action, and not my holding others to their commitments, that induces cooperation. See Robert Axelrod, *The Evolution of Cooperation* (Basic Books, 1984); Jack Knight, *Institutions and Social Conflict* (Cambridge University Press, 1992), pp. 130–131. Examples similar to Ulysses and the sirens show the problem with the enforcement model: Ulysses stops up the ears of his men so that they will not listen to his pleas to be freed. While all prefer to be safe, these men are not enforcers, but mute obstacles to Ulysses' changed preferences. My problem with the model as a whole is that it is simply not applicable to all political situations that emerge in constitutional democracies, as I show below. Knight gives a similar analysis: "Although we can find many such examples in isolated bargaining situations, it is difficult to find similar, more systematic technologies in those interactions likely to produce social institutions. Precommitments require either a third party with whom a side agreement can be arranged or some other mechanism that can penalize the failure to follow through with one's commitment." (p. 131)

42. Bruce Ackerman, *We the People*, volume I (Harvard University Press, 1991), p. 44.

43. Ibid., p. 59.

44. In *Intentions, Plans and Practical Reason* (Harvard University Press, 1987), Michael Bratman gives good reasons to think that precommitments are rare and overdramatize the constraining effects of complex planning, even in individual cases. Dramatic examples of precommitments are quite fascinating, he argues, "but we get a distorted view of future-directed intention if we take them as paradigmatic of intention" (p. 12). They give us a similarly distorted view of law, so much so that such models make quite mysterious how constitutions are supposed to coordinate ongoing planning or regulate deliberation more generally.

45. Beitz, *Political Equality*, pp. 22–23.

46. John Dryzek develops the notion of "discursive designs" for institutions which promote deliberation within them; see his *Discursive Democracy* (Cambridge University Press, 1990), especially chapter 2.

47. Ackerman, *We the People*, volume I, p. 47.

48. Ibid., p. 115. Ackerman sees the changes that the New Deal brought to the constitution as a struggle over how to apply the egalitarianism of the Thirteenth and Fourteenth Amendments. Earlier, judges resisted attempts to redefine and to limit property rights and kept to their narrow applications. The particular lived experiences behind these amendments allowed these judges to interpret property rights as precommited: the founding of the Republic "as a source of general principles that should be followed generally except in the special contexts regulated by Reconstruction" (p. 115). From these debates, we see that struggles for inclusion and egalitarian corrective justice are not always against universal principles but instead their particularly narrow interpretation.

49. Jürgen Habermas, *Theory of Communicative Action*, volume I (Beacon, 1984), p. 9.

50. Habermas characterizes political discourse as complex in the same way. He argued further that this discursive complexity is a decisive objection to radical democracy. My point here is that this line of argument follows from an overly impartialist view of publicity. See chapter 3 of *FG*; see also "On the pragmatic, the ethical and the moral employments of practical reason," in Habermas's *Justification and Application: Remarks on Discourse Ethics* (MIT Press, 1993).

51. As I indicated above, I borrow from ethnomethodology its notion of "accountability" of knowledgeable social actors. For a longer discussion of the problem of the reflexivity of social action in social theory, and of how knowledgeable social agency is still possible even in complex societies see my *New Philosophy of Social Science: Problems of Indeterminacy* (MIT Press/Polity Press, 1991), especially chapter 2.

52. For a discussion see O'Nora O'Neill, "The public use of reason," in *Constructions of Reason*, p. 49ff. As Habermas puts it in *The Structural Transformation of the Public Sphere* (p. 51), members of the public sphere are reflexive: they "read and discuss about themselves" and are concerned about maintaining their own public character. This self-reference has especially motivated reactions to state censorship as part of the process of self-definition of the public sphere.

53. See Raimo Tuolema and Kaarlo Miller, "We intentions," *Philosophical Studies* 53 (1988): 367–389.

54. John Searle, "Collective intentions and actions," in *Intentions in Communication*, ed. P. Cohen, J. Morgan, and M. Pollack (MIT Press, 1990).

55. *FG*, p. 210ff.

56. Searle, "Collective intentions and actions," p. 414.

57. Beitz (*Political Equality*, p. 100) considers this the core of his "complex proceduralism."

58. This conception of cooperation resembles Bruce Ackerman's idea that citizens ought to be guided by the Supreme Pragmatic Imperative to continue dialogue about the good. I shall argue that such a dialogue, if deliberative, can solve the very problems of conflict and disagreement which Ackerman suggests that citizens ought not discuss for the sake of coexistence. See Bruce Ackerman, "Why dialogue?" *Journal of Philosophy* 86 (1989): 5–22. For a criticism of this view from the point of view of a discursive conception of the public sphere see Benhabib, *Situating the Self*, p. 96.

59. For a systematic sketch of these procedural idealizations and rules see Robert Alexy, "A theory of practical discourse," in *The Communicative Ethics Controversy*, ed. S. Benhabib and F. Dallmayr (MIT Press, 1990). Alexy's basic rules include sincerity and consistency, as well as prior agreement on meanings. Pragmatic rules of justification are for Alexy similarly based on unanimity; they all begin with the locution "everyone must accept that. . . ." Apart from the basic rules, which should be formulated as maxims rather than presuppositions, public deliberation requires only norms that can be reflexively employed in public deliberation itself.

60. Hans-Georg Gadamer, *Truth and Method* (Crossroads, 1989), pp. 199–201.

61. Hence, my use of Austin's term 'uptake' includes both perlocutionary and illocutionary acts; some perlocutionary effects, such as achieving perspective taking among those resistant to it, may promote deliberation. The means available to a speaker to promote deliberation cuts across this broad distinction of speech act types, so I use Austin's more general term, "uptake." For the debates on this point see *Essays on J. L. Austin*, ed. I. Berlin (Oxford University Press, 1973).

62. See Knight, *Institutions and Social Conflict*, chapter 3.

63. John Rawls, "Kantian constructivism in moral theory," *Journal of Philosophy* 77 (1980), p. 518.

64. See Fraser, "Rethinking the public sphere. " See also Iris Young's criticism of Habermas in *Justice and the Politics of Difference* (Princeton University Press, 1990), chapter 4.

65. Klaus Günther, *The Sense of Appropriateness* (SUNY Press, 1993), pp. 15–40.

66. Henry Richardson, "Specifying norms as a way to resolve concrete ethical problems," *Philosophy and Public Affairs* 19 (1990): 284. For a fuller treatment see his *Practical Reasoning About Final Ends* (Cambridge University Press, 1994).

67. In true Hegelian fashion, Charles Taylor sees all conflicts of values as resolved in this way. See, e.g., his *Sources of the Self* (Harvard University Press, 1989), p. 91ff.

68. John Dewey, *Human Nature and Conduct* (Holt, 1922), p. 194. For a similar analysis see James Wallace, *Moral Relevance and Moral Conflict* (Cornell University Press, 1988), p. 86.

69. Michael Walzer, "Liberalism and the art of separation," *Political Theory* 12 (1984): 315–330.

70. For a study of problems in conflict resolution among adolescents who have not acquired this ability see Robert Selmen, *The Growth of Interpersonal Understanding* (Humanities Press, 1985).

71. Alfred Schutz, "The well-informed citizen," in his *Collected Papers*, volume II (Nijhoff, 1964), p. 120.

72. Jon Elster, *Sour Grapes* (Cambridge University Press, 1984), pp. 37–47.

73. This future orientation is particularly apparent in Kant's political essays, such as "What is enlightenment?" and "What is orientation in thinking?" (both in *Kant's Political Writings*). The importance of the future supports a planning theory of public deliberation.

74. See Michael Bratman's analysis of planning as a coherence constraint on future action in *Intentions, Plans and Practical Reasoning*, especially chapter 3.

75. Martha Minnow, *Making All the Difference* (Cornell University Press, 1990), part I. Minnow's positive construal of the role of "rights talk" gives them a dialogical characterization; as such, they are not removed from the public agenda. Quite the contrary, such talk places these issues in the center of many deliberative situations.

76. Minnow, *Making All the Difference*, p. 74.

77. Here Minnow's ideal solutions to difference dilemmas are often overly optimistic and costly. For example, her solution to the problem of bilingual education is to have all students learn one another's languages; this is clearly a solution that would be limited to two-language rather than the multilingual cases that are increasingly common. See Minnow, *Making All the Difference*, p. 31ff. Such idealized solutions ignore the fundamentally pragmatic role of deliberation in resolving problematic situations and restoring cooperation. I will treat issues of cultural differences more fully in the next chapter and develop workable moral compromises as solutions to such conflicts.

78. In chapter 9 of *FG* Habermas argues that debates over welfare rights show the emergence of a "new proceduralist paradigm" of legal interpretation. This may be true in the sense that they have produced a new constitutional regime in Ackerman's sense. These discussions are not some new form of deliberation but instead the ongoing task of creating new institutional frameworks in response to historical experience. It is misleading to call a self-awareness of this historical process proceduralist.

Chapter 2

1. Rousseau, *The Social Contract* (Basic Books, 1967), chapter 9, especially p. 55ff.

2. John Rawls, *Political Liberalism* (Columbia University Press, 1993), p. xxvi.

3. For a rights-based treatment of these sorts of conflicts, particularly concerning minority cultures, see Will Kymlicka, *Liberalism, Community and Culture* (Oxford University Press, 1989). My concern here is with the prior political problem of the public process necessary for identifying such conflicts as rights-based and for determining which rights are involved.

4. John Rawls, "Justice as fairness: Political not metaphysical," *Philosophy and Public Affairs* 14 (1985): 225. See also his more recent discussion of the concept of "reasonable pluralism" and overlapping consensus in *Political Liberalism*, lecture IV. The distinction between "simple" and "reasonable" pluralism, which Rawls borrows from Joshua Cohen, does not solve the problem of conflicts; it merely specifies which conflicts may not be resolvable on the basis of *existing* public justification and which ones may involve legal coercion.

5. Rawls argues for the claim that a "political conception" of justice is central to liberalism in "The idea of an overlapping consensus" (*Oxford Legal Studies* 7 (1987): 1–25) and in *Political Liberalism* (p. 150ff.). For Rawls's response to arguments against overlapping consensus as political in "the wrong way," see the last sections of *Political Liberalism*; see also "The domain of the political and overlapping consensus" (*New York University Law Review* 64 (1989): 233–255). I want to argue, against Rawls, that the problems of political disagreement are not just "rooted in the difficulties of exercising our reason under normal conditions" ("Domain of the political," p. 239). I construct different dilemmas of political reason to show specific conditions of public judgment and the political uses of reason. Properly construed, explanations of public irrationality do not necessarily impugn the reasonableness of individuals who disagree with the shared consensus, as Rawls claims in his discussion of "burdens of judgment" in *Political Liberalism* (pp. 54–66). They are at a different level.

6. Steven Holmes, "Gag rules, or the politics of omission," in *Constitutionalism and Democracy*, ed. J. Elster and R. Slagstad (Cambridge University Press, 1988).

7. Holmes (ibid., p. 56) admits that gag rules make democracies more rather than less imperfect, lack neutrality, and tend to exacerbate certain conflicts. None of the real historical cases that he mentions resolve these problems and ambiguities, including debates about slavery and abortion. Constitutions are indeed "enabling" devices and rules for democracies, but not because they really remove things from the public agenda. Rather than removing rights from discussion, the existence of courts, legislatures and other deliberating bodies changes the nature of the debate about them.

8. As do Jon Elster (*Ulysses and the Sirens* (Cambridge University Press, 1979)) and Samuel Freeman ("Reason and agreement in social contract views," *Philosophy and Public Affairs* 19 (1990): 122–157). In chapter 1 I argued that it is a mistake to see the limits of public reason in this way. More generally it is a mistake to see the rationality of future actions in terms of such dramatic examples; they ignore the simpler ways in which present intentions bind future actions in planning and deliberation. For a criticism of precommitment models as uncharacteristic of future-oriented action see Michael Bratman, *Intention, Plans and Practical Reason* (Harvard University Press, 1987), p. 12.

9. For this difference with Rawls see pp. 118–119 of Habermas's "Reconciliation through the public use of reason" (*Journal of Philosophy* 52 (1995)). For a full comparison of the conceptions of Kantian practical reason in Rawls and Habermas see Kenneth Baynes, *The Normative Grounds of Social Criticism* (SUNY Press, 1992).

Habermas's recent writings on problems of pluralism include the essays in *Justification and Application* (MIT Press, 1993) and "Struggles for recognition in constitutional states" (*European Journal of Philosophy* 1 (1993): 128–155).

10. For a discussion of the role of liberal constitutional principles in these debates generally and the specific role of the *Brown* decision for the liberal Canadian "Just Society" policy of the late 1960s to dismantle the reservation system, see Will Kymlicka, *Liberalism, Community and Culture* (Oxford University Press 1989), pp. 140–150. This policy recommended "the end of special constitutional status of Indians" (p. 142) and their integration into Canadian society. Integration is indeed often publicly desirable for citizenship, but not on the dominant groups cultural terms.

11. Kymlicka, *Liberalism, Community and Culture*, p. 136. It is important, too, that Native Americans retain full political rights in the larger political community.

12. For essays on the place of animal suffering in ritual and experimentation from different religious and cultural perspectives, see *Animal Sacrifices: Religious Perspectives on the Use of Animals in Science*, ed. T. Reagan (Temple University Press, 1986).

13. Christian Scientists have succeeded in most states to exempt themselves from legislation that would govern their practices of healing. The problem is that these compromises rely on rights of autonomous, adult patients to refuse treatment. For a discussion of the problem of children in these cases see Larry May, Challenging Medical Authority: The Christian Science Refusal Cases, Hastings Center Report 23, 1995. May proposes a compromise at the end of his essay that he believes should be acceptable to both doctors and Christian Scientists; the problem is that the compromise, involving diagnostic tools, does not yet recognize the depth of the conflict and the intertwining of moral and epistemic concerns within each group. But his proposal of construing the conflict as one concerning legitimate authority is a promising one for reaching a compromise.

14. Rawls, *Political Liberalism*, p. 220.

15. Ibid.

16. See Derek Parfit, *Reasons and Persons* (Oxford University Press, 1984), part I. My notion of liberal and communitarian dilemmas is inspired by Parfit's treatment of prudence, morality, and prisoner's dilemmas. I suggest that Parfit's account of prisoner's dilemmas has interesting implications for diverse and complex polities which he never directly explores.

17. Rawls, *Political Liberalism*, p. 243, n. 32. It is interesting that his compelling political arguments for a woman's right to choose an abortion appeals to the accepted superiority of "political values" over other values (and not the burdens of judgment). This appeal to the "political conception of justice" reduces it to a value commitment. It also seems to be unnecessary for the political liberal to rank political values above all others; it is enough that they are at least equal to other highest ranked values. Of course, in this case, they don't solve conflicts with other such values.

18. Rawls, *Political Liberalism*, p. 217.

19. Thomas Nagel, *Equality and Partiality* (Oxford University Press, 1991), p. 65.

20. Feminist critics of Habermas, such as Seyla Benhabib and Iris Marion Young, criticize notions of the generalized other and impartiality, respectively. See Young, "Impartiality and the civic public," and Benhabib, "The generalized and the concrete other," both in *Feminism as Critique*, ed. S. Benhabib and D. Cornell (University of Minnesota Press, 1987). Both of their arguments go beyond the less interesting claims that publicity or justice is simply one value among others, or that it is merely a value for a particular group. It is not clear how these criticisms avoid a radical form of the liberal dilemma, as smaller and smaller groups tend to construct more and more narrow identities. So long as people form their reasons publicly and make decisions in common, then they will have to adopt some public standpoint from which the reasons and interpretations given by others are intelligible. For a defense of the idea of a plurality of publics and the implications of conflicts in the interpretation of needs see Nancy Fraser, "Rethinking the public sphere," in *Habermas and the Public Sphere*, ed. C. Calhoun (MIT Press, 1992). The plurality of publics is, however, not sufficient for what I am calling "plural public reason," especially if each of them has a single public point of view. In democracies, as Fraser admits, there must be some institutions in which these diverse publics finally deliberate together. Only in such a diverse "civic" public sphere is plural public reason exercised.

21. Habermas already faces this problem in *Strukturwandel der Öffentlichkeit* (Opplanen, 1961) [*The Structural Transformation of the Public Sphere* (MIT Press, 1989)], in his discussion of radical pluralists like Mill and de Tocqueville. But he dismisses their objections to public reason as the result of "perspectivist epistemologies" (pp. 129–140). I am arguing that he should accept this criticism and make public reason plural in the sense that I shall define below. For a criticism of Habermas's overly strong notions of consensus and the rational will see Thomas McCarthy, "Practical discourse: On the relation of politics and morality," in McCarthy's *Ideals and Illusions* (MIT Press, 1991). McCarthy's criticism is somewhat different from mine in that McCarthy sees deep disagreements based on "comprehensive moral views" as an inevitable feature of political life and tied to the inseparability of moral evaluations from cultural frameworks. While they may be appropriate in certain situations, abstraction and impartiality cannot solve the problems of cultural pluralism in democratic theory; they rely on singular conceptions of public reason in my sense. On my view, such views ignore that abstraction can be attained in deliberation only when reasonable opinions converge. When they do not, it is itself a cause of moral loss. It is, however, often a requirement for the resolution of conflicts of interest, but inadequate to resolve most conflicts of principle.

22. Bruce Ackerman, *We the People*, volume I (Harvard University Press, 1991), p. 114ff.

23. Margaret Gilbert develops the idea of a "plural subject," in contrast to the "singular agency" of individualism. My concept of a "plural public" is somewhat different, since Gilbert analyses plural subjects as sharing a common goal. This is too strong a criterion for a plural public, and it would count as an instance of singular public reason on my view. Plural public reason does not require such shared goals, although it may produce them. Gilbert and I agree that members of a plural subject do not need to share the same beliefs. This lack of credal unanimity is important for my argument, since plural agreements do not require that culturally diverse citizens adopt jointly held policies for the same reasons. Gilbert goes so far as to say that members of plural subjects need have *no* beliefs in common. For public deliberation, this means that an "overlapping consensus" is not an empirical requirement for the shared activity of deliberating together. I agree with her to the extent that

jointly accepted public reasons need not be the reasons of any particular group or actor. See Margaret Gilbert, *On Social Facts* (Princeton University Press, 1989), p. 17ff.

24. Rawls, *Political Liberalism*, p. 220.

25. Habermas, "Reconciliation through the public use of reason," p. 117.

26. Rawls, *Political Liberalism*, p. 169.

27. Joshua Cohen, "Moral pluralism and political consensus," in *The Idea of Democracy*, ed. D. Copp et al. (Cambridge University Press, 1993), p. 283.

28. Rawls, *Political Liberalism*, p. 61. The purpose of the notion of "the burdens of judgement" is to establish the basis of a general philosophical argument for an ineliminable pluralism of "reasonable comprehensive doctrines." It shows why public reason cannot resolve all moral and political conflicts. The burdens of judgement are not simply differences of opinion, but are differences traceable to sources of reasonable disagreement. Rawls gives a rough and non-exhaustive list of such sources: complex and conflicting evidence, the significance of which is hard to assess; difficulties in establishing the comparative weight and relevance of different considerations; the indeterminacy and vagueness of moral and political concepts; fundamental differences in life experience; conflicts of values that give normative force to both sides of certain issues; and the selective character of institutions and the need to make hard decisions that cannot be made without moral loss (pp. 56–57). The conception of moral compromise that I develop below deals primarily with just those conflicts of value which Rawls describes as irresolvable.

29. Ackerman, *We the People*, volume I, p. 81ff.

30. Rawls seems to think that there is a simple choice between civility and dogmatism, where liberal civility takes contentious issues off the political agenda. But this is neither a real dilemma nor the only two alternatives. For an argument concerning mutual respect as a third and more inclusive alternative that is in many respects similar to mine see Amy Gutmann and Dennis Thompson, "Moral conflict and political consensus," *Ethics* 101 (1990): 76–86; for a similar argument made with respect to the status of radical critics in deliberation see Thomas McCarthy, "Kantian constructivism and reconstructivism: Rawls and Habermas in dialogue," *Ethics* 105 (1994): 44–63. Habermas's own dispute with Rawls concerns this same problem of contentious issues and values; see his "Reconciliation through the public use of reason: Remarks on Rawls's political liberalism," *Journal of Philosophy* 52 (1995): 109–131. As I argue below, Habermas does not go far enough in this argument: he includes all topics, even contentious ones, without modifying either the liberal notion of public agreement or the neutrality of the outcome of deliberation.

31. He calls this consensus "constitutional patriotism," which he defends most clearly in "Citizenship and national identity," *Praxis International* 12 (1992): 1–19. Habermas also consistently appropriates the Rawls's term "overlapping consensus" in all his recent discussions of pluralism and the constitutional state.

32. Habermas, *Faktizität und Geltung* (Suhrkamp, 1992), p. 411.

33. Ibid. Habermas does give a moral constraint on compromises: they "must not violate a culture's basic values" (p. 344). This criterion reflects Habermas's strategic

conception of compromise and is actually stronger than the one I an defending. It would preclude most solutions to deep conflicts.

34. Habermas argues for this view of the relation of majority and minority opinions in "Volkssouveränität als Verfahren," in *Die Ideen von 1789* (Suhrkamp, 1989). The minority keeps its "opinion" and argues for it in the public sphere, but gives into the "will" of the majority until it can form a new one. He argues for the same view of majority rule as converging toward singular agreement in *Faktizität und Geltung* (p. 220).

35. Hannah Arendt once publicly opposed "forcing" the integration of schools after *Brown v. Board of Education* as undemocratic. She did not make the case that integration was an unfair moral compromise of the "Southern way of life." It bears only a superficial similarity to the Native American case discussed above: the group that will not cooperate is the dominant and exclusionary culture. Arendt explicitly ignored the differences between forced inclusion and forced exclusion in public agreements, as well as the unequal standing of majority and minority cultures. The preservation of the majority culture's "way of life" is hardly a reason to deny others their rights. See Hannah Arendt, "Reflections on Little Rock," *Dissent* 6 (1959): 45–56. The deeper problem is that her conceptions of citizenship and of the public sphere are too communitarian and thus she is caught in what I have been calling a communitarian dilemma: unity at the price of diversity. For a discussion of this example as a failed politics of public compromise (but informed by complex awareness of tradeoffs of equality and difference) see James Bohman, "The moral costs of pluralism: The dilemmas of difference and equality in Arendt's 'Reflections on Little Rock,'" in *Hannah Arendt: Twenty Years Later*, ed. J. Kohn and L. May (MIT Press, 1996).

36. This way of reading Rawls was suggested to me by Henry Richardson.

37. My reference to the Rushdie case here is only meant to show that it is a complex case of deep conflict, and that intercultural dialogue about it will be furthered if this fact is recognized.

38. Martin Benjamin provides an excellent analysis of this more typical sense of compromise, a form that is also necessary for resolving conflicts of interests in pluralist societies. The moral issue here is how to "split the difference" without loss of integrity. I am borrowing his characterization of compromises in terms of process and outcome; moral compromises share the process of reaching a compromise but not the standard outcome of balancing concessions. See Benjamin, *Splitting the Difference* (University of Kansas Press, 1990), pp. 4–5.

39. Ronald Dworkin, *Life's Dominion: An Argument about Abortion, Euthanasia, and Individual Freedom* (Knopf, 1993). Dworkin tries to resolve this set of conflicts by widening the terms of the debate beyond individual rights or interests to include other values. Introducing "intrinsic values" outside the liberal repertoire is supposed to lead us to a new understanding of a variety of issues, where legal regulation should encompass a diversity of such conceptions of the value and meaning of human life. Whether or not Dworkin offers a convincing moral compromise is another matter, but he does offer a comprehensive framework that recognizes and encompasses both sides of the conflict. He does not surrender arguments for "privacy" entirely, while recognizing the "sanctity" of human life. Many on both sides of this dispute want to put the issue outside of all public deliberation.

40. For an excellent account of the use of this device in the Camp David negotiations see Howard Raiffa, *The Art and Science of Negotiations* (Harvard University Press, 1982).

41. See Charles Taylor, "Understanding and ethnocentrism," in *Collected Papers*, volume I (Cambridge University Press, 1985).

42. The Meech Lake accord produced a proposed constitutional amendment to the Canadian Charter that would recognize Quebec and tribal groups as "distinct societies." Similarly, during the process of unification of East and West Germany there were meetings at which the proposed adoption of an entirely new constitutional framework for Germany was proposed. Both proposals ultimately failed to be publicly accepted, not the least reason for which is the problem of legitimacy and representation in the deliberative bodies that produced them. I do not discuss this important issue here. How groups deliberate together through representatives is a difficult problem, since every cultural group also has its own sub-cultures and internal disputes about its identity.

43. Iris M. Young, "Polity and group difference," in *Feminism and Political Theory*, ed. C. Sunstein (University of Chicago Press, 1990). See also *Justice and the Politics of Difference* (Princeton University Press, 1990), especially pp. 184–186.

44. Cumulative voting procedures that grant each person multiple votes make it more likely that minorities and other disadvantaged groups will successfully elect at least one candidate and thus have a greater influence on the results of deliberation. See Lani Guinier, *The Tyranny of the Majority* (Free Press, 1994). Guinier gives the example of Chilton County, Alabama, where not a single African-American had ever been elected by majority-rule, "one person, one vote" rules. For a discussion of various alternatives for fulfilling the Supreme Court's interpretation of the 1982 Voting Rights Act as mandating "the right to full and effective participation," including the Chilton County case, see Lani Guinier, "Groups, representation and race-conscious districting," *University of Texas Law Review* 71 (1993): 1589–1642. I agree with Guinier that it is only on the basis of expecting to influence results and outcomes that disadvantaged groups will see decisions as legitimate and be willing to continue to cooperate, not on any intrinsic features of the decisions or the decision procedures.

45. Guinier, "Groups, representation and race-conscious districting," pp. 1639–1640.

46. On the concept of polyethnic rights see Will Kymlicka, *Multicultural Citizenship* (Oxford University Press, 1995), p. 31ff. On group-differentiated citizenship see Iris Young, "Polity and group difference: A critique of the ideal of universal citizenship," in *Feminism and Political Theory*, ed. C. Sunstein (University of Chicago Press, 1989), p. 125.

47. Robert Goodin, "Laundering preferences," in *Foundations of Social Choice Theory*, ed. J. Elster and A. Hylland (Cambridge University Press, 1986). This "cleansing" or filtering effect of making preferences public should not be overestimated, since it is limited to those bad reasons and arguments which other participants can detect.

48. Bernard Manin, "On legitimacy and political deliberation," *Political Theory* 15 (1987): 338–368; see pp. 360–361.

49. See Ackerman, *We the People*, volume I, p. 38ff.

Chapter 3

1. Aristotle, *Politics*, book 2, especially chapters 1–7, in *Basic Works of Aristotle*, ed. R. McKeon (Random House, 1941). This rather limited notion of equality is essential to Hannah Arendt's interpretation of Aristotle's notion of practice on p. 188ff. of *The*

Human Condition (University of Chicago Press, 1958). For an analysis and a criticism of Arendt's "agonistic" public sphere as presupposing a homogeneous, exclusive moral and political community, see Seyla Benhabib, *Situating the Self* (Routledge, 1992), p. 90ff.

2. For a definition of poverty as capability failure see Amartya Sen, *Inequality Reconsidered* (Harvard University Press, 1992), pp. 108–109. According to Sen (ibid., p. 109), poverty is "the failure of basic capabilities to reach certain minimally acceptable levels." For a similar (but more essentialist) capacity-based account of equality as a defense of social democracy, see Martha Nussbaum, "Aristotelian social democracy," in *Liberalism and the Good*, ed. R. Douglas et al. (Routledge, 1990).

3. Rousseau, *Social Contract* (Pocket Books, 1967), chapter 9, especially p. 55.

4. One common measure of "economic democracy" is the degree of acceptable inequalities in a society, such as the difference between the income of workers and management personnel within firms. See Robert Dahl, *A Preface to Economic Democracy* (California University Press, 1985), p. 108ff.

5. Rousseau, *Social Contract*, chapter 11.

6. Don Zimmerman and Candace West, "Sex roles, interruptions and silences in conversation," in *Language and Sex: Difference and Dominance*, ed. B. Thorne and N. Henley (Newbury House, 1975). See also Candace West and Angela Garcia, "Conversational shift work: A study of topical transition between women and men," *Social Problems* 35 (1988): 551–575. For a methodological caution about simply using "ordinary conversation" as a norm in such studies of larger contexts of power, see E. A. Scheglhoff, "Between micro and macro: Contexts and other connections," in *The Micro-Macro Link*, ed. J. Alexander et al. (University of California Press, 1987).

7. See Candace West, *Routine Complications: Troubles in Talk between Doctors and Patients* (Indiana University Press, 1984); see also Kathy Davis, *Power Under the Microscope* (Floris, 1988).

8. See Alec McHoul, "Why there are no guarantees for interrogators," *Journal of Pragmatics* 11 (1987): 455–471.

9. Jürgen Habermas, *Structural Transformation of the Public Sphere* (MIT Press, 1989), pp. 33–36. See also Michael Warner, *The Letters of the Republic: Publication and the Public Sphere in Eighteenth Century America* (Harvard University Press, 1990), for a discussion of the emergence of the literary public in America. It is important not to overlook Habermas's consistent provisos concerning the egalitarian character of the bourgeois public sphere as an idealization; however much he asserts that it does represent a historical realization of principles of publicity, he also says just as often that the bourgeois family remained patriarchal and that people hardly left their class privileges at the door of the salon. Warner's analysis shows how the colonial American public sphere of "letters" realized ideals of public equality more fully than any European example.

10. Habermas, *Structural Transformation of the Public Sphere*, p. 36.

11. Habermas develops the notion of an audience-oriented subjectivity, embodied in intimate interactions and the emergence of letter writing among family members as a form of subjective expression. Charles Taylor, in his *Sources of the Self* (Harvard

University Press, 1989), considers this form of expressive subjectivity and its ideal of authenticity to be one of the basic strands of modernity.

12. Pierre Bourdieu's account of implicit censorship of modes of expression, in his *Language and Symbolic Power* (Polity, 1991), is perhaps the most convincing part of his account of symbolic power: "Censorship is never quite as perfect or as invisible as when each agent has nothing to say apart from what he is objectively authorized to say: in this case he does not even have to be his own censor, because he is censored once and for all in the forms of perception and expression that he has internalized and which impose their form on all his expression." (p. 138) But this analysis needs to be restricted to public discourse; so limited, we can see that new modes of public expression need not be based upon the "unnameable or unsayable" (p. 42); innovation in public expression is continuous with quite ordinary activities of communicating needs and interests, and its analysis does not require such metaphysical hyperbole. For a criticism of Bourdieu's approach to agency see my "Practical agency and cultural constraint," in *Bourdieu: A Critical Reader*, ed. R. Shusterman (Blackwell, forthcoming).

13. Bourdieu, *Language and Symbolic Power*, p. 51.

14. For a discussion along these lines about the privileges of "unmarked" identities in the public sphere see Michael Warner, "The mass public and the mass subject," in *Habermas and the Public Sphere*, ed. C. Calhoun (MIT Press, 1992), p. 383ff.

15. See Basil Bernstein, *Class, Codes and Control* (Routledge, 1962), especially his categories of "restricted" and "elaborated" codes to describe class differences in speech. For a criticism of this distinction showing its arbitrary character see Bourdieu, *Language and Symbolic Power*, p. 53. For my purposes this sociolinguistic debate is unimportant, since the result of exclusion is the same.

16. On the concept of a "collective action frame" see William Gamson, *Talking Politics* (Cambridge University Press, 1993), pp. 6–8. Such interpretive framing is one of the critical roles of movements in the public sphere; as critics, members of a movement also may perform this function in their public expressions on both accounts.

17. For a history of attempts to make domestic violence a public problem see Elizabeth Pleck, *Domestic Tyranny* (Oxford University Press, 1987), especially her analysis of how psychiatry takes control of the "framing" of domestic violence as a social problem. For an analysis of the feminist movement's transformation of wife beating into a political issue, see Gretchen Arnold, "Political discourse and institutional change: The case of wife beating" (presented to Eastern Sociological Society, 1996).

18. Benjamin Barber, *Strong Democracy* (University of California Press, 1984), p. 170ff.

19. Habermas develops his conception of distorted communication in "On systematically distorted communication," *Inquiry* 13 (1970): 205–218, and "Kommunikationspathologien," in *Vorstudien und Ergänzungen zur Theorie des kommunikativen Handelns* (Suhrkamp, 1985). I criticize his narrow account and reformulate it more broadly in "Formal pragmatics and social criticism," *Philosophy and Social Criticism* 12 (1986): 332–352; see also my "Critique of ideology," in *Philosophy of Language: An International Handbook*, volume I, ed. M. Dascal et al. (de Gruyter, 1992), and "Communication, ideology and democracy," *American Political Science Review* 84 (1990): 93–104.

20. Habermas, "Kommunikationspathologien," in *Vorstudien*, p. 373.

21. Habermas, *Theory of Communicative Action*, volume II (Beacon, 1987), p. 287.

22. Peter Bachrach and Morton Baratz give this analysis in *Power and Poverty* (Oxford University Press, 1970). In "Communication, ideology and democracy" I recast the concept of non-decisions in terms of public discourse and deliberation.

23. For the development of this idea see Habermas, *Legitimation Crisis* (Beacon, 1977), p. 14ff and p. 85ff; see also "Wahrheitstheorien" in *Vorstudien*, pp. 128–186, especially his assertion that the ideal speech situation is "neither an empirical construct nor a mere construct, but rather an unavoidable supposition reciprocally made in discourse. . . . It can, but need not be, counterfactual" if it is a norm effectively operating in communication (p. 181). For a full discussion of how the construct of ideal speech situation fulfills "general symmetry requirements" presupposed in communication see Thomas McCarthy, *The Critical Theory of Jürgen Habermas* (MIT Press, 1978), pp. 305–310.

24. Rawls, *A Theory of Justice* (Harvard University Press, 1971), p. 226. See also Kenneth Baynes's discussion of this aspect of Rawls's egalitarianism on p. 159 of *The Grounds of Social Criticism* (SUNY Press, 1992).

25. Here I adopt Sen's definition of poverty (the "failure of basic capabilities" to reach a minimal level) to the domain of political equality. See Sen, *Inequality Reconsidered*, pp. 108–116.

26. For an analysis of these cycles based on the contractualist demand for "economic arrangements no one can reasonably reject," see Partha Dasgupta, *An Enquiry into Poverty and Destitution* (Oxford University Press, 1993), p. 27ff.

27. Rawls, *A Theory of Justice* (Harvard University Press, 1971), p. 312. John Stuart Mill also thinks that natural differences in ability cannot be eliminated and thus must be incorporated into democratic arrangements.

28. Rawls, *A Theory of Justice*. For a similar criticism of Rawls on "natural" inequalities see G. A. Cohen, "The currency of egalitarian justice," *Ethics* 99 (1989): 906–944.

29. Cohen, ibid., p. 914.

30. See Jürgen Habermas, *Faktizität und Geltung* (Suhrkamp, 1992), p. 367ff. Broader lists of such "facts" about complexity include the need for experts and elites, the incapacities of the masses, the "inefficiencies" of popular decision making, and many more. For a comprehensive examination see chapter 3 of Danilo Zolo, *Democracy and Complexity* (Pennsylvania State University Press, 1992).

31. See Bernhard Peters, *Integration moderner Gesellschaften* (Suhrkamp, 1993), chapter 5.

32. Habermas, *Faktizität und Geltung*, p. 396.

33. Sen, *Inequality Reconsidered*, p. 63. Earlier Sen had formulated a basic condition of individual rights, the "liberalism condition," which states that there must exist at least two social alternatives for freedom of individual choice, that is, two possible complete descriptions of alternative social outcomes. See Sen, *Collective Choice and Social Welfare* (Oliver and Boyd, 1979), p. 79.

34. Sen, *Inequality Reconsidered*, p. 69.

35. Sen, *Poverty and Famines* (Oxford University Press, 1981).

36. For an account of the role of voluntary association for democratic self-governance in complex societies see Joshua Cohen and Joel Rogers, "Secondary associations and democratic governance," *Politics and Society* 20 (1992): 393–472. This role is heightened, I am arguing, by the power asymmetries and prevalent inequalities in civil society. The target of corrective measures must also be the associations formed by disadvantaged groups.

37. Talcott Parsons held that social integration must work through consensus, but distinguishes other forms of integration that do not require explicit cultural mechanisms of shared value orientations, or "system integration." See chapter 1 of his *System of Modern Societies* (Prentice-Hall, 1971).

38. Bourdieu, *Language and Symbolic Power*, p. 59ff.

39. Paul Willis, *Learning to Labor* (Saxon House, 1977).

40. Oskar Negt and Alexander Kluge, *The Public Sphere and Experience* (University of Minnesota Press, 1994). For a detailed account of the clubs, associations and public spaces of the English working-class movements see E. P. Thompson, *The Making of the English Working Class* (Penguin, 1963). Negt, Kluge, and Thompson all raise interesting historical questions—e.g., to what extent is a "public sphere of private persons" specific to a particular class and its culture? Until quite recently, there has been a lack of comparative research on the public sphere.

41. Jo Freeman, "The origins of the women's liberation movement," *American Journal of Sociology* 78 (1973): 32. See also Doug McAdam, *Political Process and the Development of Black Insurgency 1930–1970* (University of Chicago Press, 1982), pp. 15–16.

42. Freeman, p. 32.

43. Joseph Gusfield, *The Culture of Public Problems: Drinking-Driving and the Symbolic Order* (University of Chicago Press, 1981). Gusfield (pp. 8–11) notes one of the "moral" roles of such movements is to assign responsibility for such problems.

44. There is a persistent confusion about the distinct roles of the public sphere and civil society among theorists who see a democratic potential primarily in civil society. See Jean Cohen and Andrew Arato, *Civil Society and Political Theory* (MIT Press, 1992), especially their criticisms of Habermas's writings on the public sphere. There are also prevalent confusions caused by the use of the term "publics"; here we need to clearly distinguish sub-publics from the larger civic public, the public of citizens. Without such a civic public, however attenuated, there are no real sub-publics either.

45. See Aldon Morris, *The Origins of the Civil Rights Movement* (Free Press, 1984), p. 24ff.

46. William Gamson, *The Strategy of Social Protest* (Wadsworth, 1990), p. 137ff.

47. Mayer Zald and John McCarthy, "Resource mobilization and social movements," *American Journal of Sociology* 82 (1977): 1216.

48. William Gamson and Emile Schneider, "Organizing the poor," *Theory and Society* 13 (1984): 569.

49. Current constitutional debates about "race-conscious" redistricting reflect this tension. One problem with many criticisms of this practice is that they ignore the fact that redistricting is a common practice used for many different political purposes. Its purpose in many cases is to influence outcomes causally (such as in guaranteeing a particular seat for a particular party). If we want to avoid such causal mechanisms in order to promote deliberation and fairness, we should do so across the board. Such criticisms of race-specific uses of redistricting should also make us think about eliminating other forms of causal influence, such as asymmetries of power.

50. Charles Beitz, *Political Equality* (Princeton University Press, 1989), p. 180. Beitz also identifies completeness, coherence, and a full range of alternatives as basic standards for fair agenda setting in institutions.

51. James Fishkin (*Democracy and Deliberation* (Yale University Press, 1991), p. 37) defends a rather strong standard of completeness: an agenda is incomplete if it does not contain an argument or consideration put forward by "one participant or another;" similarly David Braybrooke ("Changes of rules, issue circumscription, and issue processing," cited by Fishkin) holds out a norm of "logically complete debate" giving each participant "the same complete information about the track of the debate." While both admit Robert Dahl's caveats, such as the limitations on time due to "the need for a decision," they insist on completeness as a regulative ideal. Such a norm is unnecessary, however, not merely because of practical constraints, but because it could not in the end serve to promote better deliberation or even to guide it. On the contrary, this idealization misleads us about what makes political decisions more credible. Both Fishkin and Braybrooke accept the need for narrowing of agendas as part of the deliberation-promoting process.

52. As Cass Sunstein ("Beyond the republican revival," *Yale Law Review* 97 (1988): 1577–1578) puts it, our system of free expression is undermined by "government inaction that allows the political process to be excessively influenced by disparities in private wealth and private access." Owen Fiss ("Why the state?" *Harvard Law Review* 100 (1987): 788) argues that the courts be concerned with the quality of public debate, by promoting the expression of opinions and speakers "systematically ignored and slighted" by commercial market media. The greater the effects of the market on public discourse, the greater the regulatory power of the state needed to maintain free and equal access to the public sphere. But it is important to keep in mind that the state here is democratic and promotes deliberative democracy, and that its self-regulation of the public sphere is for the sake of maintaining its free and open character.

53. For a discussion of such issues of the regulation of public affairs speech, see R. Randall Rainey and William Rehg, "The marketplace of ideas, the public interest, and federal regulation of the electronic media" (unpublished). They argue that market forces are not ideologically neutral, that the marketplace is not open to diverse viewpoints, and that instruments for assessing consumer preferences do not accurately measure what is in the "public interest."

54. Alexander Meiklejohn, *Political Freedom* (Oxford University Press, 1960), p. 27. For Meiklejohn, the role of public discussion in self-governance gives it a special constitutional status.

55. Will Kymlicka makes this distinction in his "Liberalism and the politicization of ethnicity," *Canadian Journal of Law and Jurisprudence* 4 (1991): 239–256. For a similar point see Steven Lukes, "Four fables on human rights," in *Human Rights*, ed. S. Shute and S. Hurley (Basic Books, 1993).

56. Kant, "What is enlightenment?" in *Kant's Political Writings*, ed. H. Reiss (Cambridge University Press, 1979), p. 54. Here Kant speaks of "self-imposed tutelage" and of "giving one's reason over to another."

57. For a description of recent conflicts over family law in India from a feminist perspective, see Zakia Pathak and Rajeswari Sunder Rajan, "Shabano," *Signs* 14 (1989): 558–582. However, this analysis does not consider class divisions.

58. See Susan Moeller Okin, "Gender inequality and cultural difference," *Political Theory* 22 (1994): 12, and Hanna Papanek, "To each less than she needs, from each more than she can do: Allocations, entitlement and value," in *Women and World Development*, ed. I. Tinker (Oxford University Press, 1990). For similar arguments see Partha Dasgupta, *An Inquiry into Well-Being and Destitution* (Oxford University Press, 1993), p. 331ff.

Chapter 4

1. As I noted in chapter 1, Rousseau's account of the "general will" is sometimes interpreted this way; it is the core of the "civic republican" and communitarian ideas of democracy. For a historical overview of republicanism and its influence see Frank Michelman, "The Supreme Court 1985 term forward: Traces of self-government," *Harvard Law Review* 100 (1986): 4–77; also see his "Political truth and the rule of law," *Tel Aviv University Studies in Law* 8 (1988): 281–291. Proponents of "strong," participatory democracy think beyond ordinary practices of voting and representation and criticize current institutions for their "thin" standard of democratic legitimacy. Democracy is achieved only in a self-governing community, which is constituted by more than homogeneous interests. See Benjamin Barber, *Strong Democracy* (University of California Press, 1984), p. 117ff.

2. Robert Dahl and Edward Tufte, *Size and Democracy* (Stanford University Press, 1973), p. 70.

3. This distinction plays an important role in *FG*, especially chapters 7 and 8. I will discuss this distinction in the third section of the present chapter.

4. See, for example, Jean Cohen and Andrew Arato, *Civil Society and Political Theory* (MIT Press, 1992), especially chapter 1.

5. For a definition of dualist democracy in terms of this contrast between higher and normal lawmaking see Bruce Ackerman, *We the People*, volume I (Harvard University Press, 1991), p. 6ff.

6. See Danilo Zolo, *Democracy and Complexity* (Pennsylvania State University Press, 1992), especially chapter 3, for a clear statement of how functional differentiation is different from other forms of complexity, such as the segmentation of spheres of activity that are not functionally interdependent.

7. The locus classicus of this claim is *Models of Man* (Wiley, 1957), in which Herbert Simon develops the conception of bounded rationality to overcome the gap between normative rationality and the decision-making strategies of large organizations.

8. Jon Elster has made the "perverse effects" of social planning one of his major themes. See the editors' introduction to *Alternative to Capitalism*, ed. J. Elster and K. Moene (Cambridge University Press, 1989).

9. Cohen and Arato, *Civil Society and Political Theory*, pp. 24–25.

10. Jon Elster, *Solomonic Judgments* (Cambridge University Press, 1989), p. 17.

11. Ibid.

12. Charles Perrow, *Normal Accidents* (Basic Books, 1984), chapter 3. For an interesting discussion of the artificial world constructed by experimental science using this model see Joseph Rouse, *Knowledge and Power* (Cornell University Press, 1987), p. 230.

13. Perrow, *Normal Accidents*, p. 78.

14. Rouse, *Knowledge and Power*, pp. 230–238.

15. Zolo, *Democracy and Complexity*, pp. 64–65.

16. Ibid., p. 67.

17. Ibid., p. 56.

18. For example, see Carl Schmitt, *Political Theology* (MIT Press, 1983), p. 59ff. Schmitt argues that the Counter-Reformation defined protection from evil as the central political problem.

19. On the concept of information pooling see *Information Pooling and Group Decision Making*, ed. B. Grofman and G. Owen (Westport, Conn.: JAI Press, 1983). Also see *Information and Democratic Processes*, ed. J. Ferejohn and J. Kuklinski (University of Illinois Press, 1990).

20. See Bernhard Peters, *Integration moderner Gesellschaften* (Suhrkamp, 1993), chapters 5 and 6.

21. Habermas, *FG*, p. 397.

22. For Marx's account of the Paris Commune, in which he applauds the "reabsorption of the state into society," see "The Civil Wars in France," in *Karl Marx: Selected Writings*, ed. D. McLellan (Oxford University Press, 1977). In some early formulations Habermas seems to invite this interpretation, as when he insists that the ideal speech situation is not a "mere fiction." As we shall see below, he is now much more cautious. But the important distinction is between the requirements of agreement in moral discourse and the more minimal demands of political agreement. In my view, democracy does not require unanimity even as a regulative ideal, but the willingness of citizens to continue to cooperate. Even when they are losers, citizens need only have the reasonable expectation that they will be able to affect the outcome of future deliberation.

23. Peters, *Integration moderner Gesellschaften*, p. 230.

24. For criticisms of Joshua Cohen's account of deliberation along these lines see p. 383ff. of *FG*. For a criticism of a similar set of normative conditions offered by Robert Dahl, see p. 369ff. of *FG*.

25. This is Robert Michels's "oligarchic tendency" manifested in mass democracy; see his *Political Parties* (Free Press, 1958).

26. Peters uses Shapiro's arguments about expertise to substantiate his claims about the inevitability of the inegalitarian and contractual distinction between agent and principal in such relationships. See Susan Shapiro, "The social control of impersonal trust," *American Journal of Sociology* 93 (1987): 623–658.

27. Steven Shapin, *A Social History of Truth* (University of Chicago Press, 1994), p. 417. As Shapin puts it there: "For scientists' practical capacity to advance knowledge, even skeptically to check over another's claim with a view to falsifying it, depends on their ability to trust almost everything else about the science in which they do skepticism and the resources which permit skeptical activities to be carried through."

28. Shapiro, "The social control of impersonal trust," pp. 624–628.

29. Joshua Gamson, "Silence, Death and the Invisible Enemy: AIDS Activism and Social Movement Newness," *Social Problems* 36 (1989): 351–367. See also the work of Steven Epstein, including "Activists as experts: Dilemmas of democratization in the AIDS epidemic" (presented at American Sociological Association Annual Meeting, 1994).

30. Partha Dasgupta, "Trust as a commodity," in *Trust*, ed. D. Gambetta (Blackwell, 1988).

31. See James March, *Decisions and Organizations* (Blackwell, 1988); see also Peters, *Integration moderner Gesellschaften,*, pp. 237–238.

32. For a more dynamic and temporal account of intentional action, see Michael Bratman, *Intentions, Plans and Practical Reason* (Harvard University Press, 1988), p. 29ff. Peters's argument depends on an account of deliberation which is entirely too punctual and disconnected, and his criticisms do not apply to a future-oriented planning model of ongoing intentional activity (such as Bratman's), which builds temporal limitations into deliberation itself. Agents make plans, precisely in order to build in constraints on our activities over time.

33. See Michel Foucault, *Discipline and Punish* (Vintage, 1979), especially his denial that publicity works against the spread of the Panopticon (p. 208ff.). This is part of Foucault's argument against "reform," which he claims historically has intensified disciplinary power in efforts to limit it.

34. Habermas, *FG*, chapters 7 and 8.

35. Habermas, *Legitimation Crisis* (Beacon, 1975), p. 36.

36. Habermas, *FG*, p. 370.

37. Ibid., pp. 395–398. For a more expanded analysis of this argument and its implications for democratic theory than undertaken here or above see my review essay on Peters's book: "Unavoidable complexity and radical democracy," *Constellations* 1 (1995): 422–427.

38. Habermas puts the point this way in the postscript to the fourth printing: The practice of citizens giving themselves laws "requires more than a discourse principle by which citizens can judge whether the law they enact is legitimate" (p. 688); such a principle is, in my view, all that they need in cases of *moral* justification.

39. *FG*, pp. 99–101.

40. As Habermas puts it, "Parsons uses the term 'societal community' to designate the central sphere from which each differentiated social system is supposed to develop" (p. 109). Habermas is referring here to Parsons's book *The System of Modern Societies* (Prentice-Hall, 1971). For Habermas, Parsons overlooked the special, self-referential status of law in all institutionalization in modern societies. My argument is that there is no societal community in Habermas, and this has fatal consequences for the democratic character of his solution to the problems of complexity.

41. *FG*, p. 109.

42. Ibid,, p. 397.

43. Frank Michelman, "Law's republic," *Yale Law Journal* 97 (1988): 1502. See also Cass Sunstein, "Beyond the republican revival," *Yale Law Journal* 97 (1988): 1539–1590. For a fuller treatment of this point see Kenneth Baynes, "Democracy and the *Rechtsstaat*: Some remarks on *Faktizität und Geltung*," in *Cambridge Companion to Habermas*, ed. S. White (Cambridge University Press, 1995), pp. 201–232.

44. *FG*, p. 667.

45. For a clear discussion of what Habermas means by the various "uses" of practical reason, see Habermas, "On the pragmatic, the ethical and the moral employment of practical reason," in *Justification and Application* (MIT Press, 1993). The vocabulary in which these distinctions are cast is somewhat jarring to the English-language reader.

46. *FG*, p. 117.

47. Ibid., p. 111.

48. Ibid., p. 141.

49. Ibid., p. 384; also, p. 411.

50. Ibid., p. 210.

51. Habermas (*FG*, pp. 182–187) sees a tendency toward this error in Hannah Arendt's republicanism. See also "Hannah Arendt: On the concept of power," in Habermas, *Philosophical-Political Profiles* (Cambridge, Mass., 1985). For an account of the tension between deliberation and democracy in the U.S. Constitution, as well as between popular and institutional power, see chapters 1 and 2 of Joseph Bessette, *The Mild Voice of Reason: Deliberative Democracy and American National Government* (University of Chicago Press, 1994).

52. See *FG*, pp. 210–229. For a dualist (rather than two-track) interpretation of the U.S. system see Bruce Ackerman, "Neo-federalism?" in *Constitutionalism and Democracy*, ed. J. Elster and R. Slagstad (Cambridge University Press, 1988). See also Ackerman's *We the People*, volume I (Harvard University Press, 1991), especially his contrast between monistic and dualist democracy on pp. 7–33. For the use of the principal-agent distinction from contract law as a way of understanding representation as a form of delegation see Peters, *Integration moderner Gesellschaften*, p. 284 ff. The two-track model provides the basis for criticizing direct democracy as well as theories of civil society or associationalist theorists. Habermas would argue that Joshua Cohen and Joel Rogers's recent work, such as "Secondary associations and democratic governance" (*Politics and Society* 20 (1992): 393–472), goes too far in this direction in its proposals for democratic renewal. A vibrant associative life is a necessary condition of a strong public sphere, but not a sufficient condition. It does not by itself ensure that citizens will be able to engage in the sort of deliberation about interests that is necessary for the larger, civic public sphere of pluralist societies. Habermas also specifies how representative bodies can still meet the condition of "equal participation" of all citizens contained in his principle of democracy: "they must be receptive to the informal public sphere" and have election procedures that permit "the broadest possible spectrum of interpretive perspectives. . . ." (*FG*, p. 224).

53. *FG*, p. 224.

54. *FG*, p. 373. See p. 134 of Nancy Fraser, "Rethinking the public sphere: a contribution to the critique of actually existing democracy," in *Habermas and the Public Sphere*, ed. C. Calhoun (MIT Press, 1992).

55. Samuel Popkin's book *The Reasoning Voter: Communication and Persuasion in Presidential Campaigns* (University of Chicago Press, 1991) provides a detailed account of the "low-information" rationality characterizing voters' reasoning in presidential elections.

56. Ackerman, *We the People*, p. 8ff.

57. Fraser, "Rethinking the public sphere," pp. 122–128. Here, too, "counter-publics" are not sufficient for democracy for the same reason that civil society is insufficient; the plurality of publics is democratic only if they are within an open civic public sphere. Not only can "strong" public be distinguished from "weak" publics, but also specialized publics from the larger "civic" public sphere. Deliberative democracy depends on the existence of a larger, unifying civic public of all citizens.

58. "This model takes a *structuralist approach* to the manner in which institutionalized opinion- and will-formation is linked with informal opinion-building in culturally mobilized public spheres. This linkage is made possible neither by the homogeneity of the people and the identity of the popular will, nor by the identity of a reason that is supposedly able simply to *discover* an underlying homogeneous general interest. . . . If the communicatively fluid sovereignty of citizens instantiates itself in the power of public discourses that spring from autonomous public spheres but take shape in the decisions of *democratically proceeding* and *politically responsible* legislative bodies, then the pluralism of beliefs and interests is not suppressed but unleashed and recognized in revisable majority decisions as well as in compromises. For then the unity of a completely proceduralized reason retreats into the discursive structure of public communication." (*FG*, p. 228; for the whole argument see pp. 226–228)

59. "The exercise of political rule is oriented to and legitimated by the laws citizens give themselves in a discursively structured opinion- and will-formation. . . . . The rational acceptability of outcomes reached in conformity with [democratic] procedure follows from the institutionalization of intertwined forms of communication that . . . ensure that all relevant questions, topics, and contributions are brought up and processed in discourses and negotiations on the basis of the best available information and arguments." (*FG*, pp. 209–210)

60. The point of the passage in *FG* I cite here is to distinguish impartial public reason from mere compromise. "Whereas parties can agree to a negotiated compromise for different reasons, the consensus brought about through argument must rest on identical reasons that are able to convince the parties in the same way." (p. 411) This emphasis on the sameness of reasons is due to the fact, Habermas goes on to say, that impartiality "lends a reason its consensus producing force." For criticisms of Habermas's (and Rawls's) model of public reason for its failure to deal with problems of cultural pluralism see chapter 2 above; see also James Bohman, "Public reason and cultural pluralism," *Political Theory* 23 (1995): 253–279.

61. Bernard Manin, "On legitimacy and political deliberation," *Political Theory* 15 (1987): 360–361.

62. See chapter 3 of Bessette's *The Mild Voice of Reason* for this and other examples from the U.S. Congress.

63. Karl Marx, "Contributions to a critique of Hegel's philosophy of right," in Marx and Engels, *Collected Writings* (International Publishers, 1975), volume 3, p. 31. The problem that Marx is raising here is Hegel's tendency to think of agents as mere placeholders within an independent complex system of interdependent roles and functions; Hegel makes the converse of the liberal mistake of detaching rational action from the whole and makes the constitutional system itself solve problems of sovereignty and the irrationality of public opinion.

64. *FG*, p. 398.

65. Bessette, *The Mild Voice of Reason*, p. 35.

66. Weber puts it this way: through increased demands of the citizenry, "bureaucracy inevitably accompanies modern mass democracies in contrast to the democratic self-government of small homogeneous unit." But democracy inevitably conflicts with bureaucratic tendencies, given "the levelling of the governed in opposition to the ruling and bureaucratically articulated groups, which in its turn may occupy a quite autocratic position, both in fact and form." See Weber, *Economy and Society*, volume 1 (University of California Press, 1978), chapter 6.

67. John Dewey, "The public and its problems," in *The Later Works*, volume 2 (Southern Illinois University Press, 1988), p. 365.

68. Ibid.

69. This is actually quite consistent with the theory of argumentation which Habermas presents in "Wahrheitstheorien"(in *Vorstudien zur Theorie des kommunikativen Handelns*) and in *The Theory of Communicative Action*, volume I. According to that theory, argumentation is not simply a matter of logical deductions but of making a rationally

motivated assent to a claim *possible* on the basis of sufficient evidence. If sufficiency here is short of being logically compelled, however, then it must also always allow for a *reasonable disagreement.*

70. In defending a Rousseauian model of citizenship, Jeremy Waldron points out that it makes a difference whether citizens regard the majority as expressing their preferences or whether or not they judge it to be "the best way to promote the general good." My argument is similar, except that on my view a deliberative majority judges whether its decision fulfills what public reason demands. See Jeremy Waldron, "Rights and majorities: Rousseau revisited," in *Majorities and Minorities,* ed. J. Chapman and A. Wertheimer (New York University Press, 1990), p. 50ff. The upshot of our arguments is the same: we need not regard protections of minority opinions as anti-democratic or anti-deliberative, since they promote the integrity and publicity of majority rule.

71. Habermas's list of such rights seems to me to be as good as any; see chapter 3 of *FG.* These include rights that protect private autonomy, including liberties and legal protections; rights of participation in decision making and other rights which protect public autonomy; and welfare rights which compensate for those existing inequalities that might undermine the capacity for the equal exercise of these rights. But the role of such rights should not be overestimated. As I argued in chapter 2 and 3, having such rights does not solve the problems which social inequalities and cultural conflicts present for actual public deliberation. They are, however, necessary conditions for equal public standing and effective participation.

Chapter 5

1. Jürgen Habermas, *The Structural Transformation of the Public Sphere* (MIT Press, 1989), p. 37.

2. Ibid., p. 43.

3. John Dewey, *The Public and Its Problems,* in *The Later Works of John Dewey, 1925–1953,* volume 2 (Southern Illinois University Press, 1984), pp. 245–246. For an excellent treatment of this discussion, see Robert Westbrook, *John Dewey and American Democracy* (Cornell University Press, 1991), p. 302ff.

4. Dewey, *The Public and Its Problems,* p. 255.

5. Ibid.

6. Ibid.

7. J. L. Austin, *How to Do Things With Words* (Oxford University Press, 1962), p. 103.

8. Ibid., p. 105. Conventions of another sort are at work here: informal conventions that coordinate actions and solve cooperation games to the satisfaction of everyone. (See David Lewis, *Conventions* (Cambridge University Press, 1968), p. 105ff.) There are limits to the applicability of such solutions to problems of coordination, since they presuppose two conditions for success: that the solutions are equally satisfactory to all and thus that there is no problem of defection. See James Bohman, "The limits of rational choice explanations," in *Rational Choice Theory: Advocacy and Critique,* ed. J. Coleman and T. Fararo (Sage, 1992), pp. 227–228. Jack Knight's *Institutions and Social*

Conflict (Cambridge University Press, 1992) describes institutions that emerge out of such situations as the outcomes of bargaining games. Deliberative democracy attempts to make such informal institutionalization explicit, giving it a self-referential and public character that increases the democratic legitimacy of established institutions.

9. For a fuller treatment of the speech acts of social critics, see James Bohman, "Emancipation and rhetoric: The perlocutions and illocutions of the social critic," *Philosophy of Rhetoric* 21 (1988): 185–204.

10. John Searle, *Speech Acts* (Cambridge University Press, 1969), p. 60ff.

11. Habermas puts the point this way: "Through perlocutionary effects, the speaker gives the hearer something to understand which he cannot yet directly communicate. In this phase, then, the perlocutionary acts have to be embedded in contexts of communicative actions. These strategic elements within a use of language oriented to reaching understanding can be distinguished from strategic *actions* through the fact that the entire sequence of talk—on the part of all the participants—stands under the presuppositions of communicative action." (*The Theory of Communicative Action*, volume I (Beacon, 1984), p. 331)

12. Habermas, *Theory and Practice* (Beacon, 1971), pp. 37–40.

13. Michael Walzer, *The Company of Critics* (Basic Books, 1988). This involvement of critics in a public makes moot many of Walzer's objections against certain social critics; they need not be involved in current practices or traditions, but they must be involved in the formation of new ones (especially new forms of association).

14. William Gamson found this public structure of communication present even in the conversations of the focus groups he studied; the tape recorder had the effect of making even these small-group conversations about politics public. For example, in white focus groups this meant that "remarks that might be interpreted by the unseen gallery as prejudiced" were "more likely to be prefaced by disclaimers or additional remarks to make them seem less so." See p. 20 of his *Talking Politics* (Cambridge University Press, 1993).

15. Gamson, *Talking Politics*, p. 20.

16. Ibid., p. 85. See also Gamson's 1994 American Sociological Association Presidential Address, "Hiroshima, the Holocaust, and the Politics of Exclusion."

17. Joseph Gusfield, *The Culture of Public Problems: Driving-Drinking and the Symbolic Order* (University of Chicago Press, 1981), pp. 15–16. In the 1980s, public attention to drunk driving was reoriented from problem individuals toward affixing and distributing political responsibility, which government agencies, insurance companies, and the automobile and alcohol industries sought to disown. Gusfield also discusses the way in which highly tenuous measurements and stipulative definitions of alcoholism promoted "an expansion and a dramatization of the knowledge transmitted" from social science to the public (ibid., p. 60). Anything that would diminish the significance of the problem was eliminated because it would lessen the rhetorical effects of the statistics in the context of competing demands for attention, money and political commitment (p. 60).

18. Gamson, *Talking Politics*, p. 52.

19. Frederic Schick, *Understanding Action: An Essay on Reasons* (Cambridge University Press, 1991).

20. Ibid., p. 82.

21. George Orwell, "Looking back at the Civil War," in *A Collection of Essays* (Doubleday, 1957), p. 199. Schick cites this quotation on page 1 of *Understanding Action*, and he uses throughout his book as an example of what he means by an "understanding." The conception of understanding supplements the belief-desire model of action in order to explain a wider range of intentional actions, rational and irrational.

22. This term derives from Paul Chilton's "Metaphor, euphemism, and the militarization of language," *Current Research on Peace and Violence* 10 (1987): 7–19. For the use of this category to analyze a variety of discursive contexts and issues see Gamson, *Talking Politics*, pp. 25–27.

23. For such an analysis of how protest movements spread, see David Snow and Robert Benford, "Master frames and cycles of protest," in *Frontiers of Social Movement Theory*, ed. A. Morris and C. Mueller (Yale University Press, 1992).

24. Gamson, *Talking Politics*, p. 84.

25. Ibid., p. 85.

26. Martin Heidegger, "The origin of the work of art," in *Basic Writings* (Harper and Row, 1977), p. 186.

27. Martin Heidegger, *Sein und Zeit* (Niemeyer, 1929).

28. For an excellent discussion of the discourse surrounding these events mentioned here and their relation to problems of collective action and "symbolic contention," see William Gamson, "Political discourses and collective action," *International Social Movement Research* 1 (1988): 219–244.

29. In *Leviathan and the Air Pump* (Princeton University Press, 1985), Steven Shapin and Simon Schaffer point out that the methodological controversy between Boyle's empiricism and Hobbes's defense of deductivism has as much to do with politics and authority as with anything else. Richard Blackwell points out that Galileo's controversy with the Church had more to do with Biblical exegesis than with Aristotelian scientists; it was the Aristotelian philosophers, not the Church, that refused to look in the telescope. Here, too, the question of authority (that is, the religious authority of who is authorized to make interpretations of Scripture) is crucial. See Richard Blackwell, *Galileo and the Bible* (University of Notre Dame Press, 1991).

30. See Richard Rorty, *Contingency, Irony and Solidarity* (Cambridge University Press, 1989). For example, Rorty describes self-creation as "identical with the process of inventing a new language" (pp. 27–28), and irony as inventing "new final vocabularies" (p. 143). Such an idea not only overburdens art as a cultural institution but also makes innovation next to impossible and thus the product of "genius."

31. In his meta-parable "Von den Gleichnissen" (in *Sämtliche Erzählungen* (Fischer, 1970)), Kafka has one of his narrators say: "If a wise person says, 'Go over there!' she doesn't mean that we should go to the other side of the road. Instead, she means that

there is something wonderful over there, something we do not yet know about and that we cannot yet fully describe."

32. Heidegger, "The age of the world picture," in *The Question Concerning Technology and Other Essays* (Harper and Row, 1977), p. 117.

33. Hilary Putnam, *Reason, Truth and History* (Cambridge University Press, 1981), especially chapter 6. Putnam argues that "the real world depends on our values (and, again, vice-versa)" (p. 133). This is precisely the sort of relation of truth to disclosure that I want to develop here. If what is disclosed to me depends on my values and what I value depends on the possibility of having reality disclosed, the critic can both change our values in order to alter the way we look at the world and alter the way we look at the world by changing our values.

34. See Maurice Merleau-Ponty's description of the Schneider case in *The Phenomenology of Perception* (Humanities Press, 1962), p. 105ff. Merleau-Ponty uses the contrast between open and pathological cases of perception for a similar philosophical purpose throughout this work. 'Plasticity' and 'dialogue' are his descriptions of an open bodily relation to the world. However (as Mark Rollins has pointed out to me), his descriptive accounts of some pathologies are clearly empirically false and outdated, such as his claim that all forms of aphasia cause "rigid" language use.

35. Robert Nisbett and Lee Ross, *Human Inference* (Prentice-Hall, 1981), p. 167ff.

36. Pierre Bourdieu, Distinction (Harvard University Press, 1984), part III.

37. Habermas, *The Theory of Communicative Action*, volume I (Beacon, 1984), p. 331. As I argued above, when first-order communication breaks down, speakers can shift to meta-communication; this shift is often itself restricted by cognitive blind spots and communicative restrictions. Speakers then can attempt indirect forms of communication, including ones with strategic elements that have the effect of making the audience aware of the limiting conditions on mutual understanding and dialogue.

38. Dan Sperber and Dierdre Wilson, *Relevance: Communication and Cognition* (Harvard University Press, 1986).

39. As Grice puts it: "We might formulate a rough general principle which participants will be expected to observe, namely: Make your conversational contribution such as is required, at the state at which it occurs, by the accepted purpose or direction of the talk exchange in which you are engaged." ("Logic and Conversation, in *Syntax and Semantics 3: Speech Acts*, ed. P. Cole and J. Morgan (Academic Press, 1975), p. 45)

40. Sperber and Wilson, *Relevance*, p. 118.

41. Ibid., p. 125.

42. Sperber and Wilson (ibid., p. 162) put it this way: "Communicators do not follow the principle of relevance; and they could not violate it even if they wanted to. The principle of relevance is applied without exception: every act of ostensive communication communicates a presumption of relevance."

43. Here I mean to socialize Wilson and Sperber's overly psychologistic account of relevance. For a more sociological account, see Alfred Schütz, *Reflections on the Problem of*

Relevance (Yale University Press, 1970); in particular, see Schütz's notion of relevance as related to shared "stocks of knowledge."

44. Paul Veyne discusses "mental balkanization" as a strategy to preserve irrational and contradictory beliefs. "Separate but equal" is not only a paradigm case of such irrationality, it is also a cognitive strategy for self-deception contained in a slogan. The racist who subscribes to "separate but equal" believes both in the equality demanded by the Constitution and in the inequality required for justifying segregation. In such irrationalities, contradictory beliefs are separated into different modalities: for example, at a certain age children believe both that Santa Claus comes on Christmas and that their parents bought the presents. The Greeks believed in their myths in a similar way; see Paul Veyne, *Did the Greeks Believe In Their Myths?* (University of Chicago Press, 1988), p. 41ff. Mental balkanization, Veyne argues, permits "sincere (but irrational) blindness."

45. For an account of such disjunctures see Melvin Pollner, *Mundane Reasoning* (Cambridge University Press, 1987). Against Pollner, I am arguing that such disjunctures involve more than "leaps of faith."

46. The notion of truth candidates is crucial to Hacking's anti-Davidsonian interpretation of Foucault's archeology. See Ian Hacking, "Language, truth, and reason," in *Rationality and Relativism*, ed. M. Hollis and S. Lukes (MIT Press, 1982). Moreover, Hacking's emphasis on "styles of reasoning" also fits well with my rhetorical analysis of disclosive criticism. For a use of Hacking's concepts in the social sciences see James Bohman and Terrence Kelly, "Rationality, intelligibility and comparison," *Philosophy and Social Criticism* 22 (1996): 181–200

47. See Bruce Ackerman, *We the People* (Harvard University Press, 1992), p. 315ff., and Joseph Bessette, *The Mild Voice of Reason* (University of Chicago Press, 1994), pp. 245–246. Bessette sees these transformative moments as based on "popular rhetoric," a view especially close to assigning a democratic role of disclosive rhetoric in creating new publics.

48. Ackerman, *We the People*, volume 1 (Harvard University Press, 1991), pp. 6–7, 266–294..

49. Hannah Arendt, *On Revolution* (Viking, 1969); Walter Lippmann, *The Phantom Public* (Harcourt, Brace, 1925).

50. Dewey, *The Public and Its Problems*, p. 308.

51. Habermas, *Structural Transformation of the Public Sphere*, p. 181ff.

Conclusion

1. G. F. W. Hegel, *Philosophy of Right* (Cambridge University Press, 1991), section 318. See Habermas's discussion of Hegel's and Marx's critiques of the bourgeois public sphere on p. 118ff. of *Structural Transformation of the Public Sphere* (MIT Press, 1989).

2. Hegel, *Philosophy of Right*, section 318.

3. This is the main theme of Lippmann's book *The Phantom Public* (Harcourt, Brace, 1925). For Dewey's reply see pp. 362–363 of *The Public and Its Problems* (Southern Illinois University Press, 1984). Dewey reverses claims for the superiority of experts, since their knowledge derives from the *public* process of scientific inquiry.

4. Joseph Bessette, *The Mild Voice of Reason* (University of Chicago Press, 1994), p. 246.

5. Bruce Ackerman, *We The People*, volume 1 (Harvard University Press, 1991), especially p. 266ff. Sometimes this higher lawmaking begins with the people; at other times it depends on "presidential leadership" or the courts.

6. Richard Rorty, "The priority of democracy to philosophy," in *Philosophical Papers*, volume I (Cambridge University Press, 1991), pp. 180–181. As opposed to Rorty, my argument is not "thoroughly historicist and anti-universalist" (ibid., p. 180); rather, universalist norms of democracy need to be made historically practical.

7. Bessette (*Mild Voice of Reason*, p. 152ff.) notes a decline in the deliberative qualities of congressional committees created by "sunshine laws." As in bargaining, making the deliberative processes fully public may not promote rational outcomes; indeed, it may harden positions and promote opportunism. In bargaining, publicity often undermines the achievement of mutually satisfactory outcomes, because bargainers do not wish to appear to be giving in too quickly. Thomas Schelling notes this perverse consequence of publicity in some situations of conflict on p. 30 of his *Strategy of Conflict* (Harvard University Press, 1960).

8. For an account of the deliberative public opinion poll, see James Fishkin, *Democracy and Deliberation* (Yale University Press, 1991), pp. 81–104. In England the issue of crime was chosen for the deliberation. Fishkin reports that there was a movement of 18 percentage points away from prisons and punitive solutions and toward prevention and employment opportunities. See the report in *The Independent*, May 9, 1994, pp. 8–9. (That newspaper was one of the sponsors.) In this setting, at least, we do see a great deal of changes in preferences in a very specific direction. Fishkin has recently directed the first deliberative opinion poll in the U.S. (January 19–21, 1996).

9. Bessette, *Mild Voice of Reason*, pp. 147–149.

References

Ackerman, Bruce. 1980. *Social Justice and the Liberal State.* Yale University Press.

Ackerman, Bruce. 1988. "Neo-federalism?" In *Constitutionalism and Democracy,* ed. J. Elster and R. Slagstad. Cambridge University Press.

Ackerman, Bruce. 1989. "Why dialogue?" *Journal of Philosophy* 86: 5–22.

Ackerman, Bruce. 1991. *We the People,* volume I. Harvard University Press.

Adorno, Theodor W., and Max Horkheimer. 1982. *Dialectic of Enlightenment.* Continuum.

Adorno, Theodor W., et al. 1953. *The Authoritarian Personality.* Norton.

Alexy, Robert. 1990. "A theory of practical discourse." In *The Communicative Ethics Controversy,* ed. S. Benhabib and F. Dallmayr. MIT Press.

Althusser, Louis. 1971. *Lenin and Philosophy.* Monthly Review Press.

Anderson, Benedict. 1991. *Imagined Communities.* Verso.

Arendt, Hannah. 1958. *The Human Condition.* University of Chicago Press.

Arendt, Hannah. 1959. "Reflections on Little Rock." *Dissent* 6: 45–56.

Arendt, Hannah. 1969. *On Revolution.* Viking.

Aristotle. 1941. *Basic Works,* ed. R. McKeon. Random House.

Asad, Talal. 1989. *Genealogies of Religion: Disciplines and Reasons of Power in Christianity and Islam.* Johns Hopkins University Press.

Austin, J. L. 1962. *How to Do Things with Words.* Oxford University Press.

References

Axelrod, Robert. 1984. *The Evolution of Cooperation*. Basic Books.

Bachrach, Peter, and Morton Baratz. 1970. *Power and Poverty*. Oxford University Press.

Bachrach, Peter, and Elihu Bergman. 1973. *Power and Choice*. Lexington Books.

Barber, Benjamin. 1984. *Strong Democracy*. University of California Press.

Bayley, C. A. no date. "The Indian Ecumene and the British Public." Unpublished.

Baynes, Kenneth. 1992. *The Normative Grounds of Social Criticism: Kant, Rawls and Habermas*. SUNY Press.

Baynes, Kenneth. 1995. "Democracy and the *Rechtsstaat*: Some remarks on *Faktizität und Geltung*." In *Cambridge Companion to Habermas*, ed. S. White. Cambridge University Press.

Beitz, Charles. 1989. *Political Equality*. Princeton University Press.

Benhabib, Seyla. 1986. *Norm, Critique and Utopia*. Columbia University Press.

Benhabib, Seyla. 1992. *Situating the Self*. Routledge.

Benjamin, Martin. 1990. *Splitting the Difference*. University of Kansas Press.

Berlin, Isaiah, ed. 1973. *Essays on J. L. Austin*. Oxford University Press.

Bernstein, Basil. 1962. *Class, Codes and Control*. Routledge.

Bessette, Joseph. 1994. *The Mild Voice of Reason: Deliberative Democracy and American National Government*. University of Chicago Press.

Bobbio, Norberto. 1987. *The Future of Democracy*. Polity Press.

Bohman, James. 1986. "Formal pragmatics and social criticism." *Philosophy and Social Criticism* 12: 332–352.

Bohman, James. 1988. "Emancipation and rhetoric: The perlocutions and the illocutions of the social critic." *Philosophy and Rhetoric* 21: 185–204.

Bohman, James. 1990. "Communication, ideology and democracy." *American Political Science Review* 84: 93–104.

Bohman, James. 1991. *New Philosophy of Social Science: Problems of Indeterminacy*. MIT Press.

Bohman, James. 1992. "Critique of ideology." In *Philosophy of Language: An International Handbook*, volume I, ed. M. Dascal et al. de Gruyter.

Bohman, James. 1992. "The limits of rational choice theory." In *Rational Choice Theory: Advocacy and Critique*, ed. J. Coleman and T. Fararo. Sage.

Bohman, James. 1993. "The completeness of macro-sociological explanations." *Protosoziologie* 5: 80–89.

References

Bohman, James. 1994. "World disclosure and radical criticism." *Thesis Eleven* 37: 82–97.

Bohman, James. 1994. "Complexity, pluralism and the constitutional state: On Habermas's *Faktizität und Geltung.*" *Law and Society Review* 29: 801–834.

Bohman, James. 1995. "Radical democracy and 'unavoidable' complexity." *Constellations* 1: 422–427.

Bohman, James. 1995. "Public reason and cultural pluralism." *Political Theory* 23: 253–279.

Bohman, James. 1996. "The moral costs of political pluralism: The dilemmas of difference and equality in Arendt's 'Reflections on Little Rock.'" In *Hannah Arendt: Twenty Years Later*, ed. L. May and J. Kohn. MIT Press.

Bohman, James. Forthcoming. "Practical agency and cultural constraint." In *Bourdieu: A Critical Reader*, ed. R. Shusterman. Blackwell.

Bohman, James, and Terrence Kelly. 1996. "Rationality. intelligibility, and comparison." *Philosophy and Social Criticism* 22: 181–200.

Blackwell, Richard. 1991. *Bellarmine and the Bible.* University of Notre Dame Press.

Bourdieu, Pierre. 1984. *Distinction.* Harvard University Press.

Bourdieu, Pierre. 1991. *Language and Symbolic Power.* Polity Press.

Bratman, Michael. 1987. *Intentions, Plans and Practical Reason.* Harvard University Press.

Chilton, Paul. 1987. "Metaphor, euphemism, and the militarization of language." *Current Research on Peace and Violence* 10: 7–19.

Cohen, G. A. 1989. "The currency of egalitarian justice." *Ethics* 99: 906–944.

Cohen, Jean, and Andrew Arato. 1992. *Civil Society and Political Theory.* MIT Press.

Cohen, Joshua. 1986. "An epistemic conception of democracy." *Ethics* 97: 26–38.

Cohen, Joshua. 1989. "Deliberation and democratic legitimacy." In *The Good Polity*, ed. A. Hamlin and P. Pettit. Blackwell.

Cohen, Joshua. 1993. "Moral pluralism and political consensus." In *The Idea of Democracy*, ed. D. Copp et al. Cambridge University Press.

Cohen, Joshua, and Joel Rogers. 1992. "Secondary associations and democratic governance." *Politics and Society* 20: 393–472.

Dasgupta, Partha. 1988. "Trust as a commodity." In *Trust*, ed. D. Gambetta. Blackwell.

Dasgupta, Partha. 1993. *An Inquiry into Well-Being and Destitution.* Oxford University Press.

Dahl, Robert. 1985. *A Preface to Economic Democracy.* Oxford University Press.

Dahl, Robert. 1989. *Democracy and Its Critics.* Yale University Press, 1989.

Dahl, Robert, and Edward Tufte. 1973. *Size and Democracy.* Stanford University Press.

Davis, Kathy. 1988. *Power under the Microscope.* Floris.

Dewey, John. 1922. *Human Nature and Conduct.* Holt.

Dewey, John. 1988. "The public and its problems." In *John Dewey: The Later Works, 1925–1953,* volume 2, 1925–1927. University of Southern Illinois Press.

Douglas, Mary, and Brian Isherwood. 1976. *The World of Goods.* Routledge.

Dreyfus, Hubert. 1991. *Being in the World.* MIT Press.

Dryzek, John. 1990. *Discursive Democracy: Politics, Policy, and Political Science.* Cambridge University Press.

Dworkin, Ronald. 1981. "What is equality? Part I." *Philosophy and Public Affairs* 10: 185–246.

Dworkin, Ronald. 1981. "What is equality? Part II." *Philosophy and Public Affairs* 10: 283–345.

Dworkin, Ronald. 1993. *Life's Dominion: An Argument About Abortion, Euthanasia and Individual Freedom.* Knopf.

Elster, Jon. 1978. *Logic and Society.* Wiley.

Elster, Jon. 1979. *Ulysses and the Sirens.* Cambridge University Press.

Elster, Jon. 1984. "The market and the forum: Three varieties of political theory." In Foundations of Social Choice Theory, ed. J. Elster and A. Hylland. Cambridge University Press.

Elster, Jon. 1984. *Sour Grapes.* Cambridge University Press.

Elster, Jon. 1989. *Solomonic Judgments.* Cambridge University Press.

Elster, Jon, and Karl Moene, ed. 1989. *Alternatives to Capitalism.* Cambridge University Press.

Elster, Jon, and Rune Slagstad, ed. 1988. *Constitutionalism and Democracy.* Cambridge University Press.

Estlund, David. 1990. "Democracy without preference." *Philosophical Review* 99: 397–423.

Estlund, David. 1992. "Making truth safe for democracy." In *The Idea of Democracy,* ed. D. Copp et al. Cambridge University Press.

References

Ferejohn, John, and James Kuklinski, ed. 1990. *Information and Democratic Processes.* University of Illinois Press.

Fishkin, James. 1991. *Democracy and Deliberation: New Directions in Democratic Reform.* Yale University Press.

Fiss, Owen. 1987. "Why the state?" *Harvard Law Review* 100: 781–794.

Foucault, Michel. 1979. *Discipline and Punish.* Vintage.

Fraser, Nancy. 1989. *Unruly Practices.* University of Minnesota Press.

Fraser, Nancy. 1992. "Rethinking the public sphere: A contribution to the critique of actually existing democracy." In *Habermas and the Public Sphere*, ed. C. Calhoun. MIT Press.

Freeman, Jo. 1973. "The origins of the women's liberation movement." *American Journal of Sociology* 78: 792–811.

Freeman, Samuel. 1990. "Reason and agreement in social contract views." *Philosophy and Public Affairs* 19: 122–57.

Freeman, Samuel. 1991. "Contractualism, moral motivation, and practical reason." *Journal of Philosophy* 88: 281–303.

Gadamer, Hans-Georg. 1992. *Truth and Method.* Seabury.

Gamson, Joshua. 1989. "Silence, death and the invisible enemy: AIDS activism and social movement newness." *Social Problems* 36: 351–367.

Gamson, William. 1988. "Political discourses and collective action." *International Social Movement Research* 1: 219–244.

Gamson, William. 1990. *The Strategy of Social Protest.* Wadsworth.

Gamson, William. 1993. *Talking Politics.* Cambridge University Press.

Gamson, William, and Emily Schneider. 1984. "Organizing the poor." *Theory and Society* 13: 567–585.

Garfinkel, Harold. 1967. *Studies in Ethnomethodology.* Prentice-Hall.

Gilbert, Margaret. 1989. *On Social Facts.* Princeton University Press.

Goodin, Robert. 1986. "Laundering preferences." In *Foundations of Social Choice Theory*, ed. J. Elster and A. Hylland. Cambridge University Press.

Greenawalt, Kent. 1988. *Religious Convictions and Political Choice.* Oxford University Press.

Grice, H. P. 1975. "Logic and conversation." In *Syntax and Semantics 3: Speech Acts*, ed. P. Cole and J. Morgan. Academic Press.

References

Grofman, Bernard, and Gerald Owen, ed. 1983. *Information Pooling and Group Decision Making.* JAI.

Günther, Klaus. 1993. *The Sense of Appropriateness.* SUNY Press.

Guinier, Lani. 1993. "Groups, representation and race-conscious districting." *University of Texas Law Review* 71: 1589–1642.

Guinier, Lani. 1994. *The Tyranny of the Majority.* Free Press.

Gusfield, Joseph. 1981. *The Culture of Public Problems: Drinking-Driving and the Symbolic Order.* University Of Chicago Press.

Gutmann, Amy. 1993. "The challenge of multiculturalism in political ethics." *Philosophy and Public Affairs* 22: 171–206.

Gutmann, Amy, and Dennis Thompson. 1990. "Moral conflict and political consensus." *Ethics* 101: 76–86.

Habermas, Jürgen. 1970. "On systematically distorted communication." *Inquiry* 13: 205–218.

Habermas, Jürgen. 1973. *Theory and Practice.* Beacon.

Habermas, Jürgen. 1975. *Legitimation Crisis.* Beacon.

Habermas, Jürgen. 1979. *Communication and the Evolution of Society* Beacon.

Habermas, Jürgen. 1985. *Vorstudien und Ergänzungen zur Theorie des kommunikativen Handelns.* Suhrkamp.

Habermas, Jürgen. 1984, 1987. *The Theory of Communicative Action,* volumes I and II. Beacon.

Habermas, Jürgen. 1985. *Philosophical-Political Profiles.* MIT Press.

Habermas, Jürgen. 1986. "Entgegnung." In *Kommunikatives Handeln,* ed. H. Joas and A. Honneth. Suhrkamp.

Habermas, Jürgen. 1988. *On the Logic of the Social Sciences.* MIT Press.

Habermas, Jürgen. 1989. *The Structural Transformation of the Public Sphere.* MIT Press.

Habermas, Jürgen. 1989. "Volkssouveränität als Verfahren. " In *Die Ideen von 1789,* ed. Bad Homburg Forum Philosophie. Suhrkamp.

Habermas, Jürgen. 1989. *The New Conservatism.* MIT Press.

Habermas, Jürgen. 1990. *Moral Consciousness and Communicative Action.* MIT Press.

Habermas, Jürgen. 1990. "What does socialism mean today? The rectifying revolution and the need for new thinking on the left." *New Left Review* 183: 3–21.

References

Habermas, Jürgen. 1992. *Faktizität und Geltung.* Suhrkamp. (English translation: *Between Facts and Norms: Contributions to a Discourse Theory of Law and Democracy.* MIT Press, 1996.)

Habermas, Jürgen. 1992. "Citizenship and national identity." *Praxis International* 12: 1–19.

Habermas, Jürgen. 1993. "Struggles for recognition in the constitutional state." *European Journal of Philosophy* 1: 128–155.

Habermas, Jürgen. 1993. *Justification and Application.* MIT Press.

Habermas, Jürgen. 1995. "Reconciliation through the public use of reason: Remarks on John Rawls' political liberalism." *Journal of Philosophy* 52: 109–131.

Habermas, Jürgen. 1996. "Reply to Symposium." *Cardozo Law Review* 17: 1801–1880.

Hacking, Ian. 1982. "Language, truth, and reason." In *Rationality and Relativism*, ed. M. Hollis and S. Lukes. MIT Press.

Hegel, Georg F. W. 1991. *The Philosophy of Right.* Cambridge University Press.

Heidegger, Martin. 1972. *Sein und Zeit.* Niemeyer.

Heidegger, Martin. 1977. *Basic Writings.* Harper and Row.

Heidegger, Martin. 1977. *The Question Concerning Technology and Other Essays.* Harper and Row.

Held, David. 1980. *Introduction to Critical Theory.* University of California Press.

Holmes, Steven. 1988. "Gag rules, or the politics of omission." In *Constitutionalism and Democracy*, ed. J. Elster and R. Slagstad. Cambridge University Press.

Holmes, Steven. 1989. "The permanent structure of anti-liberal thought." In *Liberalism and the Moral Life*, ed. N. Rosenblum. Harvard University Press.

Horkheimer, Max. 1974. *Eclipse of Reason.* Seabury.

Horkheimer, Max. 1982. *Critical Theory.* Seabury.

Jay, Martin. 1984. *Marxism and Totality.* University of California Press.

Johnson, James. 1993. "Is talk really cheap?" *American Political Science Review* 87: 74–85.

Johnson, James, and Jack Knight. 1994. "Aggregation and deliberation: On the possibility of democratic legitimacy." *Political Theory* 22: 277–296.

Kafka, Franz. 1970. *Sämtliche Erzählungen.* Fischer.

Kant, Immanuel. 1956. *Critique of Judgment.* Oxford University Press.

Kant, Immanuel. 1965. *Critique of Pure Reason.* St. Martin's Press.

Kant, Immanuel. 1971. *Political Writings*, ed. H. Reiss. Cambridge University Press.

Knight, Jack. 1992. *Institutions and Social Conflict.* Cambridge University Press.

Kymlicka, Will. 1989. *Liberalism, Community and Culture.* Oxford University Press.

Kymlicka, Will. 1991. "Liberalism and the politicization of ethnicity." *Canadian Journal of Jurisprudence* 4: 239–256.

Kymlicka, Will. 1995. *Multicultural Citizenship.* Oxford University Press.

Lind, Allen, and Tom Tyler. 1988. *The Social Psychology of Procedural Justice.* Plenum.

Lippmann, Walter. 1925. *The Phantom Public.* Harcourt, Brace.

Lukes, Steven. 1989. "Making sense of moral conflict." In *Liberalism and the Moral Life,* ed. N. Rosenblum. Harvard University Press.

Lukes, Steven. 1991. *Moral Conflict and Politics.* Oxford University Press.

Lukes, Steven. 1993. "Four fables on human rights." In *Human Rights,* ed. S. Hurley and S. Shute. Basic Books.

Lyotard, Jean-François. 1984. *The Postmodern Condition.* University of Minnesota Press.

Manin, Bernard. 1987. "On legitimacy and political deliberation." *Political Theory* 15: 338–368.

Mansbridge, Jane. 1980. *Beyond Adversary Democracy.* University of Chicago Press.

March, James. 1988. *Decisions and Organizations.* Blackwell.

Marcuse, Herbert. 1966. *Eros and Civilization.* Beacon.

Marcuse, Herbert. 1968. *Negations.* Beacon.

Marx, Karl. 1975. "Critique of Hegel's *Philosophy of Right.*" In *The Collected Writings of Marx and Engels,* volume 3. International Publishers.

Marx, Karl. 1977. *Selected Writings,* ed. D. McLellan. Oxford University Press.

May, Larry. 1995. "Challenging medical authority: The refusal of treatment by Christian Scientists." *Hastings Center Report* 23: 15–21.

McAdam, Doug. 1982. *Political Process and the Development of Black Insurgency 1930–1970.* University of Chicago Press.

McCarthy, Thomas. 1978. *The Critical Theory of Jürgen Habermas.* MIT Press.

McCarthy, Thomas. 1991. *Ideals and Illusions: On Reconstruction and Deconstruction in Contemporary Critical Theory.* MIT Press.

McCarthy, Thomas. 1994. "Kantian constructivism and reconstructivism: Rawls and Habermas in dialogue." *Ethics* 105: 44–63.

References

McHoul, Alec. 1987. "Why there are no guarantees for interrogators." *Journal of Pragmatics* 11: 455–471.

Merleau-Ponty, Maurice. 1962. *The Phenomenology of Perception.* Humanities Press.

Michelman, Frank. 1986. "The Supreme Court 1985 term forward: Traces of self-government." *Harvard Law Review* 100: 4–77.

Michelman, Frank. 1988a "Political truth and the rule of law." *Tel Aviv University Studies in Law* 8: 281–291.

Michelman, Frank. 1988. "Law's republic." *Yale Law Journal* 97: 1493–1537.

Michels, Robert. 1958. *Political Parties.* Free Press.

Meiklejohn, Alexander. 1960. *Political Freedom.* Oxford University Press.

Minnow, Martha. 1990. *Making All the Difference.* Cornell University Press.

Morley, David. 1986. *Family Television.* Comedia.

Morris, Aldon. 1984. *The Origins of the Civil Rights Movement.* Free Press.

Nagel, Thomas. 1987. "Moral conflict and political legitimacy." *Philosophy and Public Affairs* 17: 215–240.

Nagel, Thomas. 1991. *Equality and Partiality.* Oxford University Press.

Negt, Oskar, and Alexander Kluge. 1994. *The Public Sphere and Experience.* University of Minnesota Press.

Nisbett, Robert, and Lee Ross. 1981. *Human Inference.* Prentice-Hall.

Nussbaum, Martha. 1990. "Aristotelian social democracy." In *Liberalism and the Good,* ed. R. Douglas et al. Routledge.

Okin, Susan Moeller. 1994. "Gender inequality and cultural difference." *Political Theory* 22: 4–24.

O'Neill, O'Nora. 1989. *The Constructions of Reason.* Cambridge University Press.

Orwell, George. 1957. *A Collection of Essays.* Doubleday.

Papanek, Hanna. 1990. "To each less than she needs, from each more than she can do: Allocations, entitlement and value." In *Women and World Development,* ed. I. Tinker. Oxford University Press.

Parfit, Derek. 1984. *Reasons and Persons.* Oxford University Press.

Parsons, Talcott. 1971. *The System of Modern Societies.* Prentice-Hall.

Pateman, Carole. 1970. *Participation and Democratic Theory.* Cambridge University Press.

References

Pathak, Zakia, and Rajeswari Sunder Rajan. 1989. "Shabano." *Signs* 14: 558–582.

Perrow, Charles. 1984. *Normal Accidents*. Basic Books.

Peters, Bernhard. 1993. *Integration moderner Gesellschaften*. Suhrkamp.

Pleck, Elizabeth. 1987. *Domestic Tyranny*. Oxford University Press.

Pollner, Melvin. 1987. *Mundane Reasoning*. Cambridge University Press.

Popkin, Samuel. 1991. *The Reasoning Voter: Communication and Persuasion in Presidential Campaigns*. University of Chicago Press.

Putnam, Hilary. 1981. *Reason, Truth and History*. Cambridge University Press.

Rainey, R. Randall, and William Rehg. "The marketplace of ideas, the public interest, and the federal regulation of the electronic media: Implications of Habermas's theory of democracy." *University of California Law Review*, forthcoming.

Rawls, John. 1971. *A Theory of Justice*. Harvard University Press.

Rawls, John. 1980. "Kantian constructivism in moral theory." *Journal of Philosophy* 77: 515–572.

Rawls, John. 1985. "Justice as fairness: Political not metaphysical." *Philosophy and Public Affairs* 14: 227–251.

Rawls, John. 1987. "The idea of an overlapping consensus." *Oxford Legal Studies* 7: 1–25.

Rawls, John. 1989. "The domain of the political and overlapping consensus." *New York University Law Review* 64: 233–255.

Rawls, John. 1993. *Political Liberalism*. Columbia University Press.

Rawls, John. 1995. "Reply to Habermas." *Journal of Philosophy* 52, 132–180.

Raz, Joseph. 1986. *The Morality of Freedom*. Oxford University Press.

Raz, Joseph. 1990. "Facing diversity: The case for epistemic abstinence." *Philosophy and Public Affairs* 19: 3–46.

Reagan, Thomas, ed. 1986. *Animal Sacrifices: Religious Perspectives on the Use of Animals in Science*. Temple University Press.

Rehg, William, and James Bohman. 1996. "Deliberation and discourse." *Journal of Political Philosophy* 4: 79–99.

Richardson, Henry. 1990. "Specifying norms as a way to resolve concrete ethical problems." *Philosophy and Public Affairs* 19: 279–310.

Richardson, Henry. 1994. *Practical Reasoning About Ultimate Ends*. Cambridge University Press.

295

References

Riker, William. 1982. *Liberalism against Populism*. Waveland.

Rorty, Richard. 1989. *Contingency, Irony, and Solidarity*. Cambridge University Press.

Rorty, Richard. "The priority of democracy to philosophy." In *Objectivity, Relativism and Truth: Philosophical Papers Volume I*. Cambridge University Press.

Rouse, Joseph. 1987. *Power and Knowledge*. Cornell University Press.

Rousseau, Jean-Jacques. 1967. *The Social Contract*. Pocket Books.

Scanlon, T. M. 1975. "Preference and urgency." *Journal of Philosophy* 72: 659–660.

Scanlon, T. M. 1982. "Contractualism and utilitarianism." In *Utilitarianism and Beyond*, ed. A. Sen and B. Williams. Cambridge University Press.

Schelling, Thomas. 1960. *The Strategy of Conflict*. Harvard University Press.

Schelling, Thomas. 1987. "Ethics, law and the exercise of self-command." In *Liberty, Equality and Law: Selected Tanner Lectures*. Cambridge University Press.

Schick, Frederic. 1991. *Understanding Action: An Essay on Reasons*. Cambridge University Press.

Scheglhoff, E. A. 1987. "Between micro and macro: Contexts and other connections." In *The Micro-Macro Link*, ed. J. Alexander et al. University of California Press.

Schmitt, Carl. 1983. *Political Theology*. MIT Press.

Schütz, Alfred. 1964. "The well-informed citizen." In *Collected Papers*, volume II. Nijhoff.

Schütz, Alfred. 1970. *Reflections on the Problem of Relevance*. Yale University Press.

Searle, John. 1990. "Collective intentions and actions." In *Intentions in Communication*, ed. P. Cohen et al. MIT Press.

Selmen, Robert. 1985. *The Growth of Interpersonal Understanding*. Humanities Press.

Sen, Amartya. 1979. *Collective Choice and Social Welfare*. Oliver and Boyd.

Sen, Amartya. 1981. *Poverty and Famines*. Oxford University Press.

Sen, Amartya. 1992. *Equality Reconsidered*. Oxford University Press.

Sen, Amartya. 1993. "Capability and well-being." In *The Quality of Life*, ed. A. Sen and M. Nussbaum. Oxford University Press.

Shapin, Steven. 1994. *A Social History of Truth*. University of Chicago Press.

Shapin, Stephen, and Simon Schaffer. 1985. *Leviathan and the Air Pump*. Princeton University Press.

References

Shapiro, Susan. 1987. "The social control of impersonal trust." *American Journal of Sociology* 93: 623–658.

Shklar, Judith. 1991. *American Citizenship.* Harvard University Press.

Simon, Herbert. 1957. *Models of Man: Social and Rational.* Harper and Row.

Snow, David, and Robert Benford. 1992. "Master frames and cycles of protest." In *Frontiers of Social Movement Theory,* ed. A. Morris and C. Mueller. Yale University Press.

Sperber, Dan, and Diedre Wilson. 1986. *Relevance: Communication and Cognition.* Harvard University Press.

Sunstein, Cass. 1985. "Interest groups in American public law." *Stanford Law Review* 38: 29–87.

Sunstein, Cass. 1988. "Beyond the Republican revival." *Yale Law Journal* 97: 1539–1590.

Sunstein, Cass. 1993. "Democracy and shifting preferences." In *The Idea of Democracy,* ed. D. Copp et al. Cambridge University Press.

Taylor, Charles. 1975. *Hegel.* Cambridge University Press.

Taylor, Charles. 1985. *Philosophical Papers,* volumes I and II. Cambridge University Press.

Taylor, Charles. 1989. *Sources of the Self.* Harvard University Press.

Taylor, Charles. 1992. *Multiculturalism and the Politics of Recognition.* Princeton University Press.

Thompson, E. P. 1963. *The Making of the English Working Class.* Penguin.

Thompson, John. 1990. *Ideology and Modern Culture.* Stanford University Press.

Tuomela, Raimo, and Kaarlo Miller. 1988. "We intentions." *Philosophical Studies* 53: 367–389.

Veyne, Paul. 1988. *Did the Greeks Believe Their Myths?* University of Chicago Press.

Waldron, Jeremy. 1990. "Rights and majorities: Rousseau revisited." In *Majorities and Minorities,* ed. J. Chapman and A. Wertheimer. New York University Press.

Wallace, James. 1988. *Moral Relevance and Moral Conflict.* Cornell University Press.

Walzer, Michael. 1984. "Liberalism and the art of separation." *Political Theory* 12: 315–330.

Walzer, Michael. 1988. *The Company of Critics.* Basic Books.

Warner, Michael. 1990. *The Letters of the Republic: Publication and the Public Sphere in Eighteenth Century America.* Harvard University Press.

References

Warner, Michael. 1992. "The mass public and the mass subject." In *Habermas and the Public Sphere*, ed. C. Calhoun. MIT Press.

Warren, Mark. 1992. "Democratic theory and self-transformation." *American Political Science Review* 86: 8–23.

Watzlawick, Paul, et al. 1971. *The Pragmatics of Human Communication*. Free Press.

Weber, Max. 1978. *Economy and Society*. University of California Press.

West, Candace. 1984. *Routine Complications: Troubles in Talk between Doctors and Patients*. Indiana University Press.

West, Candace, and Angela Garcia. 1988. "Conversational shift work: A study of topical transition between women and men." *Social Problems* 35: 551–575.

West, Candace, and Donald Zimmerman. 1975. "Sex roles, interruptions, and silences in conversation." In *Language and Sex: Difference and Dominance*, ed. B. Thorne and N. Henley. Newbury House.

Westbrook, Robert. 1991. *John Dewey and American Democracy*. Cornell University Press.

Willis, Paul. 1977. *Learning to Labor*. Saxon House.

Young, Iris Marion. 1989. "Impartiality and the civic public." In *Feminism as Critique*, ed. S. Benhabib and D. Cornell. University of Minnesota Press.

Young, Iris Marion. 1990. *Justice and the Politics of Difference*. Princeton University Press.

Young, Iris Marion. 1990. "Polity and group difference." In *Feminism and Political Theory*, ed. C. Sunstein. University of Chicago Press.

Zald, Mayer, and John McCarthy. 1977. "Resource mobilization and social movements." *American Journal of Sociology* 82: 1214–1241.

Zolo, Danilo. 1992. *Democracy and Complexity*. Pennsylvania State University Press.

Index

Index

Studies in Contemporary German Social Thought
Thomas McCarthy, General Editor

Axel Honneth, Thomas McCarthy, Claus Offe, and Albrecht Wellmer, editors, *Cultural-Political Interventions in the Unfinished Project of Enlightenment*

Axel Honneth, Thomas McCarthy, Claus Offe, and Albrecht Wellmer, editors, *Philosophical Interventions in the Unfinished Project of Enlightenment*

Max Horkheimer, *Between Philosophy and Social Science: Selected Early Writings*

Hans Joas, *G. H. Mead: A Contemporary Re-examination of His Thought*

Michael Kelly, editor, *Critique and Power: Recasting the Foucault/Habermas Debate*

Reinhart Koselleck, *Critique and Crisis: Enlightenment and the Pathogenesis of Modern Society*

Reinhart Koselleck, *Futures Past: On the Semantics of Historical Time*

Harry Liebersohn, *Fate and Utopia in German Sociology, 1887-1923*

Herbert Marcuse, *Hegel's Ontology and the Theory of Historicity*

Larry May and Jerome Kohn, editors, *Hannah Arendt: Twenty Years Later*

Pierre Missac, *Walter Benjamin's Passages*

Gil G. Noam and Thomas E. Wren, editors, *The Moral Self*

Guy Oakes, *Weber and Rickert: Concept Formation in the Cultural Sciences*

Claus Offe, *Contradictions of the Welfare State*

Claus Offe, *Disorganized Capitalism: Contemporary Transformations of Work and Politics*

Helmut Peukert, *Science, Action, and Fundamental Theology: Toward a Theology of Communicative Action*

Joachim Ritter, *Hegel and the French Revolution: Essays on the* Philosophy of Right

William E. Scheuerman, *Between the Norm and the Exception: The Frankfurt School and the Rule of Law*

Alfred Schmidt, *History and Structure: An Essay on Hegelian-Marxist and Structuralist Theories of History*

Dennis Schmidt, *The Ubiquity of the Finite: Hegel, Heidegger, and the Entitlements of Philosophy*

Carl Schmitt, *The Crisis of Parliamentary Democracy*

Carl Schmitt, *Political Romanticism*

Carl Schmitt, *Political Theology: Four Chapters on the Concept of Sovereignty*

Gary Smith, editor, *On Walter Benjamin: Critical Essays and Recollections*

Michael Theunissen, *The Other: Studies in the Social Ontology of Husserl, Heidegger, Sartre, and Buber*

Ernst Tugendhat, *Self-Consciousness and Self-Determination*

Georgia Warnke, *Justice and Interpretation*

Mark Warren, *Nietzsche and Political Thought*

Albrecht Wellmer, *The Persistence of Modernity: Essays on Aesthetics, Ethics and Postmodernism*

Joel Whitebook, *Perversion and Utopia: A Study in Psychoanalysis and Critical Theory*

Rolf Wiggershaus, *The Frankfurt School: Its History, Theories, and Political Significance*

Thomas E. Wren, editor, *The Moral Domain: Essays in the Ongoing Discussion between Philosophy and the Social Sciences*

Lambert Zuidervaart, *Adorno's Aesthetic Theory: The Redemption of Illusion*